5,000 DAYS OF WAR

THE FIRSTHAND ACCOUNT OF AN AFGHAN SPECIAL FORCES OPERATOR

YOUSUF SEDIQ

EDITED BY BRYAN BRAY

ISBN: 978-1-955026-90-1

Printed in the United States of America

Published by Ballast Books
www.ballastbooks.com

We love to partner with new authors and bring their books to life.
For more information, please email info@ballastbooks.com.

This book is dedicated to all of the unknown heroes who paid the ultimate sacrifice in the fight for freedom.

The content of this book reflects the views and life experiences of Yousuf Sediq. Details in this book such as times, dates, exact locations, some names, and operational information have been changed for security reasons due to the ever-evolving situation in Afghanistan. No party associated with the creation of this book has had any access to U.S. or NATO marked classified information, and all content is based on the personal experience and opinions of Yousuf Sediq.

While some details have changed, every bullet is real. These are the real-life stories of a man who was born into war and by God's grace alone was able to survive.

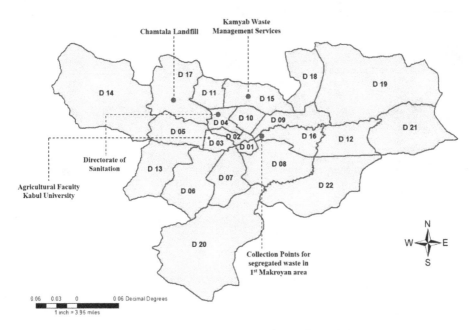

Map of Kabul broken down by police district.

Map of Afghanistan broken down by province.

Chapter 1

August 15, 2021. The enemy was at the gates of Kabul. This was the end. I had fought this fight for fourteen years. Many of my brothers-in-arms had fought it longer. I had conducted over 600 missions against the Taliban. My squadron of sixty-five soldiers had over two thousand confirmed kills on them in the last three years alone.

The Taliban did not know our faces or names, but they knew our reputation. They knew about "the Unit," and they hated us with a burning passion. They feared us, but now we were outnumbered in an impossible situation. They'd announced that if they caught any of us alive, they would publicly decapitate us, dismember us, and kill our families in a similar way.

This was the Taliban who killed children and women, bombed holy places, and murdered innocent people without any reason. This was the Taliban who forced people out of their beliefs, the Taliban who placed improvised explosive devices (IEDs) and killed civilians, and the Taliban who wanted a backward nation. This was the Taliban who oppressed innocent people, who made kids orphans, women widows, and men widowers. This was the Taliban who forced people to leave their beloved homes and immigrate through rough and steep mountains to survive. This was the Taliban who enjoyed torturing people to death. And because of them, my beloved homeland had been in forty years of nonstop war.

My soldiers and I had decided that we would not be taken alive. I had my modified AK-Draco on me and eight magazines fully loaded. I had another eight magazines in my assault pack. All sixty-five of us were ready for the final fight. We were going to kill as many Taliban fighters as we could—and die trying.

—

But, to understand how we got to this point, you first must understand where it all began. This is the world I was born into, and this is the world I survived. This is the war that nobody won.

—

My name is Yousuf Sediq. My first name is after the prophet Joseph (peace be upon him), and my last name means "honest." Based on our religion, we believe it is a child's right to be given a good and meaningful name. There are also more religious reasons behind it. Most Afghan names have a meaning. My first name is Arabic, and my last name is found in the Pashto, Dari, and Arabic languages. I was born in 1988 in a small village somewhere in northern Afghanistan. Life was simple but challenging. Looking back, I have so many good memories of my time in the village and many bad ones. I remember the gatherings, the weddings, and my friends and family fondly.

Our village was located deep down in a big valley. This valley had eighteen districts in it, and there were a number of small villages. The valley itself was very flat. The weather was bearable in the summer, but in winter, it was cold. Our village was located almost in the center of the valley, which was surrounded by mountain ranges on the left and right side. In the middle, there was a big river, a tributary that later sent its water up north to join with more significant rivers. The water came from the winter snow that melted in the spring and summer. It was pure, natural water. People were using these natural water sources for drinking and farming.

All of Afghanistan still uses natural water sources. This is especially true for villages all over the country. Our valley's history is over 400 years old, even though it has not all been recorded. What I know of it is based on the information my father collected in his memory notebook. He kept a record of everything in his notebook, especially when he was young. There was no internet, social media, TV, or radio.

To get to our village from the nearest urban area, you had to drive for three hours into the valley. Eventually, you would reach a part where you'd have to cross a small, one-way bridge. But when we were kids, we had to walk all the way to the central city (that remains unnamed for security reasons). It was a twenty-four-hour walk or ride with donkeys to travel there. People couldn't afford to buy horses.

After passing the bridge, you would encounter this beautiful village with all flat ground and green countryside. There were a small number of farms, gardens, vineyards, and groves. When you passed that village, you would see some mountains with a snug and narrow pathway between two of them. You'd pass that area, and then you'd see a few small villages, which were our villages. They were all spread out in one general location.

The houses in our valley were built on top of hills and on the sides of the steep slopes. This was done to allow for the flat ground to be better used for farming. The village consisted of eighty mud-walled homes. It wasn't easy to get clay because our village ground had rocks in some parts and dirt in others. And you couldn't just go dig into the ground wherever you wanted. There were specific locations where you could get dirt to make clay. It might sound simple, but it was really hard. We couldn't afford laborers, so we had to do it ourselves and build our houses from scratch. If you were over six or seven years old, you had to help or you would get whooped by your parents.

Afghan homes had big yards with two or three small rooms in the compound. Every room had one or two windows to bring light in the house and keep it warm in the winter. There were only a few houses that had two stories in the whole village. It was hard to afford to build more rooms. My family's house was miniscule. We had a small yard, one living room, and one tiny kitchen. We all had to live in one room, both parents and kids. We slept on mattresses.

Our parents believed that a more extensive family was better because the kids could help with farming and everything else around the house. Sons were vital to the family. We couldn't take women to the mountains to do agriculture or become shepherds. Besides, there was a lot of work to be done in the house that men couldn't do. That was one of the reasons

3

families were blessed with many children, but the main one was the lack of birth control. We didn't have birth control, and we had no knowledge of birth control either.

Nights were silent apart from the occasional rustling of the animals. Kids were tired and would go to sleep quickly. We had to be ready to do farm work early in the morning. The grown-ups would then sit together and have their social time. This often involved chatting and drinking tea. And I mean a lot of tea, like two or three teapots' worth. The grown-ups in our house were my mom, dad, older brother, and grandpa and grandma, both from my father's side. Sometimes we kids would sit and listen to their stories.

Life was difficult. We were all focused on survival. We barely had anything to eat. We had no clinics, but sickness was uncommon.

Women were giving birth to children with no problems. My father told me the story of the night I was born. He said my mom went to the storage room, and twenty minutes later, she came out with a baby in her hand. My father asked my mother, "What is in your hand?" She said, "This is your child."

This wasn't just my birth story. All the kids were born like that in our village. We were eleven brothers and sisters total, but unfortunately, two of my oldest sisters died due to starvation and poverty. I was a young child and didn't have many feelings about it, but it impacted my mother a lot. Losing two children isn't easy for any mother. I don't remember anything about them though. Life had to go on, and we had no option but to accept the hard reality. It was devastating to the family, but it was just life.

We had and still have a beautiful tradition of helping each other in good and bad times. All Afghans are like that. You would see hundreds of people coming to help during sad times, and hundreds would come to help during good times. There is beautiful unity in that. It was a feeling that was felt among the tribe or village. And if you lived in the city, your neighbors were the first to help, then your relatives, and then your tribe after them.

The village was quiet most of the time. The weekend was the only time kids had to play around and make some noise. Kids would often play in the courtyard with the other families' kids. Their favorite game was toop danda (a mix of baseball and cricket). Of course, we didn't have the money to buy a ball. We made one from pieces of cloth. We would wrap the fabric around in circles until it formed into a shape like a ball. Then, we'd give it to our mothers to sew it. The ball was hard like a rock, and we would hit each other with it. The game had no rules and no bases. It is kind of hard to explain. There is no similar game anywhere on the globe, but it was fun, and we enjoyed every moment of it. We were children and loved each other.

There was no rich or poor among us. We were all poor when it came to money, but in heart, we were wealthy. Those were good times. When we moved to the city, we got separated from our village. Later, when we grew up, we started seeing each other on different occasions such as weddings and funerals. We would play in our free time between work and school.

We didn't start school at a specific age. When we went, we would take some dry fruits for lunch. School lasted four hours, and we only had one break during that time. After school finished, we had to walk back to the village. At all times, kids went back home in little packs. We all had sticks in our hands in case we encountered wolves or other wild animals.

We would wake up at 3 a.m. in the summer and 5 a.m. in the winter to take the sheep out to the hills. We would watch over them as they fed and then come back before noon so that we would have enough time to get to school. Afghan schools mainly taught in the summer due to the terrible conditions of the school buildings. Most of the schools consisted of tents. They often didn't look like schools at all. It was more like studying under some trees in the yard. After school, we would help in the fields with our fathers. I remember I started working before I was seven and have never stopped. I believe those hard times made me the man I am today.

We had to walk three hours to get to school and three hours to get back. We didn't have the luxury of roads. We walked through hills and valleys across bare terrain. Cars didn't exist in the village, and it was nearly impossible to afford a work animal, such as a horse or mule.

We would wear whatever we had available to us. We didn't have a proper uniform; we were just happy to have clothes. We had no adequate schedule or structure for schoolwork. We still had to arrive at school early. Otherwise, we would get whooped by tree branches. I don't remember much from school lessons. Also, due to my young age, I had no plans with it and no thoughts about the system. I was a farm boy.

Due to the Taliban controlling the school system, the lessons taught were mainly religious. Talib means "Islamic student," and Taliban is the plural form of the word. The teachers were often extremist. They would teach us that a woman who wore no socks deserved to be whipped in the street. They also taught us that if we missed one of the five prayers a day, we would be flogged or beaten. If we were caught stealing, at any age, we would get our hand cut off. If we stole a second time, we would be lynched.

The Taliban were cruel and would kill you on sight without any judgment or prosecution. You can't mess with a dictator or dictatorship, and you can't bring people to practice a religion by force. This was common across Afghanistan. If you resisted the Taliban, you died. We kids didn't know what death really was at the time. We didn't comprehend it all.

No one resisted the Taliban. This was the case even though the Taliban rarely had a presence in the village itself. Villages would often enforce the Taliban rule in fear of Taliban reprisal. Stories of the Taliban killing large groups in brutal ways would make their way to the village. These stories were so compelling that many villages enforced these rules years after the Taliban eventually fell in 2001. No one knew for sure who was and was not Taliban. No one knew who would snitch to the Taliban's leaders and get many people killed.

Work in the village was difficult, and every member of my family helped. My mother had to control the chores around the house, and she helped with the farming too. Parenting, feeding, and caring for a big family is hard work. I am so grateful for my father and mother's sacrifices; they have done more than enough for us. I can't pay back their kindness.

Because Afghanistan was so mountainous, our village had one primary shepherd that would take the cattle and sheep to the green desert hills. The herds would get fed, then return. The shepherd would, in turn, receive flour from the villagers at the end of the month. My father was a shepherd. I am always grateful for his hard work and everything he did to bring food on the table in a moral way.

Our family had twenty sheep, a donkey, two cows, and chickens. We kids would work hard and help out in any way we could. We would leave the house at 4 a.m. and walk to the mountain to gather our part of the herd back from the shepherd. We only had lanterns. These were diesel lanterns, tiny ones. They definitely helped a lot, and they were cheap to buy and use. We would take the sheep miles and miles away from the village. It was all hard work. To be honest, I don't miss any part of that life. Who would miss it? A kid had no option but to work to survive and not starve to death.

Our work consisted of maintaining the farm. My brothers were tasked with gathering firewood and hooking up one of the cows to the family plow. The plow was only wood because metal was too expensive. It was used to plant seeds, mainly wheat, potatoes, tomatoes, and whatever vegetable helped our survival.

We would butcher only one sheep every fall. We hung the meat in a storehouse and let it dry until winter. It was rare to eat more than one sheep a year. Often, the meat was too expensive to eat because it was one of the only things we could barter for other items we needed. We could have killed more, but chances of long-term survival would have been less. The herd had to remain self-sustaining.

We just carried on and continued living through our struggle. The food we did have was mostly tasaw, a form of bread with salt and pepper. We cooked it in a homemade oven powered by dried wood. It tasted terrible and didn't have any smell. My mother would cook it for us. I never cooked anything. We would sit cross-legged on a cloth over the ground with all our family members. There were eight of us living in one room. We did everything there.

My dad is probably the calmest guy on earth. He has no hate for anyone. He always taught us to be respectful and kind, no matter what the other person did to us. I am not just saying all this because he is my dad. He always told me to never think about revenge if someone did anything terrible to me. I was told to be friendly and kind to them and forgive them. If you take revenge, you are as bad as they are.

7

My mother is hardworking, diligent, and intelligent. Even though she is illiterate, she has significant experience in life. She is also an excellent cook (even when she had little to work with). Growing up with my parents, we never felt that we were poor. We were always above other villagers in lifestyle. I don't mean that we were better people—we were just good at making the best out of everything.

Growing up, we learned that we had to earn our place in the village. Respect for elders is an essential value in our society. They kept the tiny community organized and disciplined. Any kid who disrespected an elder learned their lesson when they got whooped by their parents.

This teaching of respect was instilled in us from a young age and made village life peaceful. Robbery and murder were almost nonexistent. Everybody knew each other and had nowhere else to go. This deterred any wrongdoing against another family. Doing anything would turn the whole village against you, and this was enough to stop most crimes.

Village elders were our police officers, judges, and jury members. If something terrible happened, which was rare, the village elders would find a solution to sort it out. People were constantly checking with each other if something happened in the village. The first people to know about it were the village elders. They would hear about it after the morning prayer, which took place before sunrise. Mosques were our gathering areas, our courts—even weddings took place in the mosques. Of course, we didn't have any music. The Taliban were never known for their appreciation of instrumental arts.

Almost everyone was related, and everyone was friendly to each other. One time, someone brought a radio to our village from the city six hours away. People would invite him to their house for chai (tea) just so they could listen to the radio. It was interesting for all the villagers because none of us had seen radios before.

In one instance, a man tried to get in on a radio invitation by asking for a spoonful of sugar for his chai. Because food was scarce, sugar was a delicacy and carefully distributed in the village. He was denied the request because the entire house knew he had already gotten a spoonful the night before from a different home. This is how close and well connected the village was.

Most Afghans are social and caring people. We like coming together. For instance, the whole village would visit the house of a family who'd lost a loved one. They would come to embrace them and share their pain. Villagers would even stay with them and their family for three days. For the first three days, neighbors and relatives close by would bring food for the guests from their houses. We also held an annual ceremony for lost loved ones. Guests, traveling from other villages to visit the grieving, would be fed at the entire village's expense. This was common for times of grief but would vary from village to village.

As Muslims and Afghans, we have a religious tradition to feed the poor families on the third, seventh, and fortieth day. As Muslims, we believe that if someone does something good on your behalf, even after your death, Allah (God) will add it to their good deeds, and it will help on judgment day.

Afghan ceremonies were huge in sad and happy times. Weddings in our culture include everyone whether they were invited or not! It was common for 700 to a thousand people to come to traditional weddings. There would be a lot of guests that we didn't know. Poor people, beggars, neighbors, basically everyone who lived in our neighborhood would come to the wedding. If the bride and groom were rich and famous, the festivities would last for three days. If someone got married in northern Afghanistan, but their spouse was native to southern Afghanistan, their family would expect them to throw a wedding for each side of the family.

Male and female sections were separated if the wedding was in a hall. If it was in a house, the groom's house would be for the females, and three or four neighboring houses would be for the males. Neighbors would stand at the entrance of their homes to welcome the guests. Everyone was helpful. In most house weddings, we didn't have waiters to serve the food. Young males (especially the groom's friends) would stand in a line and pass the meal to each other in order to get it to the guests. Even guests standing in the line would help distribute food for the other guests.

For the female section, males would deliver the food to the doorsteps, and older females would take it from there. Female guests would help to feed the other female guests.

The groom's brothers and best friends would be there until the last moment. They would collect the dirty dishes and clean the neighbors' houses. In most cases, neighbors themselves would do it. Then, they would wash all the dirty dishes. You might think, where did all these dishes, plates, cups, and pretty much everything come from? We had stores that rented ceremonial supplies. It was cheap. We used the store's rental stuff. Then, the best friends would return everything to the store.

Generally, all Afghans like gatherings of any sort. As a kid, when I would get bored, I would walk to the hood and chill with my friends just to have company. We would sit and chat forever. We had a lot of stories. We wouldn't stop talking to one another and enjoyed every moment of it.

Sometimes I would go out with two of my best friends, Fred and Naq. We had a half-broken bicycle that we shared between us. One of us would ride it, one would sit in the back, and one would sit in front (between the wheel and seat). We would ride for thirty minutes to go to a famous Afghan soup cart. The owner had a cart and some chairs around it. He would cook one of the best soups in our area. It was a chicken soup. We would go there and buy some. We bought the cheapest version because we couldn't afford anything more than that.

Naq was living with his only brother. His mom and dad passed away when he was only a child. Fred's father passed away when he was very young too. Both of my best friends went through hard times like I did. We are still best friends to this day. They also worked as interpreters (terps) with Special Operations Forces for a few years, like I did, till they were both given Special Immigrant Visas (SIVs). They are both living in the U.S. now.

Chapter 2

My father was an army colonel in the old government. He was the communication officer for a brigade. I don't know a lot about the old government, but based on my father's stories, it was trustworthy and hardworking compared to the regime after 2001. After the fall of the old government by the Taliban's hand, my father first had to move back to the village from Kabul due to security reasons. At that point, everything kind of calmed down, and there was less of a security threat for him. It was hard to live and survive in the village, and we were running out of options. So, eventually, it was time to move back to a city, but this time, we went to Kabul, the capital of Afghanistan. We didn't have a car, so with the help of other villagers, we walked all the way from our village to the closest city, which was close to twenty-four hours of walking. Then, we asked a truck driver to take us to Kabul in the back of his truck.

When my family moved to Kabul, I was about seven years old. We stayed in my uncle's house for three months. We had no other place to go. Even though my uncle's house wasn't large, he still was hospitable and let us stay there. This is commonplace in Afghanistan. When relatives come from different provinces and villages to Kabul, the first place they will stay will be the house of their closest family member, like a brother, sister, aunt, or uncle. Like every other capital in the world, Kabul was expensive to live in. For me, city life was different, easier, and school was closer and better (though the lessons still contained extremist teachings).

Because of my father's past military career, he had to find another line of work. With the help of my uncle, my father found a job as a servant in a house in Kabul. It was a regular house but made from bricks and concrete. The owner was wealthy, and the place was expensive for that time. It had six bedrooms and a big yard and two separate bedrooms for workers like my family. We cleaned the house, brought groceries, baked bread, and cooked for them. My mom and uncle's wife did the cooking and baking. They would cook the usual Afghan traditional food. It was simple food, nothing fancy. In return, my family got a room to live in and got to eat some of the food. It wasn't a lot of food even though it was better compared to what we used to eat.

Life wasn't pleasant.

The winters in Kabul were cold, the summers were hot, and there was not much to do. My brothers and I went in search of jobs in the city. I think I was around seven or eight years old. It wasn't easy to get a job. We had no newspapers, television, or radios. There was no media from which we could see who was hiring. There was no place to put out ads for jobs. I had to go through all the shops in the city and ask them if they needed a laborer. Eventually, after three months of searching, my father found me a job.

I started working as a laborer in a big store. It was a flower store. We didn't have fresh flowers because people couldn't afford it. We only had flowers for ceremonies. The shop owner was a good guy and was generous to me. My job was to bag the sold flowers and prepare them for transportation, then fill the empty space on the shelves with more flowers from storage. I had to walk thirty-five to forty minutes to get to and from work every day and night. Luckily, my new job made it easier on the family. My mother stopped working. She was ill, and we didn't want her to get worse. The store didn't have anything useful to learn. There wasn't much chance for progression or building a career off being a store laborer. But it was still better than nothing. Besides all of that, I was happy that I had a job, and my family was happy too.

My brothers also had good luck in finding jobs. My oldest brother started working as a house painter's assistant. My second oldest brother worked in a tire shop changing tires on small cars. My third brother worked in a shoe store. I am the fourth son.

I started going to school for half the day and working for the other half. All the schools are half-day in Kabul. You either go in the morning or afternoon. Morning school was from 8:00 a.m. to 12:00 p.m., and afternoon was from 1:00 p.m. to 5:00 p.m.

I was determined and focused in my studies, hoping for a better future even though there was little hope that I would live long enough to see it. The life expectancy of a boy my age living in Afghanistan was not high. Poverty, starvation, and civil war are a few of the reasons I didn't expect to live long. The school I was going to was called Habibia School. Most of the school was destroyed in the Afghan civil war between the warlords. It was one of the best and biggest schools of its time, and we were still studying in tents. The subjects focused almost entirely on religious studies. There was no math, chemistry, physics, sports, or world history. The only school subject was the Quran, and the teachers in Kabul were also extremist. We had no option but to listen.

I know a lot about my religion, and I am a good Muslim. I pray five times a day. But unlike the Taliban, I believe in the importance of free will when praying to God. Based on what we believe, God created free will so you can choose how you want to worship your creator. I do not believe in forced worship. Religion and prayer should come from the heart. Your prayer won't be accepted if you are not praying from your heart. We have an Afghan expression saying "Khepl me Yar Sara Zele Me Pe Kando Ke," meaning "I am sitting with the love of my life, but my heart is in a trash yard." The Taliban were forcing people to practice their version of Islam, but Islam came by peace, and it should remain peaceful. What we mean with religion of peace is that God doesn't like you to pray to him if you don't want to and others are forcing you. The Taliban committed many wrongs during their regime, which we will talk about later in the book.

Afghan weekends are Thursdays (Panjshanbe) and Fridays (Juma in Pashto). These two days are holy for Muslims for two reasons. First, Muslims attend service at the mosque on Friday for prayer. Second, we believe the final day of all days will happen on a Friday. This day is usually for praying and spending time with family and friends. A lot of Afghans go on picnics on Fridays. Two of the famous places a lot of people would go to were Qargha (Blue Lake) and the Paghman district. They are both located in Kabul city and popular because people couldn't afford to go

13

anywhere outside the city. Luckily, I was off work on Fridays and would help my mom and dad with house chores.

The family's efforts with our jobs eventually paid off. We bought a house with the savings we had collected and took a loan from relatives and friends. The loan was for around 200,000 Afghani. Our income in a month was about 2,500 Afghani total ($40 U.S.). The house had two rooms but needed some construction, and because we couldn't afford to hire help, we did it ourselves. My father created the plan on how to build more rooms and expand the house. We made three more rooms. It was challenging to balance school, work, and construction. It was all hard labor. I never liked hard labor, and I still hate it. We moved right into the house after we bought it. Over the years, we worked on it to make it a better home. It still didn't have any electricity or running water.

Afghan homes were mainly made out of mud and were typically one or two stories tall. Mud isn't known for its durability or for being weight-bearing. It isn't ideal to build houses out of mud, but we couldn't afford other materials, and we had plenty of dirt. It was cheaper to repair in the event of a disaster. We used log, straw, and clay for building the house. The walls were very thick, at least twelve to twenty inches. The good thing about mud houses was that they were warm in the winter and cool in the summer. Later on, modern housing became more prominent in large Afghan cities.

—

I was eleven years old when the U.S. entered Afghanistan. Some Afghans describe it as liberation. Others describe it as an invasion and occupation. Because the U.S. had a familiar and powerful name at the time, people were hoping a change would take place and the country would be better. At that time, I was working half of the day in a clothing store and going to school during the other half. It was late 2001. We heard and saw helicopters and planes coming to Kabul. The invasion almost happened overnight. When we woke up the following morning, people were playing music and dancing on the streets. Everyone seemed happy. The Taliban regime was an oppressive regime; none of us liked it. It was a dictatorship at its peak, and the worst part of it was a bad economy.

Some soldiers came to Kabul Airport, and some went to Bagram Airfield. Bagram is a district of Parwan province, and it is located north of Kabul province. It is a colossal airbase. At the beginning of the war, it was just ruins. But later, it changed into Little America. That is what people called it. You could see Bagram Airfield from miles and miles away during nighttime.

The Russians had used Bagram Airfield when they invaded Afghanistan. It was built specifically for their invasion. My father told me they used it to provide air support to Russian troops. When the Taliban took over the Afghan government in 1996, they used Bagram as one of their headquarters. After the fall of the Taliban regime, the U.S. took over Bagram Airfield, and they used it as one of their central air bases to support troops on the ground. The U.S. also used Bagram Airfield for their operations under the broad mission name of Operation Enduring Freedom (OEF). The Taliban didn't put up much of a resistance to the U.S. They fled quickly and left the country to the U.S. and North Atlantic Treaty Organization (NATO) Forces.

For Afghans, it is always funny that invasions come and go like the wind. Many empires have once claimed Afghanistan only to find that it cannot be controlled. Alexander the Great, Genghis Khan, the British, and the Russians have tried, and now the United States would try. We have an Afghan expression: "What comes easy will go easy." It is effortless to invade Afghanistan, but it is impossible to hold it. We have witnessed this many times in the last forty years. It is always hard to keep the country together.

The Taliban regime had totally collapsed the old Afghan government. Now that the Taliban had been ousted, we had no economy, and we lost everything. What little we had under the Taliban was gone. A lot of people were living in pure poverty. Many Afghans immigrated, especially to Iran, Pakistan, Europe, and America, due to the war that was festering in the country. The U.S. started building more military bases and expanded OEF. People weren't talking about Americans much though. The only time Afghans talked about Americans was when they were looking for jobs. There weren't really any feelings about it. We were all just happy that we were freed.

America sought to establish a government and was looking for someone to lead it. It took a couple of years to get some sort of a government—a government consisting of Afghan civil war warlords who were greedy for power and corruption. It was a terrible way to establish a government. They found a man named Hamid Karzai who was from southern Afghanistan. Afghans didn't know anything about him. He was brought forward fresh out of the thin air. We didn't even know who had suggested him to the U.S. government as someone to nominate as the Afghan president. The U.S. was in power in the country, and we had no choice but to accept whomever they brought to us as a leader. We couldn't resist. Our leaders were all bought and paid for with foreign money. I mean they have been in this fight for money and power. This was an excellent chance for the warlords to get what they wanted.

Hamid Karzai was essential to the U.S. government, so protecting him was a high priority for the U.S. He was guarded first by U.S. Special Operations Forces by the unit named Operational Detachment Alpha (ODA). ODA is a twelve-man Green Beret team. Unfortunately, while Karzai was traveling through cities to become the future Afghanistan president, members of the ODA 547 were killed, and some were wounded during a friendly airstrike in southern Afghanistan. Rangers were also part of his protection team.

Despite the fact that many Afghans didn't know who he was, Karzai became the president of Afghanistan in June 2002 when the Afghan traditional assembly called Loya Jirga selected him. Lead members of the assembly were promised positions in the future government. This just proves that, from the beginning, the system was corrupt.

Hamid Karzai was one of the most corrupt presidents Afghanistan ever had. Hundreds of billions of dollars were coming into our country, but Karzai didn't use any of it for the betterment of the country's future. All he did was bluff behind a microphone. All of our leaders were busy with their personal businesses that profited greatly from the government contracts they gave to themselves. It was all a game for personal wealth, and even though U.S. military officers in the lower ranks knew about the corruption, their higher leadership refused to listen to them. With such a corrupt government and no one to fix the problem, the rich only got richer and the poor only got poorer. I was still a young teenager at the time, so I don't know the details, but this was the general sentiment of the Afghan people. Karzai was not the Afghan people's president. He was whatever the U.S. needed him to be.

Years went by, and getting a job was still tricky. The most lucrative jobs were either working for the Afghan government or working for the U.S. A career in the Afghan government was not about the knowledge you had or the skills you learned. It was about who you knew and your ability to influence that official in order for you to get employed. If you were lucky to know or be related to someone in office and get hired, the government pay wasn't great. For a regular government job, you would get paid 10,000 Afghani ($120 U.S.) a month. A teacher's salary was $100 a month. Afghan families are large, and it was hard to survive with that income alone. Those with that income, though, were better off than other citizens who had little to no chance of finding a job in that sector.

Since government leaders hired only their friends and relatives, many officers were promoted to the general ranks. We called them Machini Generals, meaning they were generals promoted by machines. They were incapable and had no experience leading an army. People weren't promoted due to merit, and because of that, no one trusted the Afghan Army leadership. Our highest-ranking officials were incompetent.

As this was occurring, the U.S. bases were hiring people who could speak English to fill jobs as terps, electricians, mechanics, and manual laborers. By 2013, we had around twenty-five thousand Afghans working at Bagram Airfield. Construction, transportation, and logistical companies started getting contracts and hired thousands of Afghans. Back then, three questions were common among Afghans. After greeting each other, they would ask, "Where do you work? How much do they pay? Are they hiring?" Of course, the questions were asked in sequence. English and computer courses started. A lot of Afghans were learning English and

17

computer skills to get a job. Thousands and thousands of Afghan boys and girls were attending these education courses. Many of them dreamed of learning English for more than just a job. Most wanted to learn the language to help at a university or to get scholarships to attend a university. They were setting themselves up for a prosperous future to support their families. This goal was rooted in tradition because most Afghan families rely on one or two males to provide for the whole family. Everyone wants to better themselves.

Chapter 3

One of the requirements to get a job in a U.S. or NATO base was speaking English. It was essential to be able to read, write, and speak the English language. You also needed computer skills like being able to use Microsoft Office (primarily Word and Excel). You would get tested on each separately.

I always wanted to work in the military. I admired the U.S. military. I was almost eighteen when I heard about the experiences of terps or people who worked for the U.S. government. Everyone was happy about the salary, food, and facilities. I always checked with friends in the neighborhood that were working with the U.S. Armed Forces. That is when I told myself that I needed to find a job at a U.S. base. Nothing could have been better than getting a job with the U.S. military. It was a dream (I thought). There were so many English courses in the big cities, and a lot of people were going to these courses. The first priority for everyone was to get a job by learning English. These jobs weren't just with the military. There were a lot of non-military organizations such as the United Nations, UNICEF, the World Food Programme, and so on.

I enrolled in an English course. I didn't have a car or ride. I was walking to most of the places I needed to go. The class was a twenty-minute walk from our house, and the classes were only one hour a day. They were from Saturday until Thursday. I studied English for eight months. We learned through a system called the International Rescue Committee (IRC). It wasn't advanced English, but it could help you start with something. While studying, I heard about this new English system that was invented by the Afghans. The class would take ten months, and it was called "the ten-month program." Yes, I know it was a very creative name.

I was halfway into the first course of IRC when I stopped and went to start the ten-month program. The IRC system was old and made back in 1990, and the new system was more updated. It was better, and I learned quicker. The IRC system would take close to two years to learn, but the ten-month program cut the time in half. The one downside was that the ten-month English training center was a forty-minute walk from our house.

I was halfway through that program and in the tenth grade of high school when I received an offer from the course owner to become the manager and study for free. The catch was that I wouldn't get paid for being a manager. I know you might ask, who works for free? It is a complicated story. I quit the clothing store when I started the new course. So, I was assigned as a manager in the English training center I was studying in. I needed to get a job, and learning English was one way to get a better job. The pay was different in U.S. bases, starting from $600 to $1,800 a month. Working with a conventional unit, you would be paid $600 to $900 depending on the company you were contracted with.

Conventional units were the U.S. Army and Air Force units that we could join out of basic training. They made up the majority of the Army and Air Force. Special Operations had the best pay. But with better pay came more risk. Special Forces had small teams. They often went after high-value targets (HVTs), and it was expected that they would see a lot of combat. Special Operations bases were also inside the most Taliban-controlled areas in the country. For civilians who had never seen war and had no combat training, working alongside the best operators in the world would be difficult and dangerous.

—

I had no political point of view back then. My main focus was just getting hired and being able to bring food back to my family. It was January 2007. I was sixteen years old and went to one of the U.S. bases in Kabul city, Police District 9 (PD 9). This was one of the famous bases in Kabul named Camp Phoenix. The Afghans called it AFSOTAR. The base used to be a Russian transport area. I went there several times and stood in line for two or three hours. PD 9 was not a really residential area. It was where a lot of construction companies were. It was a two-hour drive from our home. We would go there and stand in the line for hours to hear if they were hiring that day or not. One of the times, I had to walk all the way back home; it took me six hours. I didn't have the money to get a taxi. I had to miss work and school on the days I went to Camp Phoenix. We didn't have any information about what days they were hiring new terps.

I never liked the Afghans working in that base. Some of them were selfish and talked to us with a lot of ego. While we were standing in line, we had no choice but to listen. They would speak to us like we were low-life people because we were in need of a job, even though all of them came from families like ours. A U.S. soldier would come to the gate and say they were not hiring today.

One time, I got lucky and was allowed in for an interview, but I failed at the gate when another terp who was working there gave me three sentences to translate. I only missed one word: election console. I didn't know the meaning of this phrase. In fact, I still don't know the definition of this phrase, and I am fluent enough to have written this book in English.

"You failed," he said.

I begged him, "Please, give me a chance!"

"No. Leave!"

A U.S. soldier came in and pulled me out of the group. He told me to leave the base. The worst thing was that this wasn't part of the interview. We were just waiting to get security checked to go inside the base to do the interview there. Not only did some of the Afghans have an attitude, but some of the U.S. soldiers standing there as security had a punk attitude too. The few don't represent all, but it was disheartening.

Anger and sadness consumed me at that time, but when I grew older, I realized that God had shown me kindness by letting me fail on that day. I learned from those failures, and it helped me get better for the future I had yet to experience. I did tell my family about my failure though. It was a wrong way to kick people out of an interview, especially if it was a matter over one word.

Three months came and went, and I was still desperately looking for work. I asked everyone I knew if they had any idea where I could find a job. I asked them to call or text me if anyone was hiring. One guy told me the military was hiring down in Kandahar. It was 420 km (260 miles) away. Afghanistan is a small country compared to the United States; 260 miles is a long distance.

My journey would have to be by bus, and that would take me through three provinces that were hotbeds for Taliban activity. Most of the fight was in the southern part of the country. Provinces like Helmand, Kandahar, Zabul, Urozgan, Ghazni, Wardak. I would have to travel through Wardak, Ghazni, and Zabul. It was about a seven- to nine-hour drive by bus or a one-hour flight. Flight tickets were $100, which was very expensive, but the bus ticket was only $10 to $15.

Since Afghanistan has limited roadways, the highway I'd have to take was a high strategic priority to the United States. Any road that could support large military vehicles carrying supplies and other logistical goods was vital to the Coalition's ability to maintain operational bases across the country.

The Kabul to Kandahar highway also had many Taliban checkpoints. With the help of their informants, the Taliban mainly focused on controlling the civilian population that was traveling. If they didn't focus on the civilians, they would call out Coalition convoys in preparation for an ambush farther down the road. Informants were everywhere. Many of these informants were coerced into it, others were bribed, and some just supported the Taliban cause. The Taliban's goal was similar to that of other Afghan warlords': to gain power and rule the country. But the Taliban used the excuse of the Holy War to recruit people for this war. Many times, the bus drivers themselves were informants. The informants would report anything suspicious to the Taliban.

They would scope you out at the central bus station where the passengers were getting loaded into the buses going to different locations. If you were able to blend in with the people native to the area, it was hard for them to spot you. Wearing Afghan traditional clothing was one way of blending in with the villagers and people in the area. This clothing was a long-sleeve shirt that hung past the knees and a turban.

The Taliban had an intricate and well-practiced system. If you were flagged as suspicious by the informants, they would report that information to the Taliban in Wardak or Ghazni via a cellphone. Taliban leadership would tell their soldiers at the checkpoints to stop and check the bus that was described by the informants. The ones they looked for were people seeking to work for the Americans and the Coalition. They also looked for those who were directly working with the U.S. or Coalition Forces as a terp or a commando or with Special Operations Forces. Sometimes they would even stop you just because they didn't like you. If you were suspected of any of these, they would take you off the bus. Only the lucky would get away with being beaten and whipped; most times, you were killed. They executed you by decapitation on the side of the road with a large knife or sword in front of everyone, even in front of women and children. It was dangerous and brutal.

Any mother or father would be worried about their child traveling on one of the most dangerous roads in Afghanistan, so it wasn't unusual that my parents were scared. My safety was not guaranteed; security on the road wasn't good at all. They were also anxious because of the risk of the job I was getting myself into at Kandahar. It wasn't just the possibility of getting caught by the insurgents. There were other risks involved in it, such as getting blown up by an IED and losing body parts. Living as a disabled person in our country is nearly impossible. You can't work, and there is nothing to support vets or disabled people.

No parent wants their child in war, but one way or another, I was going to war. I was still eighteen at the time. I had no other option. I had to go do something to financially help my family. I left on the twelfth of March knowing the risk that lay ahead. I only had 1,000 Afghani, which was equivalent to $15. The bus ticket to Kandahar was 750 Afghani alone. It was a one-way ticket, and it could be a one-way trip. I didn't know if I would get a job in Kandahar. If I failed, I would have no money to come back to Kabul. But life couldn't be more of a struggle than it already was, and I had to put all the trust I had into my faith.

It was a cold winter night. There was a lot of snow on the ground, and it was freezing. The sky was clear, and you could see many of the stars. We were living in Police District 7, Kabul city. It was a sad night when I said goodbye to my family, especially my parents. My mom was crying. As a mother, it was hard for her to see her child go on a journey and not know if he would come back alive. She had no choice. My father, a respected figure renowned for his calm and patient demeanor, said, "Son, if this is what you choose, good luck and my prayers are with you."

For us Muslims, prayers mean a lot, especially coming from our parents. We believe if we have their blessings with us, God will also be with us. Respecting and taking care of our parents and family has a big reward in this world and the world after this life. In our religion, people who don't respect their parents will never be allowed to enter paradise. We are expected to care for them when they are old and sick and lack the means to provide for themselves.

I had my parents' prayers, but I was still worried. I walked to my room with a lot of thoughts. *What will happen? Will I pass? Will I survive the highway of death?* All these thoughts were keeping me awake. I was a kid with no combat experience entering a warzone. Up to this point, I had never traveled anywhere in my life. I had never been alone, so far from my family. I knew I was entering Taliban territory, traveling to a well-known U.S. base, to try to get a job working for a cause that would get me executed if the Taliban found out. I was a young, inexperienced kid going to war with the terrorists on behalf of the oppressed. I was awake until 2 a.m.

I woke up around 3:30 a.m. I had a pair of Afghan clothes from when the Taliban used to be in control. I wore those clothes to blend in with the villagers. I couldn't wear any western style clothing; it would immediately give me away as being sympathetic to the Americans. I didn't have much to take. I grabbed another pair of clothes and put it in a small backpack. That was all. I took nothing else.

I didn't want to wake my mom and dad. I couldn't bear to see them in tears again. I needed to stay strong. I quietly walked to my brother's room and wakened him. When I woke him, he asked me, "Is it time to go?"

I responded, "Yes, brother, time to go!"

We silently left the room. His vehicle was parked outside. We quietly walked to the car, then left. It was four in the morning. My brother took me to the bus station. On the way there, he gave me some advice and told me about the same journey he'd taken before me.

My brother used to be a combat terp in the western part of Afghanistan. He told me, "Do your job and always watch your surroundings while on patrol. A small mistake might cost your life."

I asked him to drop me off one mile away from the bus station for security reasons in case someone was watching the incoming cars. I hated goodbyes and had had my fair share of them the past week. It was hard telling my brother goodbye too. I knew it could be the last I saw him in this life, but I held myself together. I got out of the vehicle and said goodbye to my brother.

"You will be fine, lil bro," he said.

It was now five in the morning. Everyone and everything looked suspicious to me. I was glancing around scared but tried hard to keep myself together. I didn't want to be noticed. When I went to buy a ticket, the ticket seller looked me up and down. I was about to tell him, "What the hell are you looking at?!" but I held my tongue. I didn't want to give him any hint of my intentions. I couldn't trust anyone but myself.

He asked me, "Where are you going?"

"I am going to Kandahar."

"What are you going to do there?"

"I'm going to work with my friend who is a truck mechanic."

This was a lie. It is very common in my country for people to easily start chatting with us and asking random questions. If they aren't polite, we don't respond, but the ticket seller was being polite. I took the ticket and started walking to the departure area. So many buses and so many people were going to southern Afghanistan. I walked to the bus that was going to Kandahar, then entered and sat in my seat. I was the last one on. An old gentleman was sitting next to me. The driver informed everyone that we would depart in ten minutes.

I turned off my phone and put the SIM card in my socks. I did this because the first thing the insurgents did at their checkpoints while questioning someone was check the individual's phone and contact numbers. If anything looked suspicious, they would call the contacts, introducing themselves as the police, and tell them that the owner of this phone had a car accident and that they want to know who he was. If your story didn't match, you would be killed. There was no more questioning or prosecution. There was no court or jury. If they felt like they should kill you, they killed you.

The bus headed to the first checkpoint, which was ten minutes away from the main station. I had never been to this part of the city, so I recited my prayers. We arrived at the Kabul-Wardak gate. Kabul province has four entrances: North, which goes to the northern provinces. South, which goes to southern provinces. West to the western provinces, and east to the eastern provinces. Afghan National Police (ANP) Forces stopped us at the gate and asked the driver some questions. Finding nothing suspicious, they let us go. After twenty-five minutes of driving, we arrived in Taliban-controlled territory. We reached Pole Sorkh (Red Bridge). The Taliban usually had checkpoints here but, luckily, not that morning.

By sunrise, we arrived at Tangi Wardak. Tangi Wardak was one of the critical districts where much of the Taliban leadership resided. Tangi Valley is where Extortion 17 happened. (On August 6, 2011, thirty-eight Special Operations operators were unfortunately killed in Tangi Valley, Wardak, Afghanistan, when their Chinook helicopter, call sign "Extortion 17," was blown out of the sky).

Tangi Wardak was the area where all of the commanders, Red Unit fighters (Taliban special fighters), and foreign fighters (from Pakistani and Chechen) were staying. It was a beautiful province, but it was also a warzone. The word Tangi means "valley." This province was known for its green terrain that was flush with trees and rivers. It was filled with streams and beautiful fresh air, a marvelous place.

As we were driving, I saw a Taliban checkpoint on the road ahead. They usually consisted of three or five fighters with PKMs (7.62 belt-fed machine gun) and AK-47s. The Taliban fighters mainly used motorcycles as their form of transportation. Motorcycles only cost $300 back then for a used one and $700 for a new one. They were easy to leave around and could go anywhere in the villages. They were also a smaller, more mobile target.

The driver stopped our bus. Two scary-looking Taliban fighters walked onto the bus and started asking questions. They kind of looked like zombies. They had long hair and long beards. They wore a stinky and abhorrent sort of perfume—we call it the perfume of the dead. But they were not scary because of how they looked. They were dangerous because they could take your life at any moment without even proving you guilty of anything. The feeling was like you were walking by an execution site and didn't want to look or stare at them because they might execute you just for looking at them the wrong way. They asked random people things like, "Where are you coming from? Where are you going? What is your job? Where are you from?" They looked at me from head to toe. I acted casual. One small wrong move could cost me my head. They only asked passengers if they looked or acted suspicious, and most of the time, they had the information from their spotters who were reporting from the main bus station.

They told the driver to follow the lead motorcycle, and they led us to a village thirty minutes away from the main road. I later learned they would do this if there was an operation happening or a convoy coming down the main road. We arrived in an unknown area. It was one of the villages deep down in the central valley. The village was similar to other Afghan villages in the country. It had mud houses, farms, gardens, and dirt roads. They would usually take people to a village far away from the highway. They didn't want to alert the security forces in the area, like the U.S. and the Afghan military.

The two Taliban fighters got back on the bus and started saying, "We know who you all are. If you hand yourself over to us, we will give you a chance. But if you don't and you waste our time, you will be executed."

I was scared but told myself not to worry since I had no evidence of my intentions on me. I figured that they were just using the threat as a trick to find their enemies or raise suspicions of who might be against them. They kept calling for five minutes. They whispered something to each other, then got off the bus. When we saw they were about to leave, it was a massive relief for all of us. While they were on the bus and questioning people, it felt like walking close to an enormous burning fire. We felt like if this fire touched us, we might burn very quickly, and no one would be there to save us.

The two fighters on motorcycles led the bus back to the main road. Then, they took a different route. Once we reached the road, they left us alone. We kept driving until we arrived in Ghazni province. Ghazni security wasn't good either, but the Taliban didn't have as much control as they had over Wardak. At that time, the Taliban didn't have a lot of manpower to cover both Ghazni and Wardak, and there was a significant presence of NATO in the area.

We passed through Ghazni. The weather felt a bit warmer, and the area looked a little greener. It meant we were close to the southern part of the country. We started seeing villages. This meant we were close to the next province on our way, Zabul province. Zabul wasn't as green as Wardak. Most parts of the province looked more like desert. It was dry and didn't have as many trees or as much green terrain as Wardak or Ghazni.

We hit a traffic jam. I thought to myself, "How can there be a traffic jam on a highway?" We started hearing gunfire. One or two minutes later, we saw a large number of cars backed up on the highway. When we stopped and checked with people that were already there, they told us a U.S. convoy had been ambushed by the Taliban in Zabul province. Thinking back on it, this was probably why we were led on the alternate route by the Taliban on the motorcycle. They didn't want civilian vehicles to get in the way of their ambush or possibly trip an IED meant for the U.S.

We waited for an hour before we saw the vehicles moving again. I saw some trucks that were transporting food and fuel for Coalition Forces burned down and left on the side of the road. We couldn't see if there were any casualties. There was an extensive line of vehicles just waiting to pass by, but we had to stop and wait until the fight was over. It was common to see ambushes on the highways, and the Taliban were careless as usual. They didn't care if people were going to get hurt or killed by shooting in the direction of the road.

It was 2 p.m. when I arrived in Kandahar province. The area was called Do Rahi (which translates to Cross Section). I got off the bus in a city full of people who spoke a different language than me. We both spoke Pashtu, but they spoke a different dialect. The people had a different culture and look. This is also the city that was the birthplace of the Taliban's leader.

Kandahar province is desert-like. You only see trees or green terrain close to the villages or where people are living. The main part of the city wasn't as big as it is now. It was a smaller city at the time. The easiest way to compare Kandahar to the U.S. would be a city like Phoenix, Arizona. It has a similar type of terrain and weather. It has green areas but only in small parts. That's because of the hot weather in the province and the lack of water to farm.

I had an awkward feeling. I didn't know where Kandahar Airfield (KAF) was, and I was scared to ask local people in the area. I had no idea who was friend or foe. My friends had already told me where to go when I arrived in the city, but when you are on the ground with a death threat, a small mistake can cost you your life.

I crossed a street and saw a cab parked on the side of the road. I approached the cab driver and asked him, "How much will you charge for a trip to the airfield?"

He said, "250 Afgani."

It was a forty-five-minute trip to the airfield. I was willing to pay that much, but I had to play the game if I didn't want to get caught. I didn't want to attract any attention, and I didn't want to look rich or like a guy who had never been to Kandahar. I told him, "Oh wow, man! That is too much for me! I am unemployed and don't have that much."

There were a few minutes of bargaining. It wasn't a long conversation. I am quick at negotiating. If I tell someone a price, then I am not willing to pay more. And when I give a price, I already thought about giving that person a fair deal so they will make a reasonable profit too. That is my nature. Price rates are not set or standard in Afghanistan, and we agreed to a deal at 200 Afghani. I got into the cab, and he started driving.

The drivers navigate by memory. We didn't and still don't use Google Maps or any type of GPS in our country. The car was a 1992 Toyota Corolla that had no air conditioning. Toyota vehicles are standard in Afghanistan. They are like the AK-47: built different, built to last. These cars are tough and don't use a lot of gas—unlike American models.

I had hot air blowing on my face, but it was still better than nothing. The cab driver kept looking at me through the rearview mirror. I knew he had some questions. He waited for the moment to open that usual Afghan conversation. This conversation was one of my funniest memories from the trip. It was also a dangerous moment. I didn't know if the driver was a member of the Taliban network or not. That is why I couldn't trust anyone on the way.

The driver asked, "Where do you come from?"

"From Kabul," I answered.

"How is life in Kabul?"

"It is good, I guess."

"Why do you want to go to Kandahar Airfield?"

I wanted to play it cool and not look suspicious to him. I said, "I want to sell Afghan fast food in front of the airport."

He smiled in a weird way and said, "Are you sure you want to sell fast food there?"

I was thinking to myself, *Why didn't he believe my story!* I worried that he was working for the bad guys as a spotter. *What if he is armed and takes me to the Taliban by force?* I thought.

We passed through villages that were on our route. Finally, we arrived in a big desert with a military airfield built on it. There were no houses, villages, or people around it. I was thinking, *Where the heck is he taking me?* I wanted to ask the driver but decided not to as it might give away that I did not know the area at all.

I broke the silence. "They were talking about adding more roads to the airport. Is this still the only road to the airport?" I said this with a tone that implied my annoyance with the new government and their lack of usefulness.

"Yeah, this is the only road. I don't think they will be connecting more roads to the airport because I don't see any others close by the city!"

I kept on with my facade and said, "Nah, nah, I am sure I heard that on the news, but maybe I am wrong."

KAF was one of the largest U.S. and NATO airfields in Afghanistan. There were many military bases there, including the Afghan National Army Corps and the Afghan military apartments. The apartments were built by the Russians for the Afghan Air Force officers' families. I started seeing military towers and two Blackhawks landing in the airfield. It was huge.

I wanted to confirm with the driver that this was the airport. "These Americans took so much of our ground for their base."

"Yeah, man! Have you ever been inside?"

"No, I hate Americans and don't like to work for them."

"Yeah, they invaded our country, and they should be kicked out of this country like we kicked the Russians out of our beloved motherland."

We arrived at our destination, KAF's gate. It was located in a desert, away from villages and civilians. There was only one tiny village close to it. It probably wasn't even a village, just six or seven mud houses. They were located toward the back side of the airfield. The road was a dirt road. You would see only one or two cars pass by it a day. Other than the airfield, this was the middle of nowhere and a terrible spot to do any kind of commercial business.

I paid the cab driver.

He asked me, "Are you sure you still want to sell fast food here?"

I knew he found out I was lying, but I still stuck to my story. "Yeah! Yeah!"

When he drove off, I started laughing and said to myself, "You dumb ass. Who were you going to sell the fast food to? The camels?!"

I kept laughing for a minute or two. The Afghan National Army (ANA) soldiers that were holding security at the gate probably thought I was crazy. All the security personnel at the gate were Afghans. There were no U.S. or NATO forces among them.

I approached them, and they yelled, "Who are you, and what do you want?"

I responded, "I am here for a job interview at the Afghan National Army Corporation."

They searched me and walked me in. I was expecting to reach the ANA Corp. office in a couple of minutes, but, man, I was terribly wrong! It took me around twenty-five minutes to get to the terp camp. As I said, KAF was huge. I eventually found the building that was home to the terps. They were hiring translators and terps for Coalition Forces.

I went to the security at the gate and told them, "I have an interview appointment." This was another lie. They searched me and my backpack and asked a few questions. This interview was with the contracting company. I am not sure if they were officially registered as an American company or an Afghan company, but the owner was Afghan American. They had a small office on KAF.

They asked, "Who sent you here? How did you hear about this company?"

I assumed they were just checking if I was legitimate and not a terrorist. I answered their questions, and they seemed satisfied. After their checking procedures, they directed me to a big hall and told me to wait here.

Many stressful thoughts came to my head. It's normal to stress for a job interview, but it was vital for me to get hired here. I left school in the tenth grade, came all the way down here, went through all these risks, and worst of all, I didn't have enough money to get back to Kabul.

One of the managers came and asked me who I was and what I wanted. I told him, "I am here for a job interview, and I want to get hired as an interpreter." He told me to sit down in the waiting area. I waited for about fifteen to twenty minutes before another manager showed up. He asked me, "What's your name, and who sent you here?"

I answered, "My name is Yousuf. I was sent here by Steve." All of the Afghans working with Coalition Forces had call signs because it was hard for the Americans and the other nations' forces to pronounce or read our names. It was a kind of nickname and helped keep identities more secure over the radio and while talking to the locals.

One of the managers came to me and also asked me some questions in English—questions like "Who sent you here? How did you hear about this company, and where are you from?" Then, he told me to come to his office in five minutes.

My concern and tension exploded in me like a bomb. I started worrying and giving heed to all these negative thoughts. *What if you fail? What questions might they ask? Is it gonna be more about speaking or reading and writing?*

After five minutes, I went inside and sat down. He asked me some simple questions like how long I had been studying English and what I had been doing before coming to the company. He did all this as a form of background check.

From there, he gave me a few simple sentences in Dari and Pashto to translate into English. Then, he gave me some English sentences and told me to translate them into Dari and Pashto. After ten minutes of interview, he told me to wait outside, so I went and sat in the hall. I thought that was just the verbal interview and that I might get called for a test on paper in a few minutes. However, fifteen minutes later, he came back with a little piece of paper and told me that I had passed the interview. I can't describe the happy feeling I had when he gave me that news.

After the interview, they gave me a list of items to buy. It included shower stuff and cleaning tools. This was a requirement because most bases weren't providing shower stuff to the terps. They took me inside a barracks room and told me to pick a bed for myself. These barracks were more of a big hall with a lot of beds inside. You could choose any bed you wanted, as long as no one was using it. They all looked the same and came with an equally poor-quality mattress. This company was ripping off NATO and the terps. They charged NATO a lot of money for terps, and very little of it made its way to the terps themselves.

I went to Kandahar city the following day and bought the stuff I was told to purchase. To get to Kandahar city, I had to walk to the main entrance of the airfield, then wait for a taxi on the highway. We use Line Taxi all over the country. A Line Taxi is a specific station for a particular route between places. It works like a bus stop might in more developed countries. This is how Afghan people would travel short distances like to and from work. To rent a taxi, you either go to the specific station or stand next to the road on the route the taxis take. The driver will point with his hand or finger when he is getting close to you. That pointing is his way of asking, "Are you waiting for a ride?" You respond by shaking your hand or your head to indicate yes or no. We have been using this system for years, and we are still using the same method.

The funny story was that I only had 50 Afghani (50 cents) left in my pocket when I was back at the camp. I told myself that I was going to go to a barber shop and shave my head so I wouldn't have to deal with hair problems. Unfortunately, I lost the money and couldn't go to the barber for the next few months. My hair is curly. I'll let you imagine how that looked after a couple of months.

We were given uniforms, body armor, and a helmet. We weren't given any boots. The food was awful and unhealthy in the terp camp. It was either over-cooked or half-cooked. Even when it wasn't burnt or raw, it still lacked any taste. The cooks used a lot of unhealthy oil to cook the food. The dining facility (DFAC) was dirty. After a health inspection was done on the compound by the U.S. military, they found out that the drinking water had 60 percent bacteria in it.

None of the terps had good memories from that contracting company owned by an Afghan American. It was a small compound with a small grass area where we would all sit in the evenings. We weren't allowed to leave the camp in the morning, but they would let us go on a break from 4 p.m. to sunset. There was a little Afghan market between KAF and the Afghan ANA Corp. We would all go there to buy some drinks from the Afghan market, chill with friends, then come back by sunset. Every terp had the same idea. You would always see a crowd coming out of the camp in the afternoons.

Chapter 4

The company hiring terps was a contracting company. The way we would be engaged and sent out was by contracts. The army told the civilian company that it needed a certain number of terps with specific qualifications. The company would then find people who could serve in the role and would hire them on a contractual basis. The company made money from filling the slots. There were multiple companies supplying this need—this was just the first one I worked for.

It was March 13, 2007, when I was called into the manager's office to get my first assignment. I was told that I would be leaving for my final destination the next day. I was ecstatic. I don't know how to explain it. It wasn't the kind of excitement that might come with getting a birthday gift. I never had a birthday or received a gift, so I can't compare it to that. The excitement I was feeling was due to the possibility that I might leave this shithole. I preferred war to staying in this compound. You might imagine how bad it was.

I wasn't expecting them to give me any info about the new job because the company wasn't allowed to know what we did out there. I was assigned to work with the Canadian Special Operations Forces in the Panjwai district of Kandahar province. I packed my bag and wore my uniform and body armor. I waited in the hall of the compound.

The following day, at seven in the morning, a Canadian officer came inside the compound. When he entered the hall, he looked around and saw only me. He waved at me and asked, "Are you Yousuf?"

"Yes."

"Ready to go?"

"Let's go."

It was the weirdest experience ever. I have seen white people in the past, but doing so in uniform and speaking English for the first time was a different kind of experience that I can't express. I didn't know how we would go to the forward operating base (FOB). FOBs were bases with at least a battalion of NATO troops. The military would transport personnel either by Chinook or an armored vehicle convoy. When I walked out of the compound, I saw a convoy of fifteen to twenty LAV III (Light Armored Vehicle III, used by Canadian infantry) lined right in front of the terp compound. A soldier took me to his vehicle. The LAV didn't have doors on the side, just a ramp door at the back. These vehicles were equipped with light and heavy guns.

The vehicle had a turret with a gunner controlling it. It also had two small doors at the back end for the two gunners that would pull security for the left and right side. I am not sure how many soldiers it could transport in total. I think we had six people in the back including the soldiers pulling security. You can't stand in the vehicle. If you walk at all, you walk in a position somewhere between crouching and standing. There was a small monitor that you could use to see outside through a camera.

We drove through Kandahar city. The LAV's full speed was sixty-five miles per hour. We arrived five to six hours later at a base called FOB Wilson. Wilson was the first Canadian soldier who was KIA (killed in action) in that area, and they named the base after him. When we arrived at the base, I was taken to a connex (a large metal shipping container) that had a desk, a computer, and a bunch of military equipment in it. I was told, "This is your point of contact's office."

The point of contact (POC) walked in. "I will be your POC from now on. I will help you with logistics, leave, and any other issues you have. If you need anything, come to my office."

He walked me to the terps' tent, which was three minutes away from the POC's office. The base wasn't huge. We had twenty-four terps working on the base, but each was assigned to different platoons and teams. I went inside the tent. It was a big tent that had wood on the ground. Half of the tent was empty; the other had an Afghan carpet on the floor with military cots around the rug. Everybody had a cot. The carpet was to sit,

36

chill, play board games with friends, and pray on. It was a nice setup. I still remember the good times we all had together in that tent. We had a great brotherhood with good people around us.

When I walked in, the POC introduced me to a group of terps who were already working there and living in the tent. They were hilarious guys and started joking with me. The terps were joyful to see a new face added to the team. It was almost lunch time. The DFAC was four minutes away from our tent.

I went to the DFAC. It was my first time ever entering a DFAC in my life. There were so many fruits, such as apples, grapes, and watermelon, and so much more like Clif bars, power bars, cereals, coffee, tea, and juice. For a guy like me, who was born and raised in a poor family and who hadn't had good food for the past two weeks, I told myself, "Worror, it is your day. Eat as much as you can!" In Pashto, my native language, we use the word "worror" similar to how Americans use the word "bro" when addressing each other. I don't remember what I took, but I grabbed whatever I could carry.

We have an Afghan expression, "You are not hungry—your eyes are." In our language, it is "Chesme Gushna." We use this expression to describe anyone who is greedy. Today, this expression very much defined me.

The other terps asked, "Bro, are you going to eat all that?"

I said, "For sure!" From that whole plate, I only ate half an apple and drank one can of iced tea. I still remember that it was Snapple specifically. I looked around to see if anyone was looking at me as I threw the plate in the trash can.

The terps started laughing and said, "Buddy, we all had the same experience."

I responded, "Damn, man, this food tastes like crap. How do they cook it? Looks like it has been boiled in water and served to us."

I was spot on. I later learned that's how most DFACs cook everything. It was nothing like Afghan food. Afghan foods are cooked spicy and chubby, meaning there is plenty of oil and fat in the food.

It took a while, but later, we got used to this food. I enjoyed it even though the military food in Afghanistan wasn't fresh. Everything was stored in freezer containers for at least six months. The food was usually overcooked or not properly cooked, but life was way better than what I had known before.

For my first ever operation, I was confused and scared. I was still a teenager. I wanted to do a good job, but I had no military training. I had no experience at all. The tricky thing about these operations was that the terps were always kept uninformed about the operation. We were not even given general information about what we might do out there. I always figured it out from chatting with soldiers.

I had heard stories about terps in the past who were left behind and then tortured and killed by the Taliban. I had that fear in my head. We terps didn't have any radios to communicate with the rest of the team. We had no GPS. I didn't know anybody on the team or how they operated. It took time to get accustomed to how the team talked. Being involved with NATO forces heavily influenced my language when talking tactically. The acronyms I use have their roots in U.S. and Canadian military doctrine. Most of the Afghans working in this environment used the same acronyms and phrases as their counterparts. It was essential to integrate as much as possible to avoid confusion.

It was my fifth day of work at FOB Wilson when I went out with my team. Our convoy was prepared and ready to roll outside the wire (the military term for leaving the base). This was a joint operation with the U.S. Special Forces (SF). Canadians were using the LAVs. U.S. SF was using GMVs (ground mobility vehicles that looked like dune buggies with guns). As we rolled out of the base in the LAV, I started saying my prayers. I remember I said, "Oh Almighty God, please don't let me down. Let me be a support to my family."

We went to a village named Mushan and stayed in a small outpost overnight. The outpost was run by the ANP. Ninety percent of them were uneducated and shooting over their shoulders. I praise them for staying in that village with minimal support and no help from their chain of command. They still fought the Taliban. We had ten to fifteen ANPs, armed with AK-47s (7.62 Russian-made automatic rifles), PKMs (7.62 belt-fed machine guns), and RPGs (rocket-propelled grenades). We stayed there overnight and started our mission in the early morning. I was fearful, and worst of all, I didn't know anything about where we were going, what our target was, or what I should do. I had no clue whatsoever.

One of the Canadian team guys came and asked me, "Do you know how to use an AK?" I only saw them in the movies and used them in games, never in real life. But I still said yes. My English was weak back then. I had trouble expressing my limitations with using a rifle. "Okay, I will be back in a few minutes."

Later, the team gave me an AK-47 that I had no experience with. I was never trained with weapons. I knew that it was a weapon and it could be dangerous if you don't have the knowledge of how to properly use it, but it was better to have it and not know how to use it than be empty-handed when going to war. I took the AK and told myself, "If something terrible happens, and you are left alone, don't give the bad guys a chance to capture you alive. No matter what, they will kill you." And, of course, carrying a gun gives you the courage to fight.

As soon as I was given the AK, the soldier who brought it showed me the fundamentals. I still remember what he said: "Don't point your muzzle at somebody unless you intend to kill him. Keep your finger off the trigger at all times unless you are planning to shoot at the enemy. Do not shoot unless you are shot at." I also was given an ICOM scanner. This was a device that could be used to overhear the Taliban's radio chatter. You can press a key only to scan and listen; you can't talk back to the other side on the ICOM scanner.

We headed out of the outpost at three in the morning. Our task was to clear the area of the enemy and IEDs. My job was to listen to the Taliban talking on the radios with the ICOM. They had already reported to one another that we had entered the village. I also heard them over the radio talking about how to set up an ambush for us.

They usually talked in codes because they knew we were listening to their chatter. They had their own made-up codes. Every district and province had different codes, and there were no standard codes. We learned the codes in each area by analyzing what happened each mission after it was over. Afghanistan is very diverse. Different provinces mean different languages and cultures. It made it difficult to decipher what they were planning.

The leader of the Canadian Special Forces team was a captain. He had one strict rule: stay with him at all times. These were elite and experienced soldiers. I had not seen combat before, but my ability to translate was extremely important in this mission and those to come. Because of this, they wanted to ensure I made it to the next mission.

I was walking alongside the captain, listening to my ICOM scanner. The Taliban would talk infrequently over it. I could hear their voices followed by a bit of static from the radio waves. Their comments were unimportant at first. Then, I heard them say something that caught my attention. I turned to the captain. "Captain, the Taliban are planning to ambush us."

The captain looked unfazed. "Let me know when and where they are planning to do so."

"Roger, I will." I kept listening. We were walking through farmland near a village. It was fertile land, and the village was small with mud houses. We kept to the dirt paths between fields and spread out when the terrain allowed. We were all on guard and keenly watching our surroundings. While we were walking around a farmer's field, the ICOM chatter increased in frequency. The Taliban voices spoke codes that I didn't fully understand over the radio. I knew something was coming. The chatter became hotter and hotter until the Taliban opened fire on us.

Rounds ricocheted off rocks and made loud cracking sounds in the air. I dropped to the ground. The soil was rough and rocky, but my body armor took the brunt of the impact. My heart began to beat out of my chest, and my breathing quickened. I tried to quiet the noise and focus on the captain's one strict rule. I looked to see what the others were doing. The SF team dashed to cover and started shooting back. I saw the team leader run to a covered position behind a berm. I rushed to the captain and did whatever he was doing. I had never been in this situation before, and I was mimicking him because I didn't know what to do. The SF team was yelling at each other and pointing in various directions. I was breathing hard. The air in my lungs was filled by the smoke of the gunpowder. The SF team pointed in the directions that the rounds were coming from. A few

Taliban fighters were shooting AKs from a higher position that had some rocks as cover. The team started engaging them with their small arms.

I pulled the charging handle on my AK and chambered a round. I pointed it toward the direction of the threat and shifted my selector switch to full auto. I pulled the trigger. The AK shook and jumped so rapidly that I couldn't see anything out of my iron sights. The buttstock beat against my shoulder. The first magazine went empty in the first few seconds. I didn't really understand how to aim yet, so I just thought in my head, *Screw everything in that particular direction.* I loaded another magazine and shot full auto again. I repeated this until I had shot all five of my magazines. Thankfully, there were no villagers near the firefight. I later learned to be more precise with my targets. I quickly realized I had no more ammo and told myself, *No more full auto from now on.*

The Canadian Special Forces soldiers were laughing and saying, "This guy is going Rambo style."

The SF team brought up their rocket launcher and shot at the Taliban. The projectile hit one of the rocks near the Taliban's position and sent chunks of debris into the air. The overmatch scattered the few Taliban shooting at us, and they ran. That was the Taliban's usual tactic. It was a quick ambush, and if they got lucky and killed one of us, they would count that as a win. They didn't really want to die. They are not as brave as most of them claim.

I learned so much in the first fight. During this operation, the captain was mentoring me, telling me to not be scared when going out and to be vigilant. He told me that I can't judge people by their looks. Some looked like the Taliban, but they were just regular civilians with long beards and a turban. This look was widespread. I learned to be more calm and relaxed during a conflict. But the most important lesson I learned was to use cover during a fight.

What a fight actually looks like is not like how it is portrayed in the movies. For the first few minutes, you are trying to locate where you are getting shot from. Teamwork is the most essential factor. You can't act like a hero. It has to be a team effort; you can't win the fight alone. I learned to not do things that were beyond my ability. Sometimes, saying no can prevent a lot of bad things from happening. Never turn your back in a gunfight. And always face the enemy.

All the fear I had was gone after that one fight. Before this, I had been afraid of getting killed or losing a part of my body and existing as a man who needed help from others to live. I have compassion for people who live this way, but I never wanted that kind of life. The fear was automatically gone by the next operation. I don't know if it was because I was young and overconfident or because I just didn't have any fear. I wasn't thinking about dying at all. Suddenly, I didn't care. We didn't have any casualties in that first fight. It was just a couple of AKs shooting at us from a distance. We always knew the fight was over when it was just us shooting for a couple of minutes straight. When we stopped, no more shots were coming from the opposite direction.

We returned to the base. I was proud of myself, but we never celebrated after the fights—it would look awkward. These fights were common and regular. Still, when I came back to base after completing the twenty-four-hour mission, the feeling was incredible. I could rest in my bed, take a warm shower, and chill with friends.

There was no way to send money from Kandahar back home, so I bought a computer with my first month's salary. The computer was a DELL laptop. I got it for 800 U.S. dollars. I asked one of the soldiers to fill my laptop with movies, and I asked him to also add as many tactical videos and films as he could. You couldn't find a lot on the internet. I wanted to watch, learn, and then use what I learned on missions. It actually helped in most cases. There were few movies that were close to real-life scenarios. Documentaries were my best source of knowledge. The best ones were the International Sniper Competition that was held yearly in the U.S., British Special Air Service (SAS) documentaries, Green Beret documentaries, and anything close to real-life situations. Those operators sharing their experience were a big help. And seeing how the actors moved to cover and manipulated their rifles helped me understand how to move. I had no instructor to teach me this.

I also needed to improve my English; my comprehension and understanding skills were weak. I learned most of my English from the movies, and my knowledge of western culture came from them too. Because the soldiers I worked with then were primarily young, and for most of them, it was their first time in Afghanistan, instead of them learning about my culture, I learned about the western culture. At first, I didn't understand half of the English they were speaking. That is why, after I learned a new phrase or sentence from a movie, I would go and practice it with the soldiers. Even though what I learned didn't make any sense at first, I still did it. The English course did help, but I credit it with only 20 percent of my learned English. For the rest, I had to practice and practice to get better at it.

—

We continued doing walking patrols in the area to disrupt enemy operations. We always returned to the base at the end of the day. We didn't do a lot of nighttime ops because the unit I was with lacked high-tech night vision. I couldn't understand some of the stuff the soldiers were talking about among each other. But I was the best they could get in that area with the salary we were getting paid. No one wanted to work in these areas. The salary was miniscule compared to the job and all the risk that came with it. There was little benefit. There was no safety net for loss of life or injury, and insurance wasn't a thing. There were too many restrictions on how we lived, and they were asking civilians to do a military job that most people weren't willing to do. The most significant risk to the job was being marked as an American spy. After I started, I never went back to our village. I wanted to, but I couldn't for fear of being targeted as a spy. And that was just the dangerous nature of the job.

Days passed, and we did more patrols in the area. Day fifteen on the job, I went out on my first long operation. It was a five-day operation. I prepared by packing some Meals Ready to Eat (MREs). I had never had MREs before. My body wasn't used to it, and most of the food in them tasted worse than prison food. I also packed water, a sleeping bag, and some snacks. I didn't have any experience with extended operations.

It was early morning when we departed to go to a village to help Coalition Forces collapse one of the outposts. I had never done anything like that in my life. We departed from the base and linked up with a colossal convoy. It consisted of around forty vehicles driving just one to two miles per hour. Even though the destination wasn't far away, the estimated travel time was forty-eight hours. We also had to be observant because there were a lot of IED threats. Our lead vehicle was a Husky (a vehicle built to find IEDs by scanning into the ground). It had to drive extremely slow for the scan to work. We found over forty IEDs along the route. Each one required the entire convoy to stop and deal with it. I thank God we located each of them. The explosive ordnance disposal (EOD) teams placed C-4 (military-grade explosives that feel like Play-Doh) on every IED and blew them in place.

We arrived at our final destination and started collapsing the outpost. While the engineers were working on the base and a regular army unit handled security, we started patrolling the area. It was a flat farming area. We were going through dirt roads in small villages full of mud houses. I didn't notice many civilians around. The length of the convoy was so considerable, I think the civilians wanted to stay away from any fights that might happen between us and the Taliban.

We heard lots of chatter on the ICOM scanner but saw no action from the enemy. It was common among the Taliban to chat and talk trash about us on the radios. Most of the time, they were using that as a trick to manipulate us. Their threats were usually all lies, but we always took every one seriously. You never know what the enemy is planning up ahead. The enemy was smart because they were trained by the neighboring intelligence agencies (Iran, Pakistan, Russia, and China).

This mission was one of the hardest I had ever been through. We didn't have good sleep, and we didn't have good food. All we had to eat were MREs. My body wasn't used to eating this kind of manufactured and nutrient-dense food. I could barely find food that would work for me to eat. I couldn't trust the people in the nearby village or ask them for food either. You never know who is with you and who is against you in the village. On top of that, I wanted to chat and joke around with the team when we had the chance, but unfortunately, my English wasn't strong yet, and I was scared of losing my job. I was struggling mentally and physically.

Even if you wanted to quit, you couldn't on a mission. You had to keep going. If you did quit, there was no one to take you back. It was a big deal. If a terp quit on a mission, his team would have no way to communicate with locals. He would be blacklisted and wouldn't be allowed to get a job on a Coalition base. I never considered quitting.

We were only out of the vehicles for twelve hours over the course of the five-day operation. It was day three when the base was entirely demolished. With the mission complete, we started returning to our home base. We were back in the vehicles. Sitting and trying to sleep in those uncomfortable seats was not easy. I didn't eat or drink because I couldn't stop a long convoy just to use the restroom. I only drank one bottle of water and ate one piece of the MRE. My last meal had been twenty-four hours before. Everyone was in this uncomfortable situation, tired, starving, and really needing the bathroom.

We were ambushed on day four. It was around noon when it happened. Because we were riding in a convoy, we didn't get out of the vehicles. The vehicles were all armored, so the bullets didn't do any damage to them. We didn't stop. Where the shots are being fired at is called the X. It is always recommended to move off the X as fast as you can. When they started shooting at us, I didn't even hear them because of the vehicle's loud engine. The gunner kept shooting back, and it took only a few minutes until the ambush was over. I didn't have any reaction to it.

Thankfully, we had no casualties. We found four more IEDs on the way back, and we exploded them. It was day five when we arrived at MSG (Masum Ghar, meaning Masum mountain). There was a sizeable Canadian camp there. The first thing I did was venture on a mission of my own: finding the restroom. I had not had a bowel movement in five days. Trust me, it wasn't a pleasant experience. Later, I went on my second personal mission: getting to the chow hall.

The meal was not as good as it was at FOB Wilson, but it was way better than the MREs. We stayed at this base for a short amount of time. Our base was just a couple of hours away. After the meal, we started moving back to our base. Those five days were a hell of an experience that I don't want to have in the future. The worst part was just sitting in a slow-moving convoy. It tests your patience.

I worked with Canadian Special Forces for some time. I liked the Canadian Forces, but they had so many restrictions for terps. In general, there were a lot of issues regarding how terps were treated as I would later find out in my career.

I had served for five months when we were traveling in a wheeled vehicle convoy from one location to another. It was around nine in the morning. One of the soldiers came to me and told me to get ready. He mentioned that we were going out on a supply mission where we'd run supplies to nearby outposts. This was a short mission. The duration was always four to twenty-four hours max. As we got ready, I grabbed only my gear. Water and MREs were usually stored on the side of the vehicles during these missions. On this specific mission, we were going to an outpost in the Sinzai area. It was located between Panjwai (FOB MSG) and the Zari district (FOB Wilson). We arrived at the delivery point. This was a small outpost. It was on the side of a hill with a platoon of Afghan National Army soldiers holding it. They also had a small Canadian team with them.

Kandahar is a hot province, but the weather was nice on that day. There was a soft breeze with a warm sun in the sky. We departed from the outpost. I was quietly watching the monitor that was inside the vehicle. From that, you could see outside in case a fight broke out. We arrived at the outpost. I was chilling next to our vehicle while the team was dropping off the supplies.

After the drop-off, I got ready to return to our base. Then, we were on the road. The soldiers were talking to each other. I was listening but still couldn't understand much of their English. We couldn't see much outside due to the vehicle not having any windows and the monitor having a narrow field of view. We were on the road for about ten minutes when the vehicle hit something like a speed bump. I heard a big boom, then I was knocked unconscious.

When I opened my eyes, I found myself in a place that looked like a hospital. It was the smell that confirmed what my eyes saw. At first, I thought I was in the small clinic we had on the base, but then, I realized it looked bigger and different. I did remember the explosion but nothing else. I asked myself, *Where am I?*

I was later told that I was in a hospital in KAF. I was shocked and confused and had no idea what had happened. Based on what the doctors told me, I was unconscious for over three days. Later, I found out that we had lost two soldiers in the blast. It saddens me to this day. I had a rough time after that blast.

This is the worst experience a human and a soldier can go through. It scared me for a long time, especially when going out in vehicles on main roads and hitting any bumps on the road. I would jump, scared. But over time, I got used to it. It was another aspect of my life now.

My friends called my family and told them about the explosion. My brother called me and told me to quit my job, but I wasn't a quitter. He kept saying quit your job and come back to Kabul. I didn't want to, and I hung up on him. But he was older, and I respected him, so I used a trick I'd seen in a movie. While he was talking about my job, I said, "Hello! Hello! Can you hear me?!" Then, I hung up the phone. I sent a text to my family and told them, "My phone service is bad here. I am fine." Then, I turned off the phone. I didn't turn it on for two weeks.

Hospitals are boring. I was around people who were wounded. I couldn't see them, but there was a lot of negative energy circling in the air. It gives you a lot of negative thoughts like, *What will I do? Am I disabled? What is wrong with me?*

It was later when I experienced my first brain seizure. It was like my brain just turned off. One moment, I was thinking something, and the next moment, it was nothing. Everything was blank. I have had random seizures since that day in 2007. It still hurts when I remember it all.

The doctors wanted to send me home for leave, the military word for "time off," but I was worried about losing my job. Plus, I was worried that my parents wouldn't let me come back, especially with them knowing that I had been blown up. I was lucky to survive that explosion, but my parents would never have let me work with the military again. I was in KAF for twelve days and then returned to the FOB. I flew back to base on a Blackhawk. When I arrived at the base, my friends welcomed me back. I did tell my parents that I stayed on base and continued my work. We didn't have an excellent medical system, and we, as locals, weren't allowed to use the U.S. or NATO medical services on the airfields. I just had to learn to deal with my brain injury on my own.

I called the interpreter company and asked them to assign me to a U.S. Special Operations unit. There were too many rules with conventional units. I've never liked feeling so restricted. The company representative said, "We don't have any spots with SF."

I said, "Okay. Then, I will be looking for a different company to work with."

The company rep said with a smile, "You are always welcome here." That was all the thanks I got from them.

The bulk of the U.S. Army had a lot of rules and restrictions on what terps could do. For example, you couldn't wear uniforms during operations (which made you a more significant target for the Taliban), you weren't allowed to carry a gun to defend yourself, you weren't allowed to take a phone to talk to your family (even though you were away from home for three to four months), and you weren't allowed to have access to internet. There were many other rules, which I will explain in detail later.

Even though the U.S. Special Forces had almost the same rules as the conventional units, Special Operations soldiers were just built differently. We all know those boys are a different breed, and that's why I wanted to be in that environment. SOF units had fewer rules and restrictions. They had older and more experienced soldiers that knew the Afghan culture a bit better than other units. They had all been to Afghanistan in the past. They respected the terps more than any other NATO and U.S. forces. They were the cool guys. I am talking about the toughest and most highly trained U.S. soldiers. Brotherhood meant a lot to them. Teams were small, like around fifteen people in one base. Everyone knew each other, and they all had each other's backs.

—

The company I had worked for was only doing contracts with Coalition Forces in the southern part of the country. There was another company in Kabul located inside a U.S. military base. There were flights from Kandahar to Kabul and Kabul to Kandahar that were one hundred U.S. dollars per ticket. It was safe, and it was a one-hour flight. So, I went to this military base in Kabul to talk to the company's recruiting staff.

This was extremely difficult. They had no email, no phone number, no names posted, and you didn't even know who the recruiters were. It was a very greedy company over terps' salaries. They didn't care if terps lost their lives or became disabled. They had a contract with another greedy insurance company that, in most cases, never paid the families of terps who were killed in action. Most of the terps who were wounded were never paid the compensation they were entitled. They had no form of contract to avoid these wronged employees. They were out of reach in Afghanistan. You couldn't enter the military base in Kabul due to restrictions and security rules; you could only call them. They didn't respond to phone calls or emails, and if you kept calling them, they would either block you or change their number (SIM cards in Afghanistan were only one U.S. dollar). Worst of all, the salary for this company was 480 U.S. dollars per month, the lowest pay rate among companies that were recruiting terps.

Even with all of these conditions, I tried to apply just to work with Special Forces. I went to the company, and luckily, they were hiring on that day. They asked me to complete an English test, which included writing, reading, and listening portions. I passed the tests, and as soon as I passed, I requested to be assigned to an ODA element (Operation Detachment Alpha U.S. Special Forces). I didn't ask for a specific region in the country. As long as it was an SF team, I would be okay with it.

After two weeks, I was assigned to work with an ODA element in Camp Eggers, which was located in Kabul city and was a twenty-five-minute drive from where I lived. The camp was right across from the U.S. embassy. My job was similar to other jobs I had had. I was going out on missions with Afghan commandos. The SF element was training the commandos and conducting operations in the areas that were given to the team. I worked there for thirteen months.

After the team left, I had to get a new assignment. I called the supervisor and asked him to assign me to another SF team. They told me, "We are sorry. We no longer have a contract with Special Operations, but we do have an assignment with a conventional army unit in Bagram Airfield."

Bagram had many rules and policies. For example, you had to take a polygraph test every six months. You also had a five-hour-long counterintelligence interview, and at the end of the day, they still made their decisions based on your appearance. If they didn't like you for any reason, you would be blacklisted and wouldn't be able to work with any Coalition Forces or Afghan armed forces unit in the country.

I just didn't want to take the risk that I might ruin my career over one interview with a civilian contractor. These civilian contractors never stepped outside the base; they never went on operations. They didn't understand what we went through and how hard this job was. They were just happy to mark you as a bad guy so they could show it off as some kind of achievement. They did blacklist many Afghan locals that had been working for years and years. It was a messy system with a lot of trust issues.

I told the manager, "No, thanks. I am good. I am going back to Kandahar." He was shocked that I preferred to go to a combat area instead of taking a terp job in Kabul. He said, "It is Bagram! Everybody wants to work there! Come on!" He didn't realize that Afghans don't like to be restricted. Not all Afghans, but some like me prefer to go to a warzone.

I wanted to continue fighting alongside the coolest and most badass people on earth. I preferred the difficult times over staying on a base that was under some command sergeant major (CSM). The CSM was free to create new rules and restrictions for the terps on base that made no sense. Despite all this, I put my life on the line for the Coalition soldiers to my right and left. I would say this loud and clear: "The problem is not the soldiers. The problem is the orders given from the leader." I had my best times with the soldiers at the company grade ranks, and it didn't matter which branch of the military.

Chapter 5

E
ventually, I flew to Kandahar and went to work with the company
I was working with before. They now had contracts with Special
Forces. They were ecstatic to see me back there, and they told me,
"You don't need an interview. Just wait for fifteen to twenty days. The SF
teams need terps. Their recruiters will come, and I will put your name on
the list."

That was good news for me. The company was now paying 1,000 U.S.
dollars to people who were working with SF teams.

Later, I was in the terp camp, chilling in the shade. It was around two
in the afternoon when a manager came and said, "There are guys recruiting
for Special Operations units."

I said, "Put me on the list." I didn't tell them I'd worked with Special
Operations Forces units in the past, and I still had to go through the interview. It was the rule, and I had to respect that. I sat down in the hall and
waited until I heard my name being called.

I went into a room that was used as a meeting room by the interpreter
company I was working for. Two bearded Americans were in the room.
They were wearing civilian clothing. They looked to be around thirty-eight
to forty-five years of age. Their expressions were cold and mean. They
asked, "Are you Yousuf?"

I said, "Yes."

They replied, "Sit down."

I sat down and smiled. I was relaxed and confident. One thing I'd
learned from my past interviews was to play it calm and friendly.

They said, "Tell us about your background." I explained how I'd
started and what I'd been up to until then.

"Do you know you will be armed with an AK, and we will send you to a village alone. Can you do that?"

I already knew they would never do something like this. I replied, "Yeah, sure. As long as I am armed with an assault rifle, I can do that."

"We need more people like you."

To that, I answered, "I have a request. Assign me wherever you want, as long as the base has good food and a good gym."

They laughed. "We know the exact place for you." We shook hands, and I left the room. With that, the interview ended.

I wasn't told which base I was going to or what Special Operations team I would be assigned to. It could be Army SF, Navy SEALs, or Marine SF elements. I was told by one of the managers that I was assigned to a Special Operations unit, and I might leave in ten days. On day ten, I was told about my departure.

At departure time, I was picked up from the terp camp and escorted into the U.S. part of KAF. From there, we went to the heart of the SF Command in southern Afghanistan, Camp Brown. This was just a layover. It was around eight in the morning. After I arrived, I went to the SF DFAC to eat breakfast. The food was good, and I enjoyed it. I didn't know where I was going to end up. I thought, *What will the base be like? What will the food be like? What other facilities would be there?* I didn't expect much. Most SF bases were small, and there weren't many facilities. But a band of brothers were there, and I care about the band and brotherhood more than anything.

After breakfast, my escort came in and told me to be ready to go to the helicopter landing zone (HLZ). After grabbing my backpack, we went to load into the Chinook (CH-47s), and then we took off. We had a full flight of soldiers going to different bases. Our first drop-off wasn't my base. I couldn't see much of it. It is hard to see from inside Chinooks unless you are a gunner or sitting at the rear. The CH-47s landed, and two guys got off. After a few minutes, we took off again. We arrived at the next stop.

When the Chinook was landing, I saw a large amount of dust being kicked up by the Chinook. I said to myself, "Oh boy! Not a good sign." The HLZ where the Chinook was landing was not made with concrete.

This meant that the base was either new or it was challenging to get supplies due to the risk of IEDs on the road.

I didn't know whether this was my stop or somebody else's. Over twenty-five people were on that flight. At this moment, my escort tapped me on my shoulder and yelled next to my ear, "THIS IS YOUR SPOT, GOOD LUCK!" I grabbed my backpack, which was placed between my legs, and I started walking out of the Chinook.

As soon as I put my foot on the ground, I only saw desert to my left and right. I told myself, "Bro, they sent me to one of the most messed up bases in the whole country! The base doesn't even have gates!"

There was this guy standing in a cloud of dust that was created after the takeoff. He waved his hand in a way that said to come to him, and I walked up to the first ever Navy SEAL I had met in my entire life. He looked like every other SF operator in Afghanistan. He was a cool-looking dude with a dusty beard. He had a mean face but liked to smile. The SEAL operator asked, "Are you a terp?"

I responded, "Yes."

He started screaming, "Oh, we got a TERP! WE GOT A TERP!"

I didn't understand why he was so excited.

He said, "Let's go. I will take you to your room."

We went to my room, which was a connex but built for living. I was told by the SEAL that this was my room, but I saw another bed in there. The SEAL operator told me, "Rock Man is out on an op. They will be back tomorrow!"

I said, "Rock Man! Okay!" He left. I put my bags on the bed and thought, *Who is the Rock Man? Is he a laborer in this camp? And he lives in the terps room?* I believed that "rock man" meant a guy who breaks rocks for a living; we have them in Afghanistan. Part of me was surprised. *What is a rock man doing in this camp? There are no rocks here.* I didn't think much about it.

The camp was a mess. It was full of dirt. People were living in tents, and there were a lot of other signs that suggested that the camp was newly built. I already knew this meant that the base didn't have good food, accommodations, or showers. I didn't get the three basic things that I wanted to have while doing this job.

It was the following day when I saw a terp with a dusty face and curly beard. He was about five foot, four inches. He walked in the room and said, "Hi! Are you the new terp?"

"Yes?" I answered.

Then, he introduced himself to me. "My name is Rahman."

Rahman is a widespread Afghan and Muslim name, but because the team couldn't pronounce his name properly, they said Rock Man. I mean, it sounded like Rock Man. I told Rahman what I'd assumed he was when I heard his name. We started laughing.

We bonded quickly. Rahman was a warrior and a great human being. He was from Ghazni province, south of Kabul. He was kind and humble. We were roommates and teammates for over a year. We were both new with Navy SEALs, and we were both eager to learn. He always had my back, and I had his. We always laughed and joked about our mistakes. We shared our daily experiences to learn from each other.

Later in life, I was in Kabul when I heard shocking news from the terps I knew. I was working a different job at that time when I heard a rumor about Rahman's death. I didn't believe it, but unfortunately, it was true. In 2012, he was killed in action after stepping on an IED during an operation in Kandahar, Afghanistan. May God rest his soul in the heavens.

I was wondering why the team was so excited to see me, a new terp, working at this base. It turned out no terp wanted to work here. I soon found out the reason—because apart from the base being full of dirt and dust, the DFAC was not good. In fact, you had to cook your own food most of the time, and there were no hot showers. I was mad at first, feeling I had been swindled, or, in the Afghan language, we say, "Dupaa Shudum."

Eventually, my mind changed after doing some ops. I found that I was working with the coolest, most badass, and most down-to-earth operators I have ever seen in my entire career. I was always counted as part of the team. The team didn't care about any rules, as long as I got the job done. We used to roll out in dirt bikes, ATVs, and LATVs (which are similar to dune buggies) to start our missions. They always respected my experience and listened if I had a suggestion, especially on security matters. After every investigation of suspects we detained in the villages during raids, they asked for my opinion. I was an Afghan and knew about their body language and the tricks the Taliban used while under investigation. Above all, I had the most experience with the Afghan war among them. It was all teamwork. They were a great bunch of operators, and many of us became lifelong friends.

Eventually, that SEAL team went back home to the U.S. and was replaced with another SEAL team. They were also a great bunch of guys. Through this new team, I met my current good friend and buddy Jeff Reid, former SEAL. He is now living a natural life in Alaska, hunting for his food, growing fruits and vegetables in his backyard, and chopping wood to keep warm.

He helped me so much from the very first day we met to the day I became an operator myself. When Kabul fell, he was about to jump out of a flight to come and save me. I assured him that I was in safe hands. When I arrived in the U.S., Jeff offered for me to live with him in Alaska, but I couldn't accept due to some family factors. He opened a GoFundMe account and raised 5,000 dollars to help me start from scratch here in the United States. He is one of the friends who really motivated me to tell my story. He said, "Bro, take the chance and let others hear you. Don't let that story and life journey die within you." I am glad I listened to him and other friends of mine.

I only had one problem while working with the SEAL teams. They didn't let terps carry a gun. I mean, it wasn't the team's fault. They had orders from their chain of command to not arm the terps. This later changed.

On the first operation with the team, we were going after a Taliban commander in the Khakrez district in the Kandahar province. This operation was interesting to me. I wanted to see how Navy SEALs operate. I prepared extensively for this one. I did as much research as I could on how the SEALs operate and what I should carry with me. I was also working out a lot to help with physical challenges during an operation. I had to keep up with Navy SEALs—these guys are the Olympic athletes of the armed forces.

It was three in the morning when we lined up, waiting for the Chinooks to come pick us up. It was my first time doing a mission during the nighttime without night vision goggles (NVGs). The team had NVGs but did not have one for me. They didn't have any spare ones to give the terps. One misunderstanding U.S. soldiers had was that I didn't need an AK-47 or NVGs because I was a terp. What they didn't realize is that I knew only a small amount about the district we were operating in and that, during a Taliban ambush, they first shot the terp, then the rest of the patrol. They knew if the terp was down, the operation would get canceled because the team would face a lot of language barriers.

I didn't know the tactics the Taliban used in that district. I didn't know the codes they used on the radio or how to distinguish if they were trash talking or planning a real ambush. We had intelligence, but the live experience was something different for me.

We went on this operation, and it was similar to other operations I'd done with Canadian Special Operations Forces. The SEALs were conducting the assault and house clearing themselves and taking all the risk. Other units would have the Afghan soldiers do it instead of the U.S. forces. That was something new. I was observing and learning. It was a successful operation, and we returned safely.

I wanted to learn quickly because my nature is that I must be good at what I do. I want to be the best at my job, especially in the military. A small mistake can cost somebody's life, and I didn't want to make that mistake.

After the first two or three patrols, the SEAL team leader changed his mind about terps carrying a gun. I don't know why he changed his mind, but he did. My guess is he didn't trust me enough at first, and now, I was trustworthy in his eyes. Carrying a gun was pretty much a requirement with Special Operations units. This is because they are small teams, and if you knew how to use a weapon, it was a relief for the members who had to protect you in a firefight. My SEAL team leader said, "I will let you carry a gun, but unfortunately, we don't have a spare one." After the first twenty-four-hour operation, though, we did. We seized a Russian AK-47 from a compound. It looked like it had been recently cleaned up too.

I asked, "We got an AK-47, right, Commander?"

He laughed and said, "I remember what I told you. We have to train you first."

I went through a two-week AK-47 training. Then, Rahman and I had a competition. I won and was the first to get an AK-47. We later seized another one during an operation and gave that AK-47 to Rahman.

The first raid I ever did was with the SEALs. It was winter, and it was cold. Weather always made raids challenging if it was freezing or torrid. The biggest problems we had during winter were the cloudy, rainy, or snowy days. We couldn't have air support, and that made the job much harder.

Thankfully, the weather wasn't too bad, so we were able to have three Chinook helicopters loading operators in that first raid. We took off. As soon as the flight crew announced we were ten minutes out, I prayed to God to not fail in this mission and to empower me to beat the evil and save the oppressed. We arrived in the target area. As soon as the Chinook touched the ground, we exited the aircraft and started running toward the HLZ.

Helicopters can be heard for miles, so we usually landed a minimum of four or five miles away from the target area. This was safer for the choppers to land, and it confused the enemy (especially in the dark when they couldn't see us), making it difficult for them to determine whether our target was their village or another village close by. I could hear over my radio the Taliban's radio chatter. They weren't sure whether we landed in the area or if we just flew by the village.

We kept walking after we arrived at our target compound. We locked down the building with security forces. Locking something down means that we ensured no one entered or left the building or the perimeter. We put the ladders up against the village walls so the SEAL snipers could climb to the top to provide overwatch while the assault team breached the compound and building and engaged the enemy.

As soon as the ladders were up, our team started engaging the insurgents inside the building. When the enemy was inside a building in a village, my biggest concern was civilian casualties. While the ladder team engaged the enemy, the assault team went inside and started to clear the rooms. The whole time, I was standing close to the entrance with the commander of the team. My job was to be next to him at all times to interpret for him.

We threw grenades inside, but the Taliban kept fighting back. After fifteen minutes of shooting and clearing, the building was cleared. Three enemies were confirmed killed, and there were no civilians inside the building, which was good news.

After that, we started clearing the rest of the village house by house. We would assault a house and clear it, searching for guns and explosives and escorting the adult males outside for questioning. We usually gathered the adult males and took them with us while clearing the whole village. You would see a big line of civilians walking with the team. It was around noon when the village was finally clear. Then, we turned our attention to the adult males. We had a source with us who would mark targets for us. Then, we would separate the targets from the group and start basic questioning. The civilians would stay with us until we left the village. There were many security reasons for keeping them with us. The main one was to prevent them from reporting to other villages about the raid.

When it was dark, we started walking to our exfiltration (or exfil) area where the helicopters would pick us up with six detainees. We walked five miles to the exfil HLZ. When we arrived, we had to do a 5/25 check for IEDs and other suspicious stuff on the ground. A 5/25 check is when you intentionally look at five meters around you, then twenty-five meters around you, with a lot of patience and attention to detail before moving into an area. We looked for odd piles of rocks and freshly dug dirt. Luckkily, we found no IEDs. We got into the Chinooks, exited the target area, and returned to base.

Everything I was doing was a lesson for me. I was learning new stuff every day, from assault tactics to house clearing to what leading an operation looked like.

I have some funny stories and some sad stories from working with the SEALs. I will tell you a funny one first. I used to work out a lot. I was doing full-body workouts, strength workouts, and CrossFit. Back then, CrossFit was new. Team guys, which is what SEALs call themselves, were always encouraging me, saying, "Good job! Keep it up!" I got all the motivation you can get from some of the most badass guys on earth. I absorbed all of it and embraced the workout culture.

I remember this occurred in the afternoon. I started doing an insane leg workout. I was dragging this big-ass tire we had next to the gym. When team guys were passing by, they shouted, "Good job!" and "Awesome!" One of the team guys by the name of Mitch said, "Nice. Keep it up!" and motivated me more and more.

After the workout, I took a shower and went to the DFAC. I saw some of the guys there. We had a random chat but no word about any upcoming operation. I went to my room and watched a funny movie. It was always either *Blue Streak* or *National Security*. I used to watch them once a week. They are pure comedy. After that, I went to sleep.

It was 2:30 a.m. when someone started knocking on my door! When I woke up and opened the door, I saw it was Mitch again. I said, "Sup, bro?"

He said, "Be ready. We are leaving in one hour!"

"Bro! You saw me doing legs yesterday! My legs are sore. It hurts to walk!"

"I am sorry, bro. Totally forgot to tell you about the op."

Naturally, the operation involved an excruciatingly long walk. It was the longest walk I had ever done for an operation. I was feeling the pain in my muscles, but what option did I have? I had to do this operation. I mean, that is what they were paying me for, and there was nobody else to do it.

We departed the base at three in the morning. I couldn't feel my legs. I was limping for a mile. We were going up and down hills. Then, a mountain came our way. We climbed all the way up. We started resting and setting up the sniper rifles. I didn't know what the plan was. We, as terps, were never briefed on operation details, but I always created my own plans in case something went south. I had no radio communication with the team at all. The only communication device I was using was an ICOM scanner. The Taliban were talking on the radio, but there was no chatter about our movement. It meant they didn't know where we were, which was a good sign.

I found out our goal on this mission was to observe the Taliban's movement and activity in the area. After three hours of being out, we had no visual contact with the Taliban. We wrapped up and started returning to base. We took a different route this time. We didn't have smart tech back then, only a wristband GPS. The lead guy took us on a path that took us about one or two miles away from where we were supposed to go.

I was exhausted. The weather was scorching, and my legs were in so much pain. I was trying to keep up with some of the toughest people on earth. We finally made it back to the base. I was just feeling tired and sleepless; my eyes were red.

We had a meeting with some of the village elders and U.S. military leadership in the area. We were talking about creating local police to bring peace and stability, but the locals were afraid to do it. The Afghan locals worried it would invite more Taliban aggression, and the Afghan National Police were often known to be corrupt.

After the meeting, I went to my room and slept. I woke up ten hours later. I couldn't move my legs at all. It was the sorest my muscles had ever been in my entire life. I had to get up and go eat something. I was walking funny for the next two weeks. The team guys made fun of me with some crude humor. Thanks to Mitch, I got some muscle relief spray for my legs. Mitch is currently a mixed martial arts, or MMA, athlete and runs his show by the name *Mitch Show*. We still talk from time to time. This is one of my funniest memories from back then.

The following story happened one night. It was a different op, and this particular op was a big one. We had five Special Operations elements planning to clear an area. It was a twenty-four-hour mission. We had six Chinook helicopters loading operators. They loaded two Special Forces ODA elements and one SEAL team.

While we were waiting in the HLZ for the choppers, I turned on my ICOM scanner. The ICOM started scanning, and what I heard on the scanner surprises me to this very day. The chatter was between two Taliban groups in two different villages that were at least two hours apart. They were using repeaters—a device that pushes communication signals to each other as long as there is no high hill or mountain blocking the signal—for better communication and to report their activities to each other. We never found the repeaters. The Taliban chatter started:

"Hi and regards."

"Hi, regards, my brother."

"How is everything on your side?"

"Everything is fine."

"Some bugs flew over our village. They are coming to your village." ("Bugs" was the code for choppers.)

"Okay, brother, I will let the guys know. We will beat these invaders."

"We will be Inshallah."

A few minutes after hearing the conversation, we started hearing the choppers getting closer. I told the captain about the chatter. He said, "Roger. I will push it down the net."

One other team guy and I were loaded into the choppers with our LATVs. We took off and arrived in the target area twenty-five minutes later. As soon as the flight crew announced we were ten minutes out, I shouted, "Let's save the oppressed!" As soon as the Chinook touched the ground, we exited the aircraft. We started riding our LATVs toward the HLZ. I was loaded and ready to engage. The night was pitch black; I could barely see. I didn't have NVGs, and I was wearing my baseball cap. Our LATV was loaded to the mouth (this is an Afghan expression that means I ate so much that I didn't have space for one more bite). After the choppers took off, we started riding to go up the hill in front of us. This hill was so steep that we soon realized going up would be impossible.

We drove up to a point, and the LATV got stuck. The driver was trying to accelerate with caution, and after the first acceleration, the front of the LATV went up just a little bit. Then, he tried for the second time, and he stopped. I was thinking, "Man, the next acceleration, the vehicle is going to flip over." As soon as the thought crossed my mind, he accelerated again. I felt the front of the vehicle go up until it reached a tipping point. I grabbed the grip handle in front of me, thinking I wouldn't fall. By the middle of the first roll, I had lost control.

It was the kind of stuff you see in the movies. I braced myself like I had seen in the action scenes. I was wrong to do so. This is real life, not a movie. The vehicle flipped over once, twice, three times, and the driver fell off the vehicle. It wasn't until the fourth or fifth flip that I, too, fell off. My head and back hit hard against all the rocks that were there. I stood up quickly and saw the LATV was still rolling down the hill. The driver was looking for his helmet, so I started to help him look. When I found his helmet and NVGs, I grabbed them and handed them to him. He said thank you, and we started walking down the hill.

When we arrived at the vehicle, the team guys were surprised. They said, "Damn! You guys are still alive? We thought we lost you guys rolling down the hill."

The chief then said, "Let's get the vehicle going. If it doesn't turn on, put some explosives on it and BIP it."

BIP means to "blow in place." In this case, BIP means render the vehicle unusable so that it can't be highjacked by the Taliban. Special Forces teams regularly carried C-4 and other explosives that could be primed and used at a moment's notice.

A couple of the guys started working on the vehicle, and the rest of us started climbing up the hill. I had to go with them because I was the only terp. Rahman was on leave at that time. Man! This wasn't a hill—this was a mini mountain. When we got to the top, it was starting to get brighter and brighter out. I felt something warm on my forehead. I thought it was just sweat dripping down, so I ignored it. Plus, I had more important stuff to focus on during that time. I started listening to Taliban chatter. The chief approached me and asked if the Taliban were talking about us on their radios.

I whispered in his ear, "They know we are here, but they don't know our exact location!"

It was at this moment the chief told me, "Hold on! Hold on! Is it blood on your face?"

I said, "Really?"

I rubbed my forehead with my fingers and saw blood on my hand. I had three gashes on my head and some injuries on my back. The chief asked me if I was okay. I responded, "If I am not okay, what option do we have? None. Let's just pretend this never happened." What I meant by this was we didn't have another option but for me to continue. It was impossible to get a replacement terp in less than a month. With replacements being so rare, it was one of the biggest reasons the Taliban always targeted terps first.

The operation was supposed to be twenty-four hours, but it extended to forty-eight, then to seventy-two hours. There was no fight, but we did capture a few of the Taliban, and then, we returned to base. My injuries healed over time. I didn't use any medication. We had a limited amount of medication, and there were not many options except to just live with the pain for a few days.

I continued in my role as a terp for another nineteen months. I got bored and tired of soldiers complaining about Afghans and not trusting Afghans. At the end of the day, I was an Afghan, and they were all my people. Not all of them were the Taliban or bad guys. And besides, every Coalition soldier chose to be here and not by any Afghan's choice. We didn't send an invitation, and they weren't drafted.

Like this one time, we were sitting in our small DFAC, and a civilian contractor (who'd recently come to our base to work as a mechanic) started talking badly about Afghanistan. He was saying things like, "This country is a craphole with a bunch of stupid people."

I got angry and asked him, "What do you mean?"

He said, "Oh, I don't mean to be rude."

I said, "You were rude, buddy, whether you like it or not. And how many provinces have you been to?"

He said, "Kandahar Airfield and this district."

I said, "And this is the whole country?"

He went quiet. Legend says that he is still silent to this day.

Chapter 6

To be honest, when you are putting your life on the line and people still have trust issues with you, you get disappointed. Alongside that, there are so many unnecessary rules and restrictions for the terps:

1. We weren't allowed to have phones on base. They were worried that we might leak operation information, even though they told us one hour prior to the departure that we were going out on an operation. I mean, if we wanted to leak any information, we could easily do it. One could effortlessly smuggle a phone inside the base.

2. Some contracting companies didn't allow terps to wear military uniforms, despite the fact that the more you looked like a U.S. soldier, the safer it was for you during an ambush.

3. I mentioned previously in the other stories that the Taliban's first target was the terp. Terps who lost their lives were sent home in coffins. There was no money given to their families. They had no insurance whatsoever. The U.S. government claims that they have given insurance money to the contracting companies, but we as terps never received a penny.

I spoke with a lot of terps who were wounded, blacklisted, and fired from their jobs, and I talked to some of their families. They all had complaints about how unfair and unreasonable it was that they were kicked out of jobs. I do know terps who were kicked out of the base in the middle of nowhere in the middle of the night in Taliban territory. They served honorably only to be betrayed by the U.S.

4. If a terp was wounded during an operation, most of the time, they would be fired with a lame excuse. I was lucky my brain injury wasn't apparent, and you couldn't see it like other injuries. Otherwise, they would have laid me off too.

One reason the company would fire a wounded terp was because of the risk. We were officially signing up to be killed or injured, and maybe we'd get lucky and survive. If a new guy came in and saw a wounded terp and heard the horror stories of war, he would quit right away. Another reason was that they didn't want to get sued by a wounded terp. Once a fired terp was out of the gate, there was no way they would let him back in.

It happened to three of my friends. One is currently in Arizona. He submitted a lawsuit to sue the insurance company because of his knee injury. He is presently half disabled. He can't walk or stand for a long time. He can't easily drive, and he is having a tough time.

Another was a friend of mine who is currently living in Canada with his Canadian wife. He was kicked off the base at 2 a.m. by a Special Forces major. The major had been engaging in sexual relations with an Afghan American female civilian on the base who was being paid around 160,000 in U.S. dollars a year to provide cultural advice and translation for the Special Forces soldiers. But she wouldn't go on missions because they were too dangerous. We terps were paid a fraction of her salary and took all the risk.

To make some more cash, this friend started a side business that supplied the ODA elements on the base. He was making some pretty good money for an Afghan. The female decided that she wanted part of it, but this friend refused to give her part of the business. In retaliation, the female told the Special Forces major to fire him, and he did. The team tried to talk to the major to defend him, but he wouldn't listen.

My friend asked the major, "Where can I go? This town is full of the Taliban and ISIS. At least let me stay overnight."

The major responded, "I don't care. Get off my base. It is none of my business what will happen to you."

My friend is lucky he got paid and used some of the money to pay the ANA to keep him on their base for the rest of the night. He has nightmares and PTSD. He was under investigation for two weeks after his U.S. visa was canceled. I am not blaming his team. It was an individual that stepped on all of his hard work and sacrifices and marked him as a bad guy.

Most people who were working as counterintelligence contractors lacked compassion and were cruel to the locals, even though these locals were the ones risking everything for a few hundred dollars per month. And these locals were kicked out of the base for no reason.

Last time I talked to my friend, he said, "I have all the information on the major who did this to me. It is okay if I was powerless back there and he felt empowered and did what he could to me. But here, there are human rights courts, and I will drag him to international court."

Unfortunately, a lot of bad things happened to locals, especially to terps, but nobody listened to their stories. Thankfully, I can use this book to tell some of these stories now.

Again, I, on behalf of the terp community, am not blaming everybody. There were a few individuals who were bad, but most of the people we worked with were great guys, and most of the terps are still in contact with the teams they worked with. I just have to mention some ugly truths.

5. The Taliban hated us the most and wanted to kill us first during an ambush, yet terps didn't have anything to defend themselves with. What the team leaders told us was, "If troops are in contact, terps just go hide in a ditch or under some sort of a cover."

6. On top of everything, every five or six months, they would send us to a questioning interview and CI (counterintelligence) screening that was conducted by U.S. intelligence contractors. That interview would take up to four hours. Most of the questions were about being part of any terrorist group. Most terps were blacklisted for minor matters.

"Why didn't you tell us you bought a new SIM card or phone?" the interviewer asked.

The interviewee shrugged. "I bought one because my old phone broke. Do I have to tell you when I buy anything? Do you need to know when I get new underwear too?"

"Why is your mom's cousin working with the Taliban?"

Again, the interviewee shrugged. "I have no access to my old village, and I have more cousins than I can count. How do you expect me to stop my cousin from joining the Taliban? He thinks of me as a target and an infidel." (Infidel refers to a nonbeliever of Islam.)

"Why did you post a comment on social media that looks like you are supporting the Taliban?"

"I go on missions almost every day that result in many Taliban dying. What do you believe more? My actions or your opinions on what you thought I meant to say through my posts?"

"Why do you commute by bus, and the Taliban haven't killed you? You might be connected to them!"

"Well, if you would like to send me a limousine and an armed escort, I would be happy to stop taking the bus. Are you saying that because I am still alive I am Taliban? I see that you are living, so are you Taliban then?"

This was the level of questioning we went through. The people conducting the CI interviews were not the most intelligent workers. For details as small as these, terps would get blacklisted and fired from their jobs.

I remember this one time that I had a CI test while I was sick. I got a cold with a fever and a cough three nights prior to the interview date. I became ill because I'd had to sleep in the rain during a recent operation. A lot of soldiers had colds, and even though I was not feeling well, I couldn't change the interview date. That was way above my power, and I couldn't miss the interview. If I did miss it, that would raise a lot of security questions, and my American supervisor couldn't do anything about it either. A few minutes into my interview, I started coughing. There was a big glass pane between me and the interviewer, who was an older man. He started yelling, "Are you sick?"

I responded, "Yes."

He kept going. "WHO TOLD YOU TO COME TO MY OFFICE WHILE BEING SICK? YOU KNOW I CAN BLACKLIST YOU IF I WANT TO!"

I apologized and tried to calm this clown down. He had the power to blacklist me, and he would put on my background "Blacklisted for Security Reasons." It was usually for petty issues. They could even blacklist you if you refused to go on a mission. We don't know why you could be blacklisted for that. This was never an agreement, and nobody signed such a document, but refusing to go on a mission would get you blacklisted. I remember the contract stated that if you refused to go on a mission, you would be fired. But nothing said blacklisted.

This one other time, I had a polygraph test. I went through the test and stayed as calm and as relaxed as I could. They failed me but didn't tell me why I failed. I found out through the team captain, who told me, "They said your heart graph was not going up or down. It was suspicious for them." He laughed and continued, "They are a bunch of dumb civilians, and yet they feel proud to fire you guys. We know how important you guys are for the U.S. mission in Afghanistan."

People like that captain and the other team guys were the only reason I stayed in as a terp for that long. I felt a deep sense of honor and pride for my job when he said that. At the end of the day, these were the people who mattered to me, not the guys I saw every six months during an interview. However, the trust issues would push me to the edge of my patience and stop me from what I was doing.

One day, I'd had enough of it, so I decided to stop working as a terp. It's a job I loved from day one, but it looked like God had a greater plan for me. My SIV was approved at that time, so I could have gone to the USA, but I changed my mind and planned to stay in my homeland.

I wanted to do something good for the future of my country to make it a better place. I was okay if this dream would cost me my life. The Afghan armed forces leadership was shamefully corrupt, and I wanted to change what I possibly could. Somebody had to do something. I didn't want to work as a soldier in the Afghan conventional units. Even within the Afghan armed forces, I wanted to work with the best of our armed forces.

I had moved back in with my family in Kabul. I saw some ads about the Afghan government recruiting for Special Forces, so I decided to join that program. First, I had to enlist in the Afghan Armed Forces. I kept it a secret from my family this time. I didn't want to keep giving them news that they didn't like. After I woke up, I changed and walked out of my home to go to a recruitment station. I already had the address from a friend of mine. I took a cab, and after I arrived, I got out of the vehicle and walked into the station. I saw a recruiter and stopped and talked to him. I told him I had extensive experience and that I'd worked and operated alongside some of the best units on earth. I didn't want to go back to the regular force. I told him to "sign me up for the SF teams; otherwise, I won't waste my time or yours."

The recruiter told me, "We usually don't recruit directly for the SF teams, but I can make an exception due to your background and experience."

The training for Afghan soldiers was often rudimentary. Drills for Special Forces were intense. We had fourteen weeks of marksmanship, squad tactics, air assault, and live-fire exercises. We went through medical and physical tests at the beginning. After we passed that, we took a written test to check our education level. After a week of waiting for the results, I received a call and was told to pack my bag. I went to Camp Morehead, which was the birthplace of the Afghan Commandos.

We'd started with 240 people, and only fifteen of us passed. The selection was hard and wasn't what I expected. I had the mentality to stay strong and keep going.

When we passed the selection course, we started our actual training. It never got any easier, but it was fun for me. We were waking up at four in the morning to start doing physical fitness training until 6 a.m. After that, we would eat breakfast at the chow hall, then go to our daily training. We had small arms training, then moved into RPG and Mark-19 training where we used the two weapon systems to launch grenades. We practiced missions from walking patrols to close-quarters combat and compound clearance. We completed the course and graduated as non-commissioned officers (NCOs) at the rank of sergeant (E-5).

I was assigned to Bravo Company, 3rd Battalion, 3rd Special Forces Group. We were getting deployed to different parts of Afghanistan. The work was excellent. We were doing night raids, clearing operations, and supportive operations taking over Taliban controlled villages. Our operations were conducted alongside U.S. Special Operations Forces. These soldiers were usually SEALs, Green Berets, and sometimes Marine Special Operations Command (MARSOC). We would get sent to different provinces with different teams to operate jointly. The command would usually send us to locations where large clearing operations were required. We had an advantage over our NATO Special Forces counterparts. We had Afghan faces and spoke the language of these villages. But with NATO forces came NATO firepower. Combined, we had a greater chance of success in rooting out an enemy that hid within the civilian populations.

We typically didn't have a specific target. Sometimes our advising team would have to bring pictures along to identify some of the targets we might find in the area. Their intel was from either International Security Assistance Forces (ISAF) or NATO. Most of the time, the intel wasn't accurate. It always had problems. We would change the whole course of the operation based on our own assessment instead of the intel. If we were supposed to land on the south side of the village and clear west, we would land in the north and clear east. It depended on the fights we expected to face and the enemy movement our eyes in the sky saw on the ground. Operations usually lasted forty-eight to ninety-six hours.

I worked with great soldiers during my time. They were hardworking and constantly training to get better. But, in spite of that effort, we all had one big problem. Public officials had a lot of influence in the command. You wouldn't get promoted unless you knew people in the system. If you were part of a team that raided a target, and that target had influence in the government, you would face a lot of problems. The first thing would be parliament representatives showing up at the unit's gate asking for you. They would call your chain of command and demand that you release the target you'd just risked your life to capture. If you said you would release them, everything would stay calm. If you said you wouldn't and instead sent the target to be prosecuted, you would get replaced or removed from your post. Basically, your hands were tied behind your back.

One time, we captured the Taliban's lead media guy who was recording executions, suicide bombings, and ambushes on video and then posting them on the internet. He was caught with his computer that was full of evidence. There was even a video of him executing an ANA soldier. As soon as he was captured during a night raid, he was brought back to the base for further investigation. He was brought in at seven in the morning. I was sitting with my commander at 9 a.m. when parliament reps started calling him on his phone and telling him, "This guy will be released whether you want it or not, but if you do release him, we will be in debt. And we help people that are good to us."

The unit commander hung up the phone, looked at me, and asked, "Damn, what should we do?"

I said, "Let's complete his case quicker and then send him to court. Then, they will send him to prison." But unfortunately, we were wrong. As soon as we sent him to court, he was released for lack of evidence. Apparently, a computer full of videos of him and his crew killing people wasn't enough evidence. The truth was, he was released by the influence of the Taliban in government.

My dream was to be part of something great. I wanted to give myself to a worthy cause that helped bring peace and stability to my country. Of course, I was still working to feed my family, but by this time, there were plenty of other jobs I could have taken. I still loved this one. Many times, I was told to quit. I couldn't walk proudly with my uniform on. It had to remain a secret. I couldn't inform my relatives and friends about what I did for a living. It was an awful feeling.

My line of work barely had any supporters. Most hated us because of whatever beliefs they had. Many of these people were illiterate. Because of that, they were easily manipulated and didn't understand what the U.S. was doing in Afghanistan. They thought it was dishonorable to work in the army. This was due to the U.S. government paying the military's salary. People considered most Afghans who worked in the government to be "infidel slaves." But we still kept fighting and tried to help civilians as much as we could.

The Taliban had significant influence in the Afghan government. They knew people from low-level soldiers to parliament representatives. If you did an operation that would result in HVTs being killed, they would drag you to court for war crimes. You would receive direct calls from the Taliban telling you to stop the raid or to release their guy that you captured during last night's raid. If you didn't comply, you would lose your job. The Geneva Convention, our rules of engagement, and guarding the so-called human rights of the Taliban were the most significant mistakes the U.S. made in Afghanistan. The U.S. should have never taken it easy on the Taliban after the initial invasion.

Following those rules has given too many rights to insurgents and made them equals to U.S. soldiers. I do remember, back in 2009, we were told by the chain of command that if there was one soldier and one insurgent wounded, the insurgent would be medevacked first if his wounds were deemed more severe. In my opinion, if a suicide bomber is arrested, he must be prosecuted in accordance with due process and the law. I believe such a crime warrants the death penalty. But instead, Taliban were taken to prison. Then, they regrouped in the prisons and had enough time to talk to their leaders, who could pull some strings to get them out. After they were released, they would become more extremist due to being with others like them in the prison. When they got out, they would even be given a promotion in the Taliban's ranks.

When the Taliban lost power in 2001, after the U.S. invasion, some went back to their villages. Others went to Pakistan where they had terrorist training camps. The U.S. made a major mistake by leaving these terrorists alone. When the U.S. shifted its focus and invaded Iraq in 2003, the Taliban started training for a new kind of war. Instructors from the Pakistani Inter-Services Intelligence (ISI) were busy training the Taliban on guerilla warfare. Pakistan, as our neighbor country, always had their problems with us. They never wanted to see a developed Afghanistan. The last thing they wanted was a competent government and a united people on their western border. It helps them when Afghanistan is infighting because a divided country is no threat to them.

The Taliban learned how to build IEDs and shoot AKs, PKMs (Russian light machine gun), and DSHKAs (Russian version of U.S. 50 cal heavy machine gun). They learned how to place IEDs on roads, destroy buildings, conduct executions, run an underground network, and establish concealed communications between calls. We were receiving information from our sources 24/7 about the Taliban's plans, attacks, and training. They studied the capabilities and operational tactics of the U.S. military and used the time to plan assassinations and suicide bombings. I learned about all of this from personal experience and the Taliban posting their document clips of how they planned the attacks.

The Taliban came back more robust and more lethal. They increased their use of violence against the Afghan population. They were conducting suicide bombings and high-profile attacks (HPAs) on civilian sites in cities, executing captured prisoners, destroying roads, and targeting U.S. and NATO forces either by ambush or by placing IEDs in the streets. These attacks were more violent when their targets were the Afghan military and government. It was not a fair fight.

The institutional pressure to preserve the Taliban's rights went so far that it restricted our ability to fight them. This caused multiple problems that deeply affected Afghan soldiers. If we killed them instead of capturing them, we were committing war crimes. That was the problem we had to deal with.

Getting fired was the least of our worries while organizing missions against the Taliban. You were lucky to simply get fired. If you were unlucky and didn't plan well for your operations, it was common to be imprisoned or assassinated by the Taliban for conducting a successful operation. Luckily, I always planned my operations well enough that I survived all this corruption.

So many people quit their jobs due to these challenges and problems. In July of 2012, that's what I did. I left the army to see if civilian life was any better.

It was September of 2012 when I heard about Task Force 241 (TF-241), the Afghan tier one operating unit. I had been out of the armed forces for over a month, and I was working as a translator in an office close to ISAF HQ, next to the U.S. embassy. A great friend of mine by the name of Sultan told me about the task force. I knew Sultan from when he was in the Afghan Army Special Operations Forces as our intelligence officer. When he told me about TF-241, I was like, "No, bro, we are the only top tier one unit in the country." I knew all the Special Operations units operating in the country, including the ones from the Coalition Forces, but I had never heard of this task force.

"What is this TF-241? It's my first time hearing about it."

"You know me, and I don't lie or bluff to you."

"Yeah, I do know you."

"Give me your résumé."

"No, bro. You are either joking or want to prank me. I don't know." I laughed.

Sultan said, "I swear, bro. I'm not joking with you."

I said, "Okay. I'll think about it."

I still didn't take him seriously. I thought about it when I went home, and I did some research. Nothing popped up. I asked other friends, and they didn't know about it. Then, I thought to myself, *Okay. Let's just send him your résumé and see what happens.* I trusted him—this was the type of guy that I trusted with my life. So, I emailed him my résumé.

Sultan called me and laughed. "I got you, bro. I was just joking with you."

I said, "You piece of crap."

We had a laugh about it, but suddenly, his tone changed. "No, I am serious. I just needed a laugh. Wait two months. You will receive a call from an unknown number. They will say we are from the task force. Talk to them and see what they're going to tell you."

I asked him, "How are you so certain that I will receive a call?"

"Because you're shortlisted. They want people with your skills and experience."

"Okay, fine. Let's see what this task force is."

Just as he said, two months later, I received a call from an unknown number. I was asked, "Are you Yousuf?"

"Yes. Who am I talking to?"

"We are calling from the office." They asked me about my friend who was working there. "How long have you known Sultan, and do you know what he does for a living?"

"I don't know what Sultan does for a living. I only know he works somewhere in the government."

The guys from the task force told me to come to a location at a specific time and that they would send me the address and a link-up password in a text. When I was leaving for the initial test, I lied to my boss and told him that I was going to the U.S. embassy to cancel my U.S. visa. By the time I left to go try out for the task force, I had already spent a month working in that office. The policy was to give one month's notice before quitting; otherwise, you wouldn't be paid. I didn't officially quit, though, because I didn't know if I would pass the first test.

It was around mid-November, and it was cold. I had a quick breakfast and swiftly left home early in the morning. I took a cab to my destination. It was a two-hour cab ride. When I arrived, I got out of the cab and started to look at my surroundings. I was just being extra cautious.

There was a white van at the location with two guys in it. They had trimmed beards with black shades and looked like they were in the military. As soon as I saw them, my gut told me that it was them. They were staring at me. They got out of the vehicle and walked toward me. I was standing in a kind of defensive stance in case it was a setup. I wanted to be able to get away or fight back if this went south. I didn't have anything such as a gun or knife to defend myself.

When they approached me, they asked, "What's your name?"

"Yousuf."

"What's the password?"

"Blackbird."

They introduced themselves with two fake names and said, "We are from the task force. Are you ready? Have you brought the proper documents?"

"Yes, I am, and I have the proper documents with me."

"Get in the back of the van."

The van had two seats on the side and held some military equipment. The windows were blocked, so I couldn't see where we were going. I was taken to an unknown location. Once we entered the base gate, they dropped me off at the security checkpoint and placed me in a hall with twenty other people. We were screened with counterintelligence. Then, they put us through a physical test. We had to run eleven kilometers in forty-five minutes without gear and ninety with tactical gear and equipment. The shooting test was hitting twenty-seven out of thirty rounds from one hundred yards with iron sight on a small box target. We did pushups, sit-ups, and pullups. Then, at the end of it all, we went through a drug test and medical examination. All this was just the beginning.

After we were done with the tests, they put us all in different cars and dropped us off somewhere close to downtown Kabul. We were told we would receive a call if we were selected. We were also told not to talk about this to anyone, even our family members.

After I was dropped off, the only thing I was thinking was, *So far, it looks good, but it is too early to judge this task force*. It was two days later when I received a call from an unknown number. After verification, I was told to pack a bag with no electronic devices, such as phones, USB connectors, cameras, or laptops. I just brought a pair of clothes and shower stuff. I was given a different address this time. It was once again time to give goodbyes.

I didn't tell any of my family members anything, except I told my father. I did this because my father was an army veteran who understood the stakes. I told him where I was going and what this new job was. The only reason I shared this information with my father was for security. I wanted him to know where I was in case something happened to me or to my family.

My father said, "Keep this job a secret. Don't tell anyone, not even your brothers. If you can't keep your secret, don't expect others to keep it for you. If family and friends ask you where you work now, tell them that you are a security guard with a huge company and say that, because it is too far away, you only go home once or twice a week."

It was December when I left the house. I woke up that morning and did my early prayer. After the prayer, I grabbed my backpack. The sun was still down. I quietly stepped out of the house and started walking. It was tranquil, and the weather was kind of chilly. There were not many cars. When I got to the main road, I took a cab to the destination. I was thinking to myself, *What are you trying to get yourself into this time?* But I remember, as a kid, I always wanted to be at the top of what I did. My nature is such that if you give me something and I don't get it done, I feel like I owe you something. I don't like the feeling of owing someone anything, and I can't sleep well if the task is not completed.

It is a common thing for humans to have a lot of thoughts about a new place they are going to. Many people have questions like: What will the site look like? How is the new job going to be? How are the accommodations? How is the food? How is the environment? For me, it had become more of: What sort of job do they do? What kind of missions do they do? How do they operate? How do they breach and clear? How long do they stay out in the target area? What's the salary like?

At the beginning of my military career, it was all about the money. I had a big family to feed, and I was born and raised in a poor family. When I was just halfway through this career, my motives changed. It was now about honor and love for my people and nation.

It was around 8 a.m. when I arrived, and the sun was already up by that time. I was thirty minutes early. I looked around and saw a white Toyota Corolla waiting for me. After confirmation, we headed out, and this time, I could see where we were going.

It was an hour-and-twenty-minute drive to our destination. I was in the back seat of the car, and two guys were up front. I was talking to myself, wondering if I should ask these guys about the questions I had. I was also wondering if I shouldn't ask about the questions in case it might look like I was an amateur in this business. I decided it was best not to ask.

Anyway, we arrived and entered the base's gate. I got out of the car for a security check, and afterward, they put me in this room with three other guys. It was a meeting room that probably was used to meet with some visitors at the gate. I recognized the three guys from our first interview. We waited for thirty minutes. They came and picked us up and escorted us into the unit. Hereafter, we were taken to the barracks.

The barracks was a hardstand building built of bricks and concrete, which was uncommon in Afghanistan. The U.S. bases I was in never had brick buildings; they were either tents or connexes. We went in and saw nobody else but us four. Later, I found out that three hundred applicants had applied for the task force with SF and commando backgrounds, and after the process of vetting, background checks, and physical tests, we were the only four who were selected for this unit. We were each given a room with a shower and a bed. They were separate but in the same building. From there, they took us to the armory and the logistics room. We received our training and physical fitness training uniforms. In the evening, they took us to a barbershop to trim our hair down so that we looked like FNGs (Frickin' New Guys), a term used mainly in the U.S. military.

The base was extensive, and it wasn't until late evening that we went to the DFAC for dinner. That is where I saw most of the operators, hardcore, badass-looking guys; you could see most of them were warriors.

Since this was an Afghan unit, the food was Afghan food. It was cooked entirely differently from the food I ate in U.S. bases. After dinner, we walked back to our rooms. One instructor came and walked us to this classroom, and he taught us about the rules and regulations of the unit. Breaking them had different punishments. The punishments were losing a part of your salary or your leave, and for some, the penalty was getting fired from the unit. There were a lot of rules—I don't want to get into all of them. I will just mention a few of them: no drugs, no fights, no bad behavior, no stealing, no lying, no leaking information about the next op, no telling people about your job, and much more.

At the end, the instructor told us that we were in training, and there were certain restrictions on what parts of the base we could go to. We had numbers assigned to us; I was number four. Then, we walked back to our room, which was right across from the classroom. It was our first night, and it was late. I was ready to go to bed when an instructor walked into our hallway and called my number.

"Yes?" I said.

"Come outside."

While walking outside, so many thoughts came to my head. *Why did they only call me? Is it the drug test? But I don't smoke! What is going on?*

When I walked out, I saw a man standing in the dark, but I couldn't see his face. The instructor told me to go talk to him. I started walking, and the instructor left. When I got closer, the face looked familiar to me. At this moment, the guy in the dark walked into the light. I couldn't believe who I saw. It was my old buddy, Sultan!

I laughed and said, "You work in the task force? You son of a bitch!" We started laughing. "I have one thousand questions."

Sultan said, "I know, bro. I know."

"Let's start with the task force. Tell me everything I need to know."

Based on the unit policy, we weren't allowed to talk to the unit members and ask them questions when we were in boot camp. This was in case you failed at the end of the training (the less you knew, the better it was), but this was just between me and him.

When he told me everything about the task force, I realized Task Force 241 was something different. It had been formed by the U.S. Special Operations Forces back in 2001 at the beginning, and it had started without a name. It was meant to remain anonymous, but because of the scorpions painted on the trucks, the unit became known as the Scorpions. Later, it was officially named Task Force 241.

There were many good things about this unit. The pay, support, accommodations, and benefits were good. Everything in the task force was transparent. There was no corruption. The greatest thing about the unit, though, was that it was directly controlled by the Afghan president. This meant you wouldn't get in trouble for conducting an operation. It was a small unit somewhere in Afghanistan, and it was entirely classified by the Afghan government until late 2020.

Joining the unit wasn't easy. Neither the president nor the vice president could influence the unit on who to hire. This was one of the biggest reasons the unit had better achievements on our operations. It didn't matter how strong or powerful you were or how many government officials you knew. You couldn't get into the unit unless you knew a guy who already was working in the task force. He would have to recommend you, and you would have to have two or three months of background check by the U.S. embassy. If you ended up being clean—that is, you had no connection to bad guys, their family members, or anyone who talked to them—you were able to join.

You wouldn't hear about it on the news, TV, or social media. It had a restrictive policy. If you got caught telling people about the unit and what they did, you would be imprisoned. You weren't allowed to use your phone for work, so you would be given a work phone with a fake identity. You were not allowed to take pictures or videos, and if you got caught taking a photo or a video, you would be arrested.

It wasn't as simple as just being arrested, though. You would also be put through an investigation. Then, you would be fired and eventually sent to jail. When going home, you would leave your badge at the gate and take a white badge with your picture and your name on it. You would get searched entering and exiting the unit. It is common to smoke Hashish for many Afghans, but every month, you would be sent to do a drug test. The drug test was random and happened unexpectedly.

I know you might say, "So many rules!" But these rules and policies were the main reason that the unit was kept alive and secret. You could find the smartest, most loyal, and most patriotic Afghans in this unit. I am not saying this just because I was a part of it. This was best proven when the Afghan government fell. We operated for fifteen days during the Taliban regime and never surrendered to them.

—

It was 5 a.m. when one of the instructors came and woke us up for the PT on the first day of training. The instructor came in and started screaming, "EVERYBODY GET UP—BE READY IN THREE MINUTES! We are going to make that blood flow."

We all quickly got up, put on our PT uniforms, and went outside the barracks. We lined up out in front in formation. The instructor took the lead, and we started marching forward, then running. I almost passed out on the first day of the PT. It had been a long time since I'd run consistently. As I've said before, I am the type of guy that will push myself all the way. I don't tap out, even if it means I pass out.

After PT, we went to the DFAC for breakfast. The breakfast was excellent compared to the other units I had visited or worked with. But when I work out or do cardio, I have no appetite whatsoever. I couldn't eat much. I just had a cup of coffee with some bread and butter. We only had twenty minutes to eat. After that, we went straight into changing from PTs to our boot camp uniforms and put on our gear. Then, we went to the armory and grabbed our rifles. From there, we went to the range to zero our weapons.

Our instructor showed us the drill, and we practiced dry runs (training with no ammunition). Then, we went live. They didn't know about my background. On the first beep, we started, and on the second beep, we stopped the shooting. We were shooting at a target ten yards away. I am a super fast shooter. It's a skill that has saved my life many times. I would fire as fast as I could while being accurate and effective. I always liked to go fast on the trigger. The beep went off, and I started popping rounds down at the target. I got six shots off at three targets in two seconds. It was quick.

The instructor said, "I hope new cadets learn the training as you did."

I told him, "Sir, I was in the SOF units."

"I see."

We were told about some more rules on the base. Then, the instructor said, "Don't worry. You will be hearing more and more rules throughout your training period. Remember, the unit stands tall because of these rules. Listen to them very carefully and obey them. We don't have such a thing in this as, 'Oh sorry, sir, I didn't know about it.' You will be promoted based on your performance and obedience to these rules."

The remainder of the first day was easy. We did a three-mile run in the afternoon, then went to our rooms. I took a thirty-minute nap and told myself, *Be ready for more things to come your way.*

We went to the DFAC, ate dinner, then went back to our rooms. We were just chilling in our barracks, and it was around 8 p.m. when two guys came in. They called all of us out and told us to be ready for the advisors to interview us.

I remembered the conversation I had with my buddy Sultan on the first night at the unit. He told me, "Bro, when the advisors come to interview you guys, show yourself and show your talent to the advisors. The only reason they will interview you guys is to look for skills, potential, and courage. They will decide what squadron or part of the unit you will work in."

Because I wanted to be in a combat squadron, I said to myself, *Bro, play it cool and play it like an operator.* I thought about my experiences with the SEALs and thought, *Be like that.* I grabbed all the documents I had, including eight medals and coins from different Special Operations commands I'd operated with. I also wore my shirt that had the Navy SEALs logo on the chest.

It was 9 p.m. when I was called into the office. I walked in with a lot of confidence. Two U.S. advisors were sitting with one Afghan colonel. I said, "Hello," and briefly introduced myself. Then, I asked them, "Do you want to see the certificates or the medals I got when working with Coalition SOF teams?" These medals and coins were given to me at the end of each deployment that I did with SOF teams. Two were for exemplary leadership, and three were for good performance. Two of them were sent to me by Chris Kyle's foundation as appreciation for working alongside Navy SEALs.

"Let's see the medals—we have seen plenty of certificates so far."

I handed them the box that I had my medals in. They started looking at them. I didn't explain to them about the coins. The signs and logos on the awards and coins were enough to tell the story about where they came from.

"It looks like you worked with some badass people."

"I tried my best to keep up."

"Where did you get the shirt from?"

"I used to work and operate with Navy SEALs. I directly worked with Team Four and Ten and did joint ops with Team Seven."

Nodding with approval, one of the advisors said, "Thank you for your service." I later found out he was a SEAL Team Six member. He was only there for a short time.

They all asked me some questions, and then they told me, "We know you have worked for the cause and did a lot of great stuff in the past, but here, we start from zero."

When I left the Army Special Operations Forces, I was a sergeant first class (E-7), but the rule in this task force was that I had to start from zero, which I agreed to by saying, "I am fine with it."

"Why are you fine with it?"

"No matter how good I am, I am still willing to learn more and more. We can never be perfect, but we can be great at something."

"We like your reasons and your character." From there, they thanked me and instructed me to go back to my room. They said to not talk to my friends about the stuff we'd talked about. I acknowledged them and went to my room.

On the way back to my room, I thought to myself, *The last time two advisors told me that they knew the best place for me, I ended up in the middle of nowhere. Hopefully, they will assign me to a good place this time.* Before falling asleep, I was thinking this was easy, but I didn't know the hell that was waiting for us the next day.

Our Hell Week started. This was inspired by the initial test the Navy SEALs go through, but it was not nearly as tough as theirs. The unit was mainly advised and trained by U.S. tier one units. These were Delta Force and SEAL Team Six, but we also had joint operations with British SAS and Special Boat Service (SBS) from time to time.

U.S. advisors showed up to the training. Our advisors were great warriors, and the training was tactically relevant. We started with pistols, assault rifles, snipers, and machine guns. We moved to Mark-19s, RPGs, DSHKAs, ZPUs, and SPGs.

It was a small unit but highly trained and well equipped. We were training with aim points and red dot sights during the daytime. We used IR lasers and NVGs at night. We practiced barricade shooting, house clearing, close-quarters breaching, and close-quarters combat. We shot at targets from five yards to three hundred yards. The closest targets were for assault rifles and farther targets were for sniper rifles. We practiced shooting the machine guns from different positions. We shot from the back of a vehicle, mounted and dismounted positions, and kneeling and prone positions.

The most practical training was at night. Because the task force did the majority of its missions at night, we trained a lot in the dark.

It was day five of my training, and it was a sunny afternoon. We had just finished shooting at targets seven, ten, fifteen, and twenty-five yards away from different positions. We were about to go on our afternoon break and prepare for night training when one of the instructors came to us and said, "Who is Yousuf?"

I raised my hand. "That's me."

The instructor said, "Your brother came to the gate and was asking for you!"

"My brother! At the gate?!"

To be honest, I got scared. *Why did he come to the gate? They know I am here. Is everything fine with Mom and Dad?* So many horrible thoughts went through my head in a matter of seconds. I asked the instructor, "Did he say what he needed?"

He said no, then gave me a phone and told me to call him. I called his number, but I got no response. *Oh man, I hope everything is fine*, I thought to myself. I kept calling until he picked up the phone.

I asked him, "What is going on? Is everything fine?"

My brother said, "Your old job called father a hundred times asking for you!"

"What did you guys tell them?"

"We told them that we don't know where you are and that you might not be able to make it back to work."

"Great. Tell the company that I am in some sort of family trouble, and I don't know when I will be back. Don't say a word about this job to the company!"

I had almost forgotten about my old job entirely. I did work there for one month, though. I wondered if I would ever get my final paycheck. I mean, I wasn't even sure if I was going back or not.

I remember one of the training days, the drill was shooting from a ladder. They split us into two teams. One team would place charges on the breach point, and the other team would hold the security of the compound while standing on a ladder. The ladder was set against a wall. I got up the ladder and started reporting about any movement inside the compound. As a ladder guy, my job was also to report if there were any livestock or humans close to the breach point. We were told not to directly engage and to first warn them to drop their weapons. If they didn't comply, then we could engage them.

The instructors had already placed two targets in the yard. One had a gun, and the other one had a suicide bombing vest on. I yelled, "Drop your weapons!" and waited a few seconds. Then, I reported on the radio that they were not dropping their weapons.

An instructor stopped the training. "Yousuf. What do you see?"

I said, "Two armed bad guys!"

He said, "No. Look closer."

I looked at the targets and looked back.

"Tell me what you see."

"Two armed bad guys."

He said, "No! You see two armed bad guys, but one is a suicide bomber! We don't tell suicide bombers to drop their weapon. We shoot them not in the arm, chest, or leg but directly in the head."

"Don't we get in trouble for that?" I asked.

"We don't operate like any other unit here. Shoot them in the head."

That was when I learned that the task force doesn't mess around with anyone. They get straight to the point: eliminate the threat.

The training was excellent. I learned more and more stuff every day. We did hostage rescue drills and specialized shooting practices. We also had certain days when the advisors would come to the unit to teach us some drills. Most of these special sessions involved close-quarters combat and house clearing. When I did the Afghan Army Special Operations training, we didn't do much of this kind of preparation. We did some but not as in depth as we did at this task force.

One day, we did a drill with this instructor who was excellent at what he was doing. He was a former CAG operator (known as Delta Force). I asked him, "What level of training is this?"

"What do you mean?"

"I mean, compared to your training you had back in the U.S.?"

"These are not conventional unit tactics. This is tier one training that we were taught, and now, I am teaching you guys. This is some of the most advanced stuff we are teaching you guys."

I was happy and proud that we were getting trained the way the elite units in the United States were.

It was almost the end of the training. I needed to get off the base and go to my previous company to get that one month's salary from when I worked there. I told the instructors the truth about where I was going and said to them that it was a lot of money for a guy like me. My instructor was gracious and gave me emergency leave. He told me, "Go get your money, but don't tell them you work here." The money was seventy thousand Afghani (about 1,000 U.S. dollars). The only concern I had was that I hadn't given my one month's notice before quitting. Based on the company rules and policies, if you didn't notify your office about resigning, you wouldn't get paid. So, I was thinking of a fake story that could cover the two months that I had been absent. I couldn't just tell them that I was trying out and training for a top-secret Afghan unit that nobody really knew about.

When I arrived at the office's door, the security guard asked me where I had been. I told him that I'd been in Helmand province and that I was assigned to a job from the office. I didn't need to use much of a story on the guard. After I was searched, I walked in. It was cold and even more so because the task force had shaved my head for boot camp, so I was wearing a winter hat to keep my head warm. I was still thinking of a fake story to get my money. As soon as I walked in, I had my story.

All the staff were shocked when they saw me. They all came to greet me, and everyone was asking all these questions: "Where have you been? You were gone for two months! Were you okay?"

For security reasons, I couldn't tell the truth, but at the same time, I needed the money. So, I started telling my fake story. "I went to the U.S. embassy to cancel my Special Immigrant Visa. When they took my fingerprints, I was told to wait in the waiting area. After waiting for twenty minutes, six masked gunmen walked in and put a bag over my head! They cuffed my hands and took me to the ISAF headquarters. They put me in a Blackhawk and transferred me to Bagram Airfield, and I was in detention for two months! They mistook me for a Taliban commander. They said we have similar faces!"

Some of the staff bought my story. They said, "Yousuf, that is terrible!"

One of the staff members spoke up, saying, "I don't believe you. That seems unlikely."

At that moment, I took off my hat. They saw my shaved head and were surprised. Only then did they believe my story. We don't shave our heads in the winter. Shaving is not common in Kabul.

The supervisor told me that I could still work at that office. He said he would talk to the company leadership.

I politely declined.

When the staff found out I was clean, they felt terrible for me and told me to not tell anyone about the incident because it might cause some problems for me in the future. The supervisor told me not to worry, and he said he would talk to the company's leadership and explain to them why I was absent so they would pay me the one month's salary. The money was transferred to my bank account after a couple of days. That is how I got my money.

—

I went back to the unit the following morning, and we continued training in both the day and night. It is life, and everything has its ups and downs. During the period of the training, sometimes it was fun, most of the time it was exhausting, and sometimes it was boring. Overall, this training helped a lot during my military career.

We went through all that, and at the end of the training, we had a test. If you passed, you were now part of the unit. If you failed, you were given two month's salary and sent home. The examination was physical and mental, and it involved shooting. For the physical part, you had to do a two-hundred-meter sprint in under two minutes, seventy pushups, and seventy sit-ups. Then, you had eighty minutes to do a sixteen-kilometer hell walk with full gear. The hills on this route were steep and killed our legs. We also had to climb a twenty-foot rope with our combat gear, then carry a wounded soldier a thirty-yard distance and sprint up a hill in forty-five seconds.

The mental score was given based on your performance, teamwork, and activity during the two months of training. This test was more abstract and based on the perception of the advisors.

The shooting test consisted of shooting a thirty-round magazine at targets. Each target was a black silhouette with a small box drawn on it that we called the "A" box. We had ten rounds to shoot at the twenty-five-yard target, ten rounds to shoot at the fifty-yard target, and ten rounds to shoot at the one-hundred-yard target, firing from different positions. To pass, you had to hit twenty-seven out of the thirty rounds. That was the pass requirement, and if you failed, you were done with the task force.

I had an excellent reputation with the instructors, the advisors, and the other three FNGs. I passed the test with a great score and performance. The advisors liked me for some reason. The training advisors were private military contractors (PMCs). Later, I found out I was recommended to the unit leadership by one of the U.S. instructors. He wanted me to start in a team leader role. This instructor used to be a Navy SEAL, and he knew some of the guys I'd worked with in the past.

Based on the unit rules, new guys couldn't be put directly in leadership positions, no matter whether they were leading two men or one hundred men. The only reason they didn't let new guys run in leadership roles from the start was because of the difference in operating procedures compared to other units. It took time to learn these procedures, and leaders had to earn their spot. I was told that I had six months to prove I was worthy of this position and power. I used those six months and volunteered to participate in another four weeks of SWAT course training. I did this even though I was just out of training.

I felt I needed to prove myself. In the SWAT course, we did fast roping and shot MP5s. Most training drills were hostage rescue situations. We focused on reading target buildings, breaching, clearing a room with two men and four men, and more. I did the best I could to learn and demonstrate my best performance. I was going to the range every afternoon, shooting from different distances and working on various drills. I would use the search engine Google and the video platform YouTube to view tactical videos from former tier one operators. Of course, these were not from just some random YouTubers.

As I had learned, actual combat is way different from what we see in movies and games. So, hearing about their experiences helped a lot. I would watch a video, then work on the drills in my free time. I didn't have much free time, but one hour a day would still work for me. Sometimes I would go to the range and watch the advisors training, then practice the same drills. Sometimes I would just walk up to them and ask if I could shoot with them. They would be all for it. When you love something, you learn it very quickly, and I loved this job. Naturally, I was a quick learner. Most advisors were impressed, but you can't be great all the time. You fail, you mess up, you make mistakes, but you still learn from your failures.

I did have failures in life, but thankfully, they weren't big or messy. Still, they were failures, and I needed to learn from them. I had many close calls throughout my career. Many almost resulted in my death. Being in combat for thirteen straight years will do that to you. Being a soldier will get you to different places with a lot of high ups and low downs.

One of the close calls was when I was in the SWAT course. We were clearing this compound, and I was the first guy going into the room. When we breached, it was a hallway. We quickly cleared it. Then, I took the left room with one other guy and the other two took the right. I walked in a ready-to-action position. I saw two targets on my right. When I walked in, I started popping rounds at the target on the left, leaving the second target for the other soldier. While I was shooting rounds, I moved myself to the left so my buddy could have a clear line of sight. Based on what we were trained to do, we needed to be in a straight line, but the soldier was one step behind me. He almost shot my right elbow off. I called a cease-fire.

I yelled at the soldier, "What the heck are you doing?"

He said, "I'm sorry."

"Being sorry doesn't do anything. Practice more, and if this happens in real life, it might get you or your buddy killed!"

The instructor walked in and asked, "What is going on?"

I didn't rat on him and lied instead. "His weapon jammed." I didn't want him to be punished, and I also didn't want him to be neglected in this line of work. But he learned and became an excellent breacher later in his squadron.

—

The unit standard operating procedure (SOP) for TF-241 was going after suicide bombers, major organized crimes (such as weapon and drug smuggling), terrorist gatherings, HPAs, HVTs, and many other types of counterterrorism operations. I have been with a lot of units and have done many types of operations, but this unit was a different breed. The task force wasn't messing around with bad guys. We rolled out every night to kill or capture terrorists. Then, we returned to base and did it again the next night. We would go out in the dark and return to base before sunrise. We had great support in this unit both in the air and on the ground. Our orders were directly from the Afghan president.

TF-241 was a brotherhood that I had never before experienced.

When we were going to target areas, the Taliban would run away to the hell they came from. We were operating inside and outside of Kabul province. The Taliban placed their spotters in the areas where they could report our convoy's movement. They had limited success. We were like the ghost that the enemy never saw coming. We were our enemies' worst nightmare and the oppressed people's beautiful dream.

Chapter 7

I was in a support squadron at the beginning. This squadron was different from other squadrons. Its task was to provide backup soldiers and heavy weapons and mortar support during an operation, which was highly effective during an operation when you didn't have air support. There wasn't an assaulting team in the squadron. That was the part I didn't like. Assaulters were the guys breaking down doors, entering breaches, and taking out the bad guy in close combat. That's what I wanted to be. I liked being at the tip of the spear.

The first operation I ever did with the task force was one I had to force my way onto. Since I was recommended by the advisors to start as a team leader against the usual protocol, there were some people who weren't happy. The U.S. Special Forces community is small and very close to each other. Because I had worked with so many teams, I had some level of reputation in the U.S. Special Operations world. I am not sure exactly how I was recommended, but it was either because a friend of the advisors vouched on my behalf or because I showed a high level of proficiency during the training.

Some of the soldiers were upset, but they had no choice but to accept it because it was above their pay grade. When leadership makes a decision, you can't reject it. This is how the military works. Because of that specific reason, my squadron leadership wouldn't give me any chances to prove I belonged in the position I was assigned to. They wouldn't involve me in the operations and leadership training. I could easily see that the squadron commander didn't want me around. I wanted to go out on an operation to prove to them that I was capable of this position and that I wouldn't let them down. So, I became friends with the operational commander, and I asked him to put me in an operation. He told me that he would, but somehow, he either forgot or he didn't believe in my experience and chose not to. I asked him the following night for the next operation.

I got a bit serious and told him, "If you don't put me on this operation, I will be mad."

He got serious too and said, "Why are you so interested in going out? Are you tired of your life?"

"I know what is out there. I know all the risks. This is the job I signed up for. Don't even put me among the assaulters. Put me as the backup team or with guys that only pull the security. Whether I go now or later, I will be going on missions eventually, and I just want to be ready for it."

He agreed to put me on a mission. It was mid-February. I remember it was freezing. I was called on the radio and told to come to the briefing at 1500. My name was on the list for tonight's mission. I grabbed my notebook and went to the tactical operations center (TOC).

The technology there was new. The satellite imaging, the offline tactical military maps on smartphones, different coded radios, and small drones for operations were far more advanced than anything I had previously worked with. We didn't have most of this technology back in the Afghan SF units. This was because of the support the task force had from Afghan and Coalition sites.

I went into the TOC and said hi to some of the guys I was introduced to. I stood in a corner of the briefing room. The commander and the advisor came in and started the briefing. The target was one of the Al Qaeda network leaders. He was meeting with insurgent leadership in Maidan Wardak province, which is located on the west side of Kabul province. Security wise, Wardak was one of the worst provinces, and it regularly stayed at war with U.S. and Coalition Forces from day one. But it had a beautiful, mountainous countryside. The target was staying in Tangi Valley, Sayedabad district. Taliban leadership headquarters and main strongholds were in this valley. We had operations all over the country, but mainly, they were around Kabul province. I had personally never operated in Wardak province with any prior unit, and I had zero information about it.

I was attached to the security team. Our job on this team was pulling security for the leadership during an operation. We were not bodyguards but secured their area so they could talk with air support and coordinate elements on the ground. Before the briefing ended, the lead advisor emphasized, "If you see an armed insurgent, don't hesitate to engage him. Find a cover and use it." When the briefing finished, we were dismissed.

The departure time was after sunset, and our hit time to return to base was at seven in the morning. I only had three hours to prepare before leaving. I went straight to Sultan's room to ask him any questions about what to expect. It was far from my first time in a fight, but TF-241 was something different. Sultan told me, "Let's go to the DFAC. We will eat and I will walk you through this whole process."

We went to the DFAC, and while eating dinner, Sultan started explaining. "We line up with our vehicles by the unit's gate. When you get to the gate, find the squadron's deputy commander (D-Com). The D-Com will tell you which vehicle you will be riding in. Lock and load before you hop in the vehicle. Once we are out of the gate, muzzles are out of the window, and when we get to the target and the convoy stops, they will call it on the radio. When the convoy stops, get out of the vehicle and go up front." He paused and asked, "You will be security tonight, right?"

"Yes."

"Okay. You will be on the rear side of the line. Up front is where the assaulters will be. Because we are wearing NVGs, everything looks green. Just mark your team or the guy in front of you. You will be fine for the rest of it."

"What are the rules of engagement? Will I get in trouble if I kill a bad guy?"

"Bro, you are in the task force. Rules of engagement are different here. You see a bad guy with a gun, be positive he has a gun and just drop him. Nobody walks out of their homes during our raids unless they have intentions of ambushing us. No one likes seeing civilians get caught in between. In my experience, anyone outside is trying to kill you."

"You sure?"

"Bro, they know we don't mess around. They know they can't influence us through the Afghan government or parliament reps. First, they try to run away before we arrive. Second, they will surround themselves if they are about to get caught. But if they don't want to surround themselves, they will fight. Most of the time, they just run away. But when they stay, they want to fight. We are in a war. We are the military. We are not the police. We don't always go in to arrest them. Most of these guys will be released through the corrupt judgment system we have."

Some of you reading this might say, "Just shoot them." Others might say that you can't just shoot a bad guy. You might think of human rights and the rules of the Geneva Convention or how the good guys in movies always manage to shoot the bad guy in the shoulder. But just like how I found out the hard way that what is in the movies isn't real, you'll find out war isn't that clean. We don't have time to disarm the bad guy, hold them hostage, and determine whether they deserve death. We can't just shoot them in the legs. Our job is to eliminate the threat and trust that those who are determining our targets are doing it right. This is how we fought back. The Taliban and Al Qaeda didn't hesitate to kill combatants and civilians alike. Stopping them meant saving lives.

We finished dinner and went back to our rooms. I started preparing for the mission. I wasn't scared of the fight. I was worried about making a mistake, and if I did make one, it would be taken seriously, especially by the people who were already unhappy about me working as a team leader. I had to stay relaxed no matter what happened. I calmed my mind and always prayed to God.

Because it was a cold night, I wore some warm clothing under my uniform. I set up my body armor and checked my radio, batteries, and NVGs. I checked my gun by going to the range just to shoot some rounds. I checked the laser and other tech on the gun. I set up the pouches on my body armor the way I wanted to for this mission. I usually never carried more than four magazines on my vest, but I packed eight mags this time. The task force issued eight mags, and that's what the rest of the soldiers carried. We weren't allowed to load tracer rounds because it would give away our positions during the night. After I was geared up, I went to the gate.

Before I asked the D-Com what vehicle I was riding in, one of the soldiers came to me. "Hey, man! You're the new guy?"

I said, "Yes."

The soldier said, "Come with me. You are in my vehicle. Mark it. I don't want you to get lost when coming back in the morning."

All the vehicles had marks and numbers on it. This one was A16.

A voice came over the radio. "Net call! Net call, lock and load, departing in ten minutes." This was the moment. You could hear every gun loading at the same time. You could feel the freedom. It's a feeling I can't fully explain.

The last call was for everyone to get in the vehicles. You could hear the radio confirmations on the net. "Departing! Departing!" Vehicles started moving one by one. They moved slowly to create spacing. We rolled out of the gate. It was a long convoy of great warriors, my countrymen, going after some bad guys. It was dark, and the NVGs were down over our faces. From the light of the NVGs glowing in our eyes, we looked green like devil hunters. It can only be described in one word: badass.

Riding out on this mission was the most fantastic feeling I ever had. Even though I had done similar stuff in the past, I had never done it with this number of vehicles and operators. The unit had three squadrons, and all three of them were rolling out. We were moving in blackout drive, meaning lights off and wearing NVGs, for the first mile. When we were on the main road, we turned our lights back on. If you were a civilian car coming our way, the only thing you would see from a distance was green lasers hitting your car. People knew it was a military convoy. It translated to *pull over—or else*. We were probably the first unit to use so many green lasers.

Back when I was in Afghan Army SF, the gunner would just shout at the drivers to get out of the way. Even Kabul's crazy drivers got the hint to pull over. If they didn't, we would throw a water bottle at their windows. It was a cheap, harmless way to get them to move. Getting drivers to move immediately wasn't as much of a problem for other units since the security threat wasn't as high as it was on TF-241.

My barrel was out of the window. When we were going through the city, you could see happiness on most people's faces. That meant they were supporting the government and were happy to see the enemy crushed. Of course, some weren't happy because they had relatives in the Taliban, and they knew when a convoy this big was coming after someone, it might be their last night on earth. When we arrived at the Kabul-Wardak gate, a voice spoke over the radio. "Net call! Net call! Blackout. Blackout." This meant we were in Taliban territory and the use of any light was prohibited. Things were about to get real serious.

Scanners were always on when departing from the gate. The Taliban scanner chatter started: "A raid is on its way."

They called themselves Mujahedin (Holy Fighters). They were talking about our convoy, but they didn't know where we were exactly. They had spotters that reported our convoy, usually at gas stations or bread bakeries. They kept asking each other, "Where are they? Do you see them?"

We kept driving. The gas stations were right on the side of the road. Their main communication tools were ICOM radios and sometimes phones. They were asking for our location to determine where we were going so they could tell the insurgents in the area to leave or hide. Usually, all the Taliban would start hiding as soon as they knew about the raid coming to their area, but sometimes we caught them off guard. We arrived in the target area. Again, a voice came over the radio: "Net call! Net call! Stopping point. Stopping point."

We got out of the vehicles. I checked my gear and equipment. I was all set. I took a few steps back and took a picture of the vehicle in my head. I started walking to the front of the formation as quickly as I could. I saw a line and went to stand there. Two minutes passed, and we were almost ready to start walking to the target compound. I noticed a bunch of guys behind me. I said to myself, *Oh boy, looks like you are standing with the wrong group.* I asked one of the last guys, "Are you an assaulter?"

The assaulter said, "Of course. What did you think? Do I look like a clown?"

I was definitely standing with the wrong group. I quickly took off and went all the way to the rear side of the line. One of the commanders stopped me. "Tell me who you are and where are you going."

I said, "I am security."

The commander got mad and said, "Go to the rear side of the group. We will have a talk when we get back to base." The good thing was it was dark, and he didn't know who I was. He thought I was one of his soldiers.

One advisor was in front of me. I asked him a question with broken English. I didn't want them to know I understood and spoke English. If they knew that I understood English, the advisors might be more selective with the secret information and fresh intel they communicated out loud. I was there to hear, watch, and observe—and I wanted to listen to it all. This is how I asked him. "You advisor?"

The advisor said, "Yes."

"Me security, security." I used body language and signs.

The advisor told me to stay behind him and pull the security in the back. I marked his image in my mind and the appearance of the guy in front of him. He had a patch on his backpack. Otherwise, everyone looked green and the same. The NVGs I had on made it even worse. They were one of the worst pairs of NVGs I had ever used, but I was confident. I'd previously done similar night raids as a terp with the U.S. SOF units, and I'd done them without NVGs too.

We started walking. I was just focused on my surroundings; that was the only thing I had in my head. I was prepared for the enemy to ambush us any moment. You never knew what could happen in the next few steps.

It was a quiet night. It was cold, and there was snow on the ground. You could hear the footsteps of all the soldiers. We received a call over the radio. The plan had changed. We had intelligence, surveillance, and reconnaissance (ISR) watching over the village and a US AC-130 gunship overhead. Every building in the village had been given a name; they were all displayed on our Android Team Awareness Kits (ATAKs). This was a military version of Google Earth (an internet-based platform for satellite imagery) that worked offline. You didn't need an internet connection. The imagery had to be loaded manually. It was one of the most significant pieces of technology created for the Special Operations Forces and military units. The ISR reported some movers to the north of our target compound. Afghan homes are big and usually have more than one house, which is why we called them compounds. The movers were reported on our original route. Getting into a fight with movers before we hit the target would mean our target would likely escape. We changed to our alternate route.

We had three assault teams and three security teams because we were raiding three targets at the same time. Around three hundred warriors went on this mission. The scanner chatter was frequent and frantic. I could sense the fear the Taliban had from the raids. We got to our first target, but we had to wait a few minutes until the other teams had locked their targets. The plan was to do simultaneous explosive breaches. Almost all our breaches were explosive breaches. There were a lot of reasons for it, the main one being security. It was way too dangerous to send a guy over the wall to open the door. Also, it is hard to communicate and call out stuff in a warzone. The blast of the breach would initiate the sounds of battle. We were well prepared for these operations and already had our plans. The movers at the compound did not. Limiting their ability to communicate gave us another tactical advantage.

The assault commander passed to the squadron commander over the radio, "Commander! Teams are ready, and all assaulters are in position to place charges and breach the compounds."

We, the security team, were up front and had already locked and contained the compound. Nothing was getting in, and nothing was getting out. We were watching the alleyways and the footpaths coming into the building in case the Taliban called for backup. Once the security teams were set, the team lead reported that the building was locked down. That is when the assaulters went to their assault position by the compound. Ladders went up. The ladder guys climbed them and started reporting on the target. They would usually report the interior design of the structure, any movement inside the building, and especially any suspicious activities. This could include a lot of action in the rooms, people peeking from windows, lights being turned on and off, a lot of talking, people holding weapons, and many more things. We were operating in a neighborhood full of people who wanted to kill us, either by shooting, placing IEDs, or blowing up their own body to kill us. However, the ladder guys called NSTR, meaning "nothing significant to report."

Breachers then went up to the doors and placed an explosive charge. As soon as they were set, they reported to the commander. The commander started the countdown. "Five. Four. Three. Two. One." BOOM! The explosives went off. Everyone in the village, including the Taliban, were alerted to our presence in their village. They all knew we were here. Buildings in Afghan villages are all mud houses. Most are over one hundred years old. Due to their construction, the explosions created a big cloud of dust at the main entrance both inside and outside of the compound. It was dangerous to go through that kind of entrance with NVGs. You couldn't really see anything. This is why the ladder teams were so important. They could provide cover fire for the assault teams that had to push through the breach point with limited vision. The ladder guys who came down from the ladder during the explosion then went back up to pull security. This was in case the target or his fighters made any moves. If they did, the ladder guys could engage the enemy on the peripheries under strict fire control measures.

While that was happening, the assaulters, who had already waited a few seconds for the dust to settle, started to run through. Assaulters breached and started clearing the building. It was executed with elite precision with mere seconds between steps. It was embedded in our minds from our military instructors to never stand in front of the breach point, whether it be a door, a gate, or a window. When the assault team goes in, it is one person to the left, one person to the right, and so on, never staying in front of an opening. You must move fast and clear your corners for you and your team's safety. After that door is blown, if the enemy wants to stand and fight, rounds of AK-47 ammunition will be heading your way at the breach point. Once a fight breaks out, you are fighting not one, not two, but many fighters inside the compound.

For this operation, once the assaulters were in, rounds started popping off all over the compound. This was the moment things became a sort of controlled chaos. All elements were on different radio channels. I quickly changed my channel to hear what was going on inside the building. One guy with an AK-47 came out of his room and was about to send a machine gun burst into the entrance, but he was killed before he could do any harm to our guys.

There is a reason that the terrorists always shoot at the doors. It happens so often it can be considered a standard assumption when in this kind of fight. These are guys who are terrified of losing their life, either by dying or going to prison forever. Think how you might react if a team of deadly tactical force burst into your room. Now think how the terrorists would probably fight back. The answer is that they will likely hide in their room and wait for us. They will wait until they hear our footsteps. This is because they can't see through the door, and they are scared. They will assume we are behind the door; then, they will open fire at the door. They'd hope to kill one or two of us before they die. That is the ideology most criminals have, especially the group we were fighting against. They didn't care if they died in this war. They accepted this fate even if they were scared of it.

The assault had gone on for two minutes. You could hear more and more gunshots ringing out. Most people know the sound of a gun from being behind one or from watching movies. It sounds like a large pop. But when you're on the wrong end of a muzzle or ricochet, it sounds like a whistle or a zing.

We, as security, were still oriented outside the compound. The building had six rooms, and shots were coming out of all six rooms. The assaulters couldn't push any farther into the building. The chatter on the scanner was also loud. In these types of situations, the Taliban weren't talking in codes. If they were screaming, that meant one of their men was down. They were screaming and saying goodbye to their buddies over the ICOM.

Our lead advisor said, "We can't take the risk of going farther into this compound. It isn't worth the risk, and I wouldn't exchange the life of one of our operators for one hundred insurgents. We will call an airstrike on the compound."

Airstrikes were called by our U.S. advisors and carried out by the U.S. Air Force. The call came in on the radio telling our guys to pull back and that air support was dropping a five-hundred-pound bomb on the building. We pulled back about half of a mile from the target building. You might wonder why we distanced ourselves that far from the airstrike. We know from past experiences that once a bomb is out of the plane, there is no way to control it. If you are close to the target, you might get hit too or fragments might catch you. And the biggest reason of all, of course, is that it is a freaking bomb. The farther you are from the blast site, the safer you will be.

The bomb was in the air. It was called out when it was one minute away from the building. When it was seconds away, you could hear it. It sounded like the air was ripping in two. It hit the building, and the bomb destroyed the whole compound. Seeing the damage made me want to stand farther away the next time. The building was now just a massive pile of dirt.

Once that bomb hit, the village turned to hell. ISR reported more fighters were coming on motorbikes from different villages. We had an AC-130 overhead ready to engage targets. An AC-130 gunship is a heavily armed, long-endurance, ground-attack variant of the C-130 Hercules transport. It is a fixed-wing aircraft, and it carries a wide array of ground-attack weapons that are integrated with sophisticated sensors, navigation, and fire-control systems. The AC-130 asked for approval from the command on the ground to engage. It was approved, and that beast started engaging insurgents. It made a magnificent sound that can only be described as *bbbbbrrrrrrrrrpppppp*. It killed over twenty insurgents that were coming toward our troops, either by motorcycles or on foot.

After fifty minutes of engaging targets, we went back to do a battle damage assessment (BDA) to confirm whether our target was among the guys who'd died. The bodies were scattered across the rubble with large gashes across them and chunks of red flesh thrown about the wreckage. After the BDA, we used DNA to confirm that our target was killed. Ten of his fighters were also killed. That confirmation was a mission accomplished. We then collected whatever we could from the building, which looked like it was being used more like a headquarters than a regular compound. After the sensitive site exploitation (SSE), we kept clearing more buildings nearby.

Clearing mosques was common. If there was a mosque on our route to the next target, it had to be cleared. We moved in and cleared it. We never used explosives to breach a mosque. It always had a lot of windows, and we could clearly see the inside. The reason we had to clear it was that insurgents were using mosques as places to sleep and hide. This was especially true in winter. It was warmer in mosques, and it is a holy place, a place with no owner. The Taliban didn't want to stay in their own houses because they didn't want anything to happen to their own homes. But they were okay if they caused a holy place to be destroyed. They aren't good Muslims.

Mosques are very holy. We call them God's house on earth, a place of worship and prayers. It should have never been used as a shelter for the Taliban to sleep or teach their extremist thoughts. But since people were scared to tell them that, the Taliban used the mosques as much as they could. If we engaged or bombed them in there, the Taliban would use that as a tool to recruit more young Afghans to their cause. They would usually tell them, "All these soldiers are infidels! They destroy the mosques for no reason!"

Unfortunately, holy places had been bombed in the past based on wrong information or incorrect intelligence. Now, when clearing mosques, we would see signs of insurgents in four out of five sacred sites. We would see leftover ammo or explosives, documents, and much more. We cleared most parts of the village, but we had no other engagements or firefights that night.

It was freaking cold. But it didn't matter if the weather was cold or warm as long as the weather was clear for the air support. If air support was able to operate, then we were operating. We always had to depart the village before the sunrise though. After the sunrise, it would become difficult to recognize the Taliban due to increased civilian activity in the area. The Taliban were too scared to wear a uniform, so they blended in with villagers during the day. For that reason, the best option was to return to the base early. It was around five in the morning when we wrapped up the operation and started back to base. While walking back to where we had our vehicles lined up, my NVGs began blinking.

Oh boy! I thought. *That is not a good sign!* The warning was that my batteries were low. I quickly checked my pocket and pouches and didn't find any spare batteries. I said to myself, *Bro. You messed up. What will you do?* Among our gear we also had flashlights that were attached to our helmets. Some had them attached to their rifles.

While walking back, I slowly pulled out the batteries from my flashlight. I told myself that NVGs were more critical than the flashlight, which I wouldn't be using almost at all the rest of the night. The flashlight was infrared (IR), meaning it couldn't be seen with the naked eye. I replaced the NVG batteries with my flashlight batteries while walking and without anyone noticing. I would have been in trouble because you could always just go to the logistics or communication office, and they would give you spare batteries. It was a lesson learned. I always remembered to carry extra batteries and ammunition.

We got back to the vehicles. The scanner chatter was still hot. The Taliban were screaming, "Don't let them leave in peace! We have to kill them all!"

I thought, *It looks like we killed an important leader or member of their group.*

We started departing from the area. While on our way back to base, ISR and the AC-130 were still above our heads. They might have gone for a refuel and come back. You could still hear ISR reports over the radio. They were mainly talking about movers up ahead, close to the main road. Then, we heard ISR reporting five guys with shovels and something like a bag. They were watching three miles ahead of us. We were still driving until the ISR said that it looked like they were placing something on the ground. This was the moment I was confident they were placing an IED for us. The following report came in: They were dragging some sort of wire from the road to the tree line six hundred yards away.

The squadron commander stopped the convoy half a mile away from the identified location. Based on an EOD report I heard over the radio, it looked like a wired IED, which can be dangerous until either the wire gets disconnected or we kill or arrest the guys controlling the trigger. The gunship was asked to drop rounds at five men. After the confirmation with the squadron commander, the lead advisors gave the approval to the gunship to start engaging the movers. The sound from it was blaring, and it was like music to my ears. After three or four minutes, ISR reported there was no sign left from the movers. We couldn't see the movers either, but we could see the sparks of rounds hitting that specific area. It looked nice through the NVGs. After that, we had our EOD team push up front with a security team to place charges on the IED or whatever explosives they had planted there for us. EOD reported that it was an IED and that it looked big. It was too risky to disconnect the wire and pull the IED out of the ground. We had no option but to place a C-4 charge on it and explode it.

The commander gave the EOD team lead the confirmation, and a charge was placed. The timer was set for three minutes. We stayed far enough away, then detonated the IED and started moving. There was no time to conduct a BDA of the dead insurgents. It was close to sunrise, and we needed to leave the area. It was going to be a challenge to control the traffic on the road. Kabul has no regulation or proper traffic rules, and even if it did, drivers don't obey the laws. For that reason, it makes the roads very hard to control.

We left the area and entered Kabul's gate. By the time we were in Kabul city, the sun was up. It was around 7:30 a.m. when we finally arrived at the base. When we entered, we parked on the side of the road and unloaded our weapons and rolled into the unit. After, everyone went to their rooms. Overall, it was an excellent experience to help me get to know the unit and how it operates. The task force exceeded my expectations, and I felt proud to be a part of such an organization.

Chapter 8

I went to my room and took off my gear. After a shower, I went to the DFAC to have my breakfast and also listen to the stories of what the boys encountered on the mission. There was always a hunger within me to increase my experience and better my understanding of our rules of engagement. I grabbed a cup of tea and sat at the table where the soldiers were seated. Everyone was talking about their individual side of the experience and what they had seen. Some compared last night's operation with previous operations and mentioned what went well and what needed work. It was an informal way of mentoring each other. It was just soldiers' thoughts, but I was listening to them carefully so that I could learn and understand more about this unit. There were a bunch of stories from different guys in each of the assault teams. At the end of the day, one guy was never the hero. It was and is always about teamwork. Teamwork makes the dream work, like they say in America.

I learned a lot. Before, I'd never had such excellent and continuous air support above us during an operation. The task force's air support was with us from the start to the end of the op. The air support definitely wasn't Afghan. It was all American aircraft and pilots. Even the SEALs and other American SF teams I'd worked with did not have this level of support.

When I got back to my room from the DFAC, it was past 8 a.m. Because I was exhausted, I went to sleep in seconds. It was 2 p.m. when I woke up. I was still tired. My back and legs were sore, and I had a slight headache. It had been a while since I had done ten hours of walking, but it was a great experience. After I got up, I took a fresh, cold shower. It helped to wake my body up quicker.

Part of my plan for the day was to go to the DFAC to hear more about how many insurgents had been killed during last night's operation. First though, being the social person that I am means I dislike eating alone, so I headed to the rooms of the guys who were in Charlie Squadron to check if they wanted to get some lunch. I always liked the guys in Charlie Squadron. I thought they were the coolest guys on base.

I went to the Charlie Squadrons' room and saw a couple of them were awake. I asked them, "Are you guys going to lunch?"

"Yes," one of them said. He got up and went to wake the others. I didn't want to wake them because they weren't my friends yet, and I didn't know them well.

We went to the DFAC and had plenty of chats. Every story told put more questions in my mind. The Charlie guys were more than happy to answer anything I asked them. Later that day, one of them sat with me from eight at night until three in the morning, sharing all his stories. I enjoyed every bit of it. At the end of the conversation, he said, "Bro, let's go to sleep. We might have another mission later today."

I learned a lot—it was like a class for me. I still remember most of the stories he mentioned. It was a good conversation.

One of the guys that I had just become friends with came into my room and said, "Hey, bro, there is going to be an operation in the city. Ask the commander to put you on that op. It will be a fun experience."

I thanked him, and he left the room. As soon as I heard about the mission, I went to the operational commander again and asked him to put me on this operation too.

His face was surprised. He looked me up and down again. "Aren't you tired from last night's operation?"

"I am, but I want to go out again."

"Don't get yourself exhausted. We have these operations every day, nonstop." But he put my name on the list for this operation.

This one would be low-vis, meaning low visibility—similar to an undercover FBI operation or when you have a Special Operations squad operating in civilian clothing. These were highly successful operations most of the time. They had a lot of achievements with less effort. I liked that you didn't need fifty vehicles to do them either. You didn't need to be in full gear, and, of course, they were less dangerous.

A short briefing was done, and I found out that we were going out with twelve vehicles. Because I had never done undercover operations before, I had no expectations. Based on what I learned after asking the other soldiers, it was similar to a night operation but just a little different because it was done in the city and not a village. As I mentioned before, I needed the experience, and I loved this job. I was also hoping to learn more about the TF-241.

The target was an insurgent commander who was also a Taliban financial chief for that province coming from Kapisa province (a province located northeast of Kabul province). He was a terrorist key commander, and we needed to take him down. We weren't going after him though. He was coming to us. That was the fun part and what got me excited for this operation. In my head, I was in a movie again, but this time, it was a spy film. But again, life isn't a movie. And, man, I was so wrong. This mission was very dull. It was not some Jason Bourne or James Bond stuff.

At the end of the day, our task force was part of the Afghan National Directorate of Security (similar to a mix of the FBI/NSA/CIA and the Department of Homeland Security). We were a small task force in the country, but the primary department was running interior and exterior intelligence for the whole country. We never did these types of jobs back when I was in the special forces. The Afghan Army SF operations were only military and combat focused.

We all gathered close to the gate. The commander and the advisor did a ten-minute briefing. We were all handed a picture of the target. The target had long hair, a beard, and a face that looked mean but suggested he was just a useful idiot with no knowledge in his brain. That was my first thought when I saw the photo.

We were told that a team was tracking his phone and that he had just entered Kabul city. There was a tracking system, and once it locked someone's number, it would track them as long as it could. They also said we were doing a snatch and grab mission. I didn't know what the hell that meant. Later, I found out that "snatch and grab" meant we went into the city and kidnapped our target right from the sidewalk or wherever he was. We loaded our rifles and pistols. The modes of transportation were civilian vehicles (Fords, sedans, Toyotas, trucks, vans, and other cars that can easily blend in the city with the other people). Everything was covered. We all had scarves to cover our necks so people didn't see the radio wiring and headphones on our ears. And we were all wearing baggy Afghan clothes to cover the body armor.

I didn't do much to disguise myself. I just wore regular Afghan clothes. I didn't need a disguise because I looked like any other Afghan in the city. Everybody was assigned to a specific vehicle in the convoy, and everyone had a particular job and assignment in the team. I was just going as backup. We all loaded into the vehicles, and I got into the one that was assigned to me. They were expecting me, and as soon as I got in, we started rolling out. I didn't know any of the guys in the vehicle with me, but I decided to ask them questions about the mission. They were helpful and explained the whole thing to me. After that, I was ready to play along. The target was marked and locked.

The commander called, "Departure. Departure," on the radio.

One car left the base, and the rest of the cars didn't move! It felt weird. Usually, we moved together. I didn't say anything. I didn't want to say something that might make me look stupid. Three minutes later, another car left. Another three minutes, and then another one. I later found out that we were using this trick so cars coming out of the base didn't look like a convoy. It was a smart move.

Police District 1 is where you could find the busiest part of Kabul city, and unfortunately, that's where our target was. It was challenging to find our bearded target among a thousand other bearded people. And let's not forget that these targets were competent and well trained. They knew about the tracking system that the U.S. and NATO were using. We lost our target's phone signature, so we were in the dark about his current location. We were circling around in the city for a couple of hours until we locked on to this guy's phone again. After we locked him, we had to get out of the vehicles and start searching for him on foot. We couldn't pull people over and match their face with the picture we were given. We had to be discreet about it. We had to look all over for this guy.

I was with the Global System for Mobile (GSM) communication team. GSM is a digital mobile network that is widely used by mobile users around the world. The GSM guy looked at the device, then glanced back up. He scanned around. "Bro, the system shows him here, but I can't seem to locate him."

We were looking up and down, left and right, to find the target. I happened to be looking in one specific direction when I noticed a guy was looking at me. As soon as I looked at him, he got into a cab. I told the GSM guy, "That looks like him. That is him." Wasting no time, I ran to the cab and reached to my side. I had no option but to pull my pistol and stop the taxi. The taxi driver was quick to take his hands off the wheel. His actions immediately told me he didn't want trouble. I told the taxi driver to pull over, and he obliged. Then, I grabbed our target and got him out of the car.

Our target was hysterical and asked, "What did I do? Who are you guys?"

I told him, "Zip your mouth and shut up!"

I didn't know what our rules were when arresting targets in the city, and I didn't know what we were supposed to tell them. One thing I knew, though, is that it definitely wasn't what U.S. law enforcement uses when they read your Miranda rights and say stuff like "You are under arrest, and you have the right to remain silent." We weren't dealing with preteens shoplifting. We were dealing with terrorists in a warzone area, and the rules were different.

The rest of the team was there in seconds. We cuffed our target, put a bag on his head, and got him in the car. The commander asked, "Who arrested him, and how was he arrested?" Everybody pointed at me and said that I did it. The commander asked me, "Are you the new guy they are talking about?"

I responded, "Yes."

"Okay. Good work."

I was confused about what he meant by that. I didn't think about it much. After that, we returned to base. The guys told me that it was not common for the commander to ask that kind of question. I wasn't nervous, but there were some questions in my head. I said, "I hope I am not in trouble." I did not know what I could be in trouble for, but I was still too new to get a read on the situation.

When we arrived, it was late in the afternoon, nearly sunset. The squadron commander called me on the radio and told me to come to the TOC. I got worried and immediately wondered to myself if I had done something wrong. I hoped that I was not in any sort of trouble. It got me curious about what was going on. I started walking to the TOC. I was hoping to see someone I knew on my way to ask him about my call to the TOC, but I didn't see anyone. Eventually, I said to myself, "If you made a mistake, don't argue. Just apologize and say, 'I am new,' and tell the leadership it won't be repeated. But if it is something different, then let's see what it is." When I arrived at the door, I knocked.

"Come in."

I saw the squadron commanders and the advisors who were sitting around the briefing table. Because it was a Special Operations task force, we didn't have many formal things like saluting for leadership or stopping and saluting while an officer was walking by. The only time we saluted was when we had promotions or ceremonies. We also didn't have many formal meetings like this. Anyone would assume something was wrong, and I was no exception. Over and over in my head, the same thoughts swirled around: *Oh boy! Hope no trouble comes my way. I must have done wrong when I arrested that target. I was not supposed to do that. What if it wasn't my job to do that?*

I was told to sit down, and they started asking me some questions about my background.

"Where are you from?"

"I am from northern Afghanistan."

"What is your military background?"

"Prior to this unit, I was a combat terp with Canadian and U.S. Special Operations Forces. Then, I joined the Afghan Army Special Operations Forces. I was in the service for a few years."

"Why did you leave the army?"

"Because of the restrictions on operations. If you shoot a bad guy, you will be in trouble. If you arrest a bad guy, you will be in trouble. It wasn't worth it, and after my last contract ended, I left the army."

"Who brought you here?"

I answered, "An old buddy of mine from the time when we were in the special forces."

"What is his name?"

I was talking about Sultan, and as soon as I mentioned his call sign, most of the leadership knew him already from his outstanding performance.

"What was your rank in the army?"

I said, "I had recently been promoted to E-7 when I left." They were all writing stuff down.

"How are your leadership skills?"

"I can lead a team. I was leading small teams before."

They asked me a few more questions. Then, they told me, "If you don't have any questions, you are free to go."

I said, "I actually do have something I would like to say. I have never done a low-vis operation. If I am in trouble for that, I just want to apologize and get that off my chest."

They laughed and said, "No! No! You did great. Your arrest today is one of the good reasons you are here in this meeting today. Now you can go."

I left the room. The tension in my stomach was all gone. But my thoughts immediately shifted to something else. I have a terrible habit. If I hear that there will be a surprise for me, I have to know what it is. I don't ask the person who told me, but I will ask around. I will still be happy for the surprise, but I enjoy it more when I know what is coming. I am a curious guy. I know you might say, "But that is not a surprise." I know. I'm sorry, that is how I am. I wanted to know what this meeting was about, so naturally, I started asking around. First, I went and asked my friends in Charlie Squadron. Then, I went to Bravo, then to Alpha. At this point, you might think that I knew the whole unit. I did not know the entire unit, but I knew almost everyone.

It was a small unit, and we Afghans are social in general. Once some-one says hello to us, whenever we see them again, we say hello, and that is how we become friends. People who have been deployed to Afghanistan and had encounters with Afghans might have experienced this. I know from my experience, having lived in the United States for half a year now, that this is not common in the U.S. Here, people barely see each other, and people rarely talk to each other in the neighborhood. Of course, I might be wrong, but back in Afghanistan, everyone knows each other in a village. It's almost the same thing in the city. We weren't snitching on each other. We were talking to each other and hearing each other's stories. In the neighborhood I grew up in, we even knew who worked where and how much their salary was. There is a lot more stuff that doesn't look normal for others, but it is expected in Afghanistan. It is hard to describe in a few sentences the interconnectedness of everyone at home and at work.

My friends were willing to find the answer to my query and suggested we just wait for the commanders to get back from the meeting. I knew I wasn't in trouble, but what was the purpose of this meeting? Was it called for a good reason, or was it just a random meeting? The night passed with no news, but the following day, I got a call from the Charlie boys on the radio. They told me to come to their room. I walked into their room, and as soon as I walked in, they told me, "BRO!!! We got big news for you!"

"What is it?"

"Guess."

"Bro, I have had enough surprises. Please tell me if it is good news, which it seems like it is. I will invite you guys for dinner if you tell me!"

"It is official. They are letting you start with your army rank. You're not an E-5 anymore. You're going to start at E-7."

That was big news for me. It meant I didn't have to start from scratch, and financially, it made a big difference in my salary. In the task force, we had an Afghan government salary that was fair, but besides that, we had the NATO bonus salary, which was based on our rank. This news gave me a lot more confidence in the task force. It meant if you had the skills and were professional, then that would help you go all the way to the top.

By the way, I did invite them for dinner later on my leave.

I worked in the support squadron for three months after the news. I always had problems with the support squadron's commander. I felt that he was a greedy and dumb guy. He never wanted to see me improve. Like when I was going on these volunteer missions, he would call me stupid, though, of course, not in front of everybody. He would tell me, "You are dumb. Why are you risking your life? You are making stupid decisions."

Because he was a commander, I couldn't tell him anything. But oh man, sometimes I was inches away from punching him in the face. He was walking on my nerves. He was mostly worried that I would take his job. Whatever I am, I am not a backstabber or a snitch. If I deserve your position, I'll take it over because I lead better than you. If leadership sees me fit to do so, I'll definitely take it. But if I don't deserve it, and you are better than me, then carry on. You deserve it.

As a leader and commander, it doesn't matter if you are leading two soldiers or two hundred soldiers. You are responsible for everything that happens to them because of your mistakes. As I have heard, "With great power comes great responsibility."

Chapter 9

I went on leave for ten days. The break wasn't too enjoyable because I couldn't go anywhere due to the dire security conditions in the country. I just hung around in the house with my family. Overall, it was a break from work. After the leave, I was happy to go back to work. I took the two-hour trip back to the unit. Then, I changed into my uniform and was getting ready to go to the range and do some shooting when I heard someone calling my name on the radio. It was the Bravo boys. Their commander told me to come to his room. I went there, and he told me to sit down. I sat down, and the Bravo commander asked me, "How do you like the support squadron?"

"It's not a bad place, but there's not much action in it."

"What do you mean? You get to stay on base while everybody else is going out and walking for miles and staying awake all night. And they have so much risk to their lives when they do it."

"If I cared about the risk, I would have never come to this unit. I wasn't drafted. I am doing this because I love it."

"You are my new deputy commander!"

"Wait! What! How? When?" I was shocked. "But nobody told me anything about it."

"I have been checking your background and performance since you joined the unit. You are hardworking and honest, and you are not scared to do the dangerous stuff. I like that. I don't have a deputy right now, but who better than you. You know English. You have a Special Operations background."

"But nobody told me anything about this decision."

"Because it was made this morning. Aren't you happy?"

"Of course I am, but I am a sergeant first class, and the deputy commander's position is a first lieutenant."

"Don't worry. I already recommended you for a promotion in three months. You will be a second lieutenant, and you will be able to work in an officer's position. But don't worry about that part at all because you are starting your work today."

I was really shocked. It definitely was good news, but I wasn't ready to hear it. I asked him, "Does the support commander know about this?"

"Who cares. Get some friends and grab all of your gear and bring it here. You are officially done with support. Welcome to Bravo."

I went and brought all my gear from the support squadron. I didn't have a lot, just a few things. The task force held a formation and introduced me to the squadron. They called my name, and I walked up front. I saluted the task force commander. He said, "Welcome to the task force."

I said, "It is an honor, sir." I saluted him and turned around. I walked a few steps, saluted the soldiers, and said my usual motto: "God, country, brotherhood."

Then, I walked to the Bravo Squadron's line, and the squadron commander said, "Welcome to our squadron." A new journey started for me, and it was a big one.

We had two assault teams, two security teams, and one mobility team in our squadron. The commander controlled the whole squadron, but a D-Com only directed one assault team and one security team. Of course, when the commander is not present, the deputy runs the squadron. This is a lot of responsibility. I had only been preparing for a team or group leader, not a D-Com.

The reason the commander brought up that I knew English was because we had a lot of encounters with our American advisors during training, operations, meetings, and other activities. We always had American advisors with us. It made it a lot easier for both sides when there were no language barriers. Even though we had terps working with us, direct communication with each other made things a lot easier, especially when we were in a firefight. Misinterpretation can mess up everything in an operation, and mess-ups can get people killed. I had been a terp in the past, and I knew that then. There were some badass terps with us with excellent English-speaking ability, but there were also terps who had never seen combat. They could speak English, but they didn't talk the way operators did. Knowing English and being in leadership, I helped bridge that gap.

I started my role as the D-Com. On that day, the first thing I had in my head as a man in a leading position was to work on the guys to get them better at what they did. I mean, they were good, but you have to always strive to become better. I also needed to update the training program because some drills were outdated. We had a set of training that was given to us by the S-7, or the training section. This training regimen was years old, but all of the commanders were provided flexibility and authority to dictate how we trained. The Bravo Squadron commander didn't care about what the S-7 gave us. He always told me, "I believe in you and enjoy the motivation you have given the soldiers. And that is all that matters to me." So, I used the stuff I had learned throughout my career with different tier one units like SEAL Team Six and Delta Force. I also drew on my experience in leading positions from my time with the Afghan SF. I added some more advanced tactics into the training. And I added more close-quarters shootings, fast drills, shooting on timers, and competitive shooting between the soldiers in the squadron.

One of the essential things I changed about the way we trained was focusing on the problems we had. I became like a coach. I watched my team and worked on the mistakes the team made. If we had a problem with assaulting, I would have us work more on assaulting. I would cancel all the other training and just work on that one aspect. We would repeatedly hammer it until the teams moved fluidly. This was just my strategy. I would also listen to the guys and hear their opinions on what we needed to work on. I helped them with whatever could make our job easier. I wanted achievements and successful raids, but I also wanted to protect my guys at all costs and protect the civilians in the area who could get caught between us and the targets. Safety of my team and the civilians was my number one priority.

It is hard to make an Afghan happy and satisfied at the same time. We have a joke: One man said, "I will give a sheep as a gift in my wedding to

116

every single guest to make it the most perfect wedding ever!" When guests were leaving, the groom himself was handing each of them a sheep as a gift. His aunt took one, and she said, "Son, you spent so much money on the wedding! You could have at least bought and given each of us a piece of rope with the sheep so we could take it home easier!"

I assume all humans are like that in a way, but that is the Afghan way of expressing it. Some people can never be made happy. In this context, it means that it doesn't matter how hard you work, how many bad guys you eliminate, how much human trash you clean up from the earth, how much you sacrifice, and how many people's lives are made better. If you make one mistake, all the good deeds and sacrifices will be forgotten. The bad thing about the Afghan war was it didn't matter how cruel the insurgents were and how many civilians they had killed or would have killed. If we, as Afghans, bombarded the wrong house, then riots, protests, and aggression would occur. When this happened, it was usually due to bad intel or a compromised informant. I touch on this later in the book. No one wanted it to happen, and I empathize with the victims. But we are human, and no matter how much effort we put into keeping civilians out of it, some situations were unavoidable.

The backlash from civilians was demoralizing, but we still kept conducting operations. I worked as the Bravo D-Com for one year. The whole task force had outstanding achievements during this time. We prevented so many attacks, and I loved the job I was doing. When we were training, I would ask the advisor to rate the task force and squadron's performance. The advisors were always happy with it. My first question to a new advisor was always, "First time in Afghanistan?" If not, "What provinces and what units have you worked on in the past?" Then, I would ask him, "How do you like the task force, and if you compare it to a U.S. armed unit, what unit would we be similar to?"

Ninety-nine percent of the advisors said, "You guys are similar to U.S. Army Rangers." I mean, at the end of the day, we were trained and advised by the U.S. tier one units. These were the best of the best, and the advisors had been the best of the best for a long time. And we all did Special Operations training.

We would go out every other night or sometimes every night. The task force did at least two hundred and fifty operations a year. You might say either that is a small number or that is a lot. If you say that is not that many, it tells me you have never been in the military. I know it is a lot because it was a small task force in the country operating in thirty-four provinces. We requested many times to expand the task force, but unfortunately, it never got approved. The excuse we got was a lack of budget and support, from both the Afghan and U.S. government sides. Also, you can't mass produce elite soldiers. That would come at the cost of them being elite.

—

I was in the task force for about six months when I encountered my first HPA. The entire base was whipped up into a frenzy. We received an alert that Kabul was under attack. It was a coordinated attack that involved multiple Taliban teams. We didn't know what they planned to hit. An alarm was heard across the entire base. We always trained for these kinds of situations, and we were ready for it. Countering the attack was part of our job. We were expected to be suited up with all vehicles prepared to go out the gate in ten minutes. Alpha Squadron was on leave at this time, so it was just the Bravo and Charlie Squadrons on this mission. I was still the D-Com for Bravo Squadron, and the squadron commander was in India to receive medical care for an issue his son had. That meant I was in charge; I had to lead Bravo through this one.

Our S-3 (the operations chief) gave me a quick update on the situation. He said, "Kabul is under attack at three different places: Police District 12, Police District 7, and Police District 10."

"Which district is my squadron going to?"

"You have Police District 7."

As soon as I heard that, I told my vehicle commander to move the convoy to the gate and send my vehicle to my location. I didn't want to waste time running to the vehicles. The unit's base was huge, and every second we delayed meant someone's life would be taken by these animals. My vehicle rolled up, and I got into the front passenger seat.

HPAs are carried out as a show of force. By attacking people and the government in the capital, the Taliban were showing that nowhere was safe from their reach. They wanted people to be scared of them wherever they were. HPAs typically involved a suicide bomber hitting the gate to a critical area or building. Then, a group of gunmen would go in and start shooting everyone. It did not matter if you were Muslim, Christian, Buddhist, or atheist. They did not discriminate. They even shot people's dogs. Today the Taliban can claim whatever they want to claim about these atrocities. I have seen it with my own eyes, and my people have seen it.

My vehicle approached our convoy and came to a jerking stop. There was no time to waste, and I trusted that we were all ready to roll. I called over the radio, "Departing! Departing!" The first vehicles drove out the gate, and everyone else followed. The first three vehicles had sirens blaring and lights flashing. This was supposed to help clear the path so we could quickly get to the fight, but Kabul has always had lousy traffic jams. The city had no stoplights, and traffic laws were more like suggestions. We were stuck. The soldiers in the front got out and forced people to move their cars out of the way. They shouted, yelled, pushed people, pointed weapons, and even broke a couple windows.

People who grew up in a more modern world might not understand this. At first glance, this would look like bad and violent behavior. But sometimes this minimal violence can save lives. No civilians were hurt during this. It was just done to scare them because we had no time to kindly ask them to move. I would prefer for one reckless driver to have a broken window than for another innocent life being taken because we got delayed.

It took us about thirty minutes to get to the target location. It was easy to tell we were close when the Kabul around us looked like a ghost town. The streets were empty near where the attack was taking place. There were police forces on the ground, but they were waiting for a unit like us to come and clean up the mess.

The target building was located on the left toward the south side of the street. We were approaching from the west side. I told my mobility commander to change lanes to the left side of the road so we could use another building as cover for our approach to the target building. The target building was a four-story building, and it had a fifth floor that was still under construction. There was a bank on the fourth floor and apartments on the lower floors. The Taliban chose to attack this building because it was the only tall building across from the old Afghan Parliament house. Their plan was to shoot this parliament house and the people inside.

When we got there, the crisis response unit (CRU, similar to SWAT) was already there. This was the kind of mission they trained for. Prior to that day, though, we didn't know this kind of unit even existed in Afghanistan. This illustrates the lack of communication and coordination between Coalition advisors and the Afghan government. The CRU was already getting ready to breach and start clearing the building. I told my soldiers to pull security around the building and not let anyone in or out.

First, I needed to know what was going on. At this point, I had very little information. I wanted to know what weapons they had, how many of them there were, and what had happened up to this point. I got zero information from the police force present.

I noticed a security guard standing among the police force. I got curious and went to talk to him. "Who are you and what are you doing here?"

"I am part of the security for the bank!"

"Security? How are you alive? Why did they not kill you? Quickly tell me everything that happened. Be as detailed as possible."

"We have four security guards working in the bank here. Two of us stay at the main entrance of the first floor, and two others stay up top in the bank. I started my shift at eight this morning when a van pulled up in front of the entrance to the building. Seven or eight armed men came out of the vehicle."

"What were they armed with?"

"They had AK-47s, PKMs, RPGs, and a lot of grenades."

"Did they say anything to you?

"Not much. They said, 'You are lucky. We don't want to kill you. Drop your gun and run away from here. If you look back, I will shoot you in the head.' So, I dropped my gun and ran away as quickly as I could. I called the cops a few minutes later, and they told me not to go anywhere and to stay somewhere close to the area. I have been here since this began, but nobody has talked to me."

"What floor were they on?"

"I don't know."

"How is the security at the bank? What is the door like? Can explosives get through it? Is it heavily armored or lightly armored?"

"I don't know, but it looks heavy."

I told my intelligence officer to get the security guard's information and phone number, then send him home. The CRU was taking the lead on the operation, but I still had to create a plan. I did not know how the CRU would do or if they would be successful. I wanted to be prepared for us to get called to go into the building. Since my team wasn't the main effort, I went to the command-and-control area to get a better feel for what was going on. The CRU started their assault. As soon as they entered the building, they were ambushed, and they had four soldiers down. Their team leader was wounded but still alive. Another team went in to get the casualties. They engaged in gunfire but managed to retrieve the casualties and make it out alive.

As soon as this team made it back out of the building, I sent four of my guys to talk to them and get all of the intelligence they could. Based on what they collected, this is how they were set up: They were spread out on all four floors. They also had a suicide bomber on each floor, and they had two fighters covering the stairs. When they saw anyone approach the stairs, they would engage with AK-47s and grenades. It was a good defense. If we pushed through the main door, we would get funneled in and take casualties at the doorway. If we got creative and found a way through a different floor, they could use the suicide bomber and explode that floor, causing casualties at the point of entry. We also couldn't use our full range of weapons or explosives because there was a family living in an apartment who was still there.

We called in air support in the form of Blackhawks and Apaches. They fired at select targets in the building and managed to kill two of the fighters, but there were still six more to deal with.

These attackers were also shooting at random civilians living in the area. It was a crowded neighborhood. One of the more messed up parts about it was the people who gathered to watch. I witnessed a situation where teenagers were running left and right on the street. The insurgents were shooting at them. The teenagers were about seven hundred meters from the shooters. It was a long shot, but one lucky bullet could end one of these teens' lives. I sent a team to clear away the civilians. This was no joke. This was no show. They could easily have gotten killed. My team came back and told me that the civilians were not listening. To that, I said, "Okay. If that is their choice, then that is their choice!"

Five hours passed, but we had no success. I had sent guys into nearby buildings to get a better angle on the insurgents. My guys were firing at the fourth floor, but nothing was working. The only way this would get resolved would be clearing it room by room, and we still couldn't find a way in.

As this was going on, I received a call from the task force commander. "There is an insurgent cell preparing another attack on the city. I need you to go to Police District 8."

"What about here?" I responded.

"The CRU will take care of it."

"That is not what it looks like so far!"

"The insurgents there are locked down and contained. They aren't going anywhere. Get to Police District 8 now!"

I told my men to prepare to leave. We left the area in our vehicles and headed to PD 8. On the way, I received another command. I was told to return to the base and that we were going to hit a group of suicide bombers in three hours. My leaders could not give any more details over the radio even though it was encrypted. I told my mobility commander to change our route back to our base.

It was late afternoon when we got back. I told my guys to resupply, refuel, and be able to get out the gate on three minutes' notice. Then, I went directly to the command center. When I arrived, I said, "What the heck is going on? Why were we pulled out of the fight?"

The task force commander spoke. "We are officially done reacting to high-profile attacks!"

"WHAT?! You are joking, right?"

"Unfortunately, no. I am dead serious. Higher brass said that we need to focus more on preventing these attacks instead of countering them. They want us to get ahead of situations like this."

"That is a lot to ask for a unit as small as us. We are just a fraction of the three hundred thousand strong army. I hope only relying on us works out. We will give it our best effort."

They changed our mission from reacting to this attack, and instead, our advisors and our operations officers began working on a plan to seize the initiative from the attackers. I received a copy and went to work on my briefing. I prepared it in twenty minutes and called my team leaders in to get briefed. I used the satellite imagery we had. It was not something secret or high tech; it was just the map from Google Earth that was updated last in 2009. A lot of infrastructure improvements and construction projects were happening in Kabul at the time. The map wasn't accurate, but it was the best we had access to. I started working with my team leaders to plan out where we would park vehicles, position security teams, place ladder teams, put up blocking positions, and set up the fire support team. We weren't allowed to use any air support in Kabul. I had to create a plan in case we started exchanging heavy gunfire. We were going to engage suicide bombers. These guys were ready to die, and they would try to take down as many of us as they could. We could not make any arrests. We had to eliminate the threat. We had to move quickly but with a lot of caution and good planning. We would survive with a bit of luck.

It is true that we signed up for this kind of job. But as they say, "Work smarter, not harder." This was especially true in our line of work because failing meant someone wouldn't be able to go home. We are humans first and soldiers second. Our families prefer to see us walk home in our uniforms, not be carried in a coffin. No family on earth wants to see that. I believe that, as a commander, if you are a good leader and create a good plan, then you can take your soldiers through death itself and bring them back alive. And if you are a leader who doesn't care about your soldiers, you will be the actual cause of their death whether it comes in war or training. So, being the interim commander, I had to make sure to bring these boys back in one piece.

We were departing in thirty minutes. I went to the command center and talked to the targeting chief. "Where did this intel come from?"

"It came directly from the ISAF intelligence section."

"It must be accurate then."

"Yes. This is the Coalition force's intelligence, and they pay good money to their sources."

"Sometimes good money can also make the source lie about the information to make it seem legit."

"I agree with you, but my guy tells me that this is good intel."

While talking to the targeting chief, I received a call saying that we needed to leave now. We would receive an update en route if any new intelligence came up about the target. I called my team leads and told them to move to the gate. We lined up, locked and loaded our weapons, then departed. It was almost dark by this time.

We arrived at the area, got out of the vehicles, and lined up to move toward the target compound. The compound consisted of one building in a somewhat condensed residential area in the city. There was an outside wall that acted as a border around the property. There was a door that served as the way to enter and exit the lot this wall surrounded. The building was two stories tall. There was a window to the left and right of the door to the building. We started our movement. We arrived, and the security team locked down the compound. The blocking position vehicles were in their position. The fire support team was ready too. The ladders went up and said NSTR. We weren't usually allowed to use explosive breaches in the city, but this situation called for us to bend the rules. We were assaulting a compound full of suicide bombers. We had to use explosives.

The charge was set on the door connected to the wall. I started the countdown to breach. "Five…four…three…two…one." The door exploded. The assault team rushed in. Four soldiers went through the door, and I followed. I had to be inside to understand what was going on so I could give good orders. Rounds started popping off from inside the rooms. We kicked in the door to the building and started clearing it. One team started clearing the left room on the ground floor while another team cleared the right. The ladder teams kept shooting at the rooms on the second floor. One of the assaulters called, "Booby trap." We all exited the building immediately. We kept shooting at the windows until everyone was out of the building.

We couldn't call an air strike and finish this fight through raw firepower. This was a residential area. I called in my mobility commander and asked him, "How many RPG rounds do we have in the vehicles?"

"We have four rounds in each vehicle." This was about eighty total.

"How many explosive charges do we have?"

"EOD says we have four twenty-pound charges."

"Get four RPG guys on the rooftop of the building across the street. Take that building down!"

We continued firing until the RPG guys were in position. They shot four RPG rounds in each of the four windows for a total of sixteen rockets. The building was still standing.

My plan changed. "Get me six men to set the twenty-pound explosives on that building!"

Six of my men took the explosives and went behind the building. They climbed to the roof, set three twenty-pound charges and their timers, then got to a safe distance. The charges exploded and brought the entire building down. A cloud of dust rose up from behind the wall.

I sent in our EOD team to clear the threat from the suicide bombers. They reported that the threat was eliminated. After that, we had the police take over at the scene, and we returned to base.

As soon as I got back to the command center, I gave a detailed report of what had happened. The lead advisor asked me to get him some names of guys who had standout performances. This kind of action was what made us who we were, and this kind of operation was an excellent opportunity to show appreciation. I gave the command team a list of men who had performed great during the raid.

The unit held a formation for us all. When I heard the command call my name, I thought to myself that my name hadn't been on the list. I thought it might have been a soldier in the other squadrons that I might not know who had the same name as me. They called my name again but with the detail of "Yousuf, the Bravo D-Com."

I responded, "Yes, sir!" and walked up to the leaders who were standing there.

I saluted the unit commander. He said, "You deserve this." I saw he had a rank patch in his hand. He pulled my E-7 rank and pressed the 2LT patch on instead.

I saluted and turned around. I walked a couple of yards and said our motto, "I will serve this country with honor."

I hadn't been expecting that at all. Thirty minutes later, I received a text from the squadron commander. The text said, "Congrats! You proved me right—thank you." I was delighted. Only a little bit of my happiness was because of the promotion. It was mainly about bringing everyone back to base alive. The smiles on their faces meant the world to me. On the other hand, I was happy I didn't fail the advisors and the squadron commander that recommended me for the rank and position. I was grateful and appreciative.

We were going on our regular leave in ten days. The commander was back four days later. He was proud and joyful. I was proud of my boys. They are the ones who made me look good as a leader. Their performance meant a lot. We went on regular leave, but this time, it wasn't bad. We had a couple of the commanders going with us. We went to the north of Kabul province to visit the beautiful nature there. We needed that refreshing weather after all.

Chapter 10

Our squadron finished our official leave period. It was time to go back to the unit. To be honest, I loved my job so much that I missed it during my leave. I am sure that most, if not every, Special Operations soldiers miss the brotherhood when away. We were supposed to be back at three in the afternoon.

I left home early and went back to the unit. It was around 9:30 a.m. when I arrived at the main gate. After getting searched, I went into the car to drive to the main part of the base, but one of the Charlie Squadron soldiers was standing there. I greeted him and shook his hand. He said, "Congratulations."

With a surprised look, I said, "Congrats on what?" and he gave me the shocking news.

He said, "You are nominated to become the Charlie Squadron commander!"

I said, "What!!! Are you serious? Are you joking with me?"

He said, "No, sir."

This was a soldier I had seen once or twice in my entire time in the unit. He definitely wasn't joking! The first thing that popped in my head was that the Charlie commander was a smart guy. I asked the soldier, "What happened to your current commander?"

He said, "Nothing. He is going to the U.S. He received an approved Special Immigrant Visa from the U.S. embassy because of his work when he was directly contracted with the U.S. government."

So many questions came to my mind, but the most important one was: *Why didn't they pick anyone from the Charlie Squadron itself?* I had only been a D-Com for about four months. To be honest, I wasn't thrilled with the decision. I was just getting used to the Bravo Squadron. I knew most of the guys in Bravo, how they operated, who had what problems, who was struggling with what training. As their lead guy, it was essential for me to know about my men. This applied from both work and personal perspectives. I wasn't ready for so many changes in such a short time. Anyway, it is just the nature of military life. You have to obey orders.

We drove in. My first priority was to find out more details about this news. As soon as I arrived to the main part of the base, the first thing I did was go to the Bravo commander's room. He wasn't there yet. I called his personal number, but his phone was turned off. It looked like he was at the gate entering the unit (we would turn off our phones to put it in a box at the entrance).

I wasn't excited about the new position, but I wasn't scared of running a squadron. I was just happy at Bravo, and I was really enjoying my time there. I went to Charlie Squadron to greet the boys and also find out what was going on. I went to their room. After greeting them, I saw that the boys weren't thrilled to see me. I said, "What is going on? How have you guys been? Been busy a lot?"

I didn't ask anything about what I had heard. I played dumb. I wanted to see who was happy and who was not. I mean, I didn't blame them if they weren't happy about it. I was still new compared to most of the guys, especially Charlie's leadership. It had taken them all years to reach the positions they held, and I hadn't been a part of the unit for very long. I said to call me on the radio when they were going to the DFAC. I had seen what I wanted to see. The changes in behavior meant they were not happy.

It is crucial for a commander or leader to have his men's support. I went to the S-1 Office, which is the administration office that handles the information for all cadet human resources, including personnel readiness, personnel services, and headquarters management. I asked the S-1 officer about what I'd heard. He wasn't really helpful. All of the reactions told me that the decision wasn't made by the Afghan leadership at all. It definitely was the advisors' leadership's decision.

As I have said, I am a curious guy. I wanted to find out who made the decision and why. Having a new guy get promoted so quickly had never happened in the unit since its establishment. It was no surprise to me that many people held bad feelings toward me because of my quick ascent.

We have greedy people, snitches, and jealous people all over the world. But I strongly believe in one thing: Don't be the kind of people I mentioned above. Be humble, generous, and optimistic. Every negative or positive thing happens for a reason.

I am a religious guy, though I am not an extreme believer. God has always been merciful and helpful to me, even though I wasn't always a good servant for God. I believe in prayers. Prayers get accepted, no matter who or what you believe in. There is a strong creator up there that looks over all of us, no matter your skin color or beliefs. He doesn't care if you are rich or poor, as long as you have a good, clean heart. Of course, there are conditions to clean your heart, which we won't discuss here. But if your heart is pure, God will always be with you. I believe that whatever he has written in my destiny is for a good reason, even if bad things happened to me. There are definitely good reasons behind these things, but because we are so focused on the negative side of it, we forget about the positive side.

When I saw all those adverse reactions from the Charlie guys, I said to myself, "If God has decided to put me in that position, I see no power on earth stopping God from doing that. But if he doesn't want me to work in that position, it won't happen." No matter how much one might snitch behind someone's back or backstab them to get something, they won't get it because that isn't God's plan. This is just my belief. This belief has always worked great for me. It might be different for everybody.

I went to see the Charlie Squadron commander. He was a great warrior. After knocking, I entered his room. He stood up, shook my hand, and hugged me. He told me, "I know you can do it."

I acted dumb. I said, "What is going on? I have been hearing some weird news going around the unit! What is going on?"

He said, "Don't play dumb, bro. I have been observing you since the day your name popped up in that leadership meeting when you walked in and talked to us. I know you have the courage and the mentality of a leader." He asked me, "Do I look like a dumb guy?" and laughed!

I said, "No, Commander, of course not."

He said, "Then, I know I picked the right guy to lead Charlie. I love this squadron. The soldiers on my team are great warriors. You know I am leaving. I wanted to leave them in good hands."

I said, "What about your D-Com? Don't you think he deserves this position instead of me?"

"My D-Com is a warrior, but he has been wounded, and I have talked to the unit commander about transferring him to an office job."

I asked, "What about the other leaders in the squadron? They are great warriors too, and they have been with Charlie longer than me."

"They have. I will be moving one of them to work as your D-Com."

I told him, "The only reason I am asking all these questions is that I don't want to lead a team that seems unhappy with me. Like they feel I have taken something that was theirs, if you know what I mean."

He said, "I totally understand you. Whether you like it or not, some people might like it, some people might not. People will talk, but it will not change anything. Your performance and actions will change their mind."

He was referring to an Afghan expression we have: "You can close the city's gates, but you can't close people's mouths."

Promotions in our unit were controlled equally by our advisors and the Afghan leadership. It was made this way to avoid any sort of corruption. U.S. involvement was necessary. First, a promotion would go to the Afghan leadership, and then it would be taken to the advisors, and then a decision would be made. You might say, "Why was it 50/50?" Well, it was because the principal salary we received was from the Afghan government, but we also received a bonus that was given to us by the U.S. government. It was essential to have the advisors involved in the process. This system was successful and kept the unit clean and transparent.

There was one slight problem with the commanders. They had language barrier problems when directly talking to the advisors. There was also a problem in the perception of our advisors. The advisors were a bunch of serious-looking guys. Most of the Afghans didn't want to have direct involvement with the advisors because they were worried about losing that extra pay. There was this idea that if the advisors didn't like you, then they would not give you the extra compensation from the

American government. It was just a misconception. But I have worked with Special Operations in the past and had no problem communicating with the advisors.

One big misunderstanding our Afghans had was about the advisors and their cursing. For me, cursing is nothing. I even used the F-word in official meetings and interviews. I was told by the U.S. officers and soldiers that I used the F-word more than an American. My response was that it helps with communication. It is a habit now (so much so that the editors had to strip it from this book).

This is how bad the misunderstanding was with Afghans in the unit. When I was new, and we were going to the range, a terp saw me speaking in English. He said, "I know you speak English and might have worked in the past with the Americans, but these people are very serious, and you shouldn't even ask them where they are from."

I responded, "Are you scared of them?"

"No! No!"

"Your face is telling me something different."

"No, I am not."

"Bro, are you dumb? Why would you ask an American where he is from? It is obvious he is from the United States of America. They are not from Russia!"

He didn't respond and left.

This was one of the reasons the Charlie commander told me that he appointed me to lead his squadron. I had been in serious discussions a few times with different Coalition officers. In general, if we are arguing about something, and I know and have seen something, no matter what you say, you can't change my mind. I know my people, and I know my judgment. I have never been afraid to speak my mind to the advisors or my leadership. But if I don't know what we are discussing, I won't even start arguing with you. I will say, "Really? I didn't know that," and move on.

Fourteen days passed, and I kept visiting Charlie Squadron and talking to the boys. The soldiers seemed happy. They slowly started to know me, and they found out I had no bad intentions and that I didn't cheat to get to this position.

It was the fifteenth day, the assignment day. A formation was held. The old Charlie commander was called up front. He was given an appreciation letter and a medal. Then, the old Charlie D-Com was called up front. He was given an appreciation letter and was introduced as the new S-7 (training officer). After him, I was called up front. I saluted the unit commander and shook his hand. He told me, "Keep up the hard work."

I responded, "I will not fail you, sir." I turned around and said our motto and walked to Charlie Squadron's formation. I stood in the line. When the formation was over, all the other squadrons went to their daily routines. The Charlie soldiers made a circle around me and the commander. We stood in the middle.

The commander said, "I am leaving. Our D-Com is gone from Charlie. He needs to rest for a while. Some of you might have questions about my decision. It was 50/50 between me and the advisors. I am certain. I believe in him. Trust me. A good decision was made here." He said goodbye to everybody and left.

I used the chance while we were all together. I told the guys, "We will work hard and show our best results as you guys did in the past." The D-Com wasn't assigned yet. I asked the soldiers, "What was in your schedule for today's training?"

One of the group leaders said, "We have GPS training today."

I said, "Let's do a short training. I need to meet with you guys and go through some of the training plans."

They did an hour of training and came back to their barracks. I went through all the challenges and problems the squadron was going through, training-wise and promotion-wise. The following day, I told the boys, "We will do a raid tomorrow. Let's mark a compound in the training area and practice assaulting it."

The building we were going to practice raiding was a shoot house that we used for close-quarters battle and close-quarters combat on a daily basis. I told them to start clearing the building. Their clearing went smoothly and nicely. I said, "Oh, good job." I knew they had done this a lot, so they'd absolutely memorized all the corners. I took the assault team and put them inside one of the rooms. I told them, "Assume, you have breached into this compound through the guestroom's window. Clear the building for me." Corners were missed this time, and it was a mess. I said, "I know, I know. Next time we are training here, we won't go through the same breach point ever again. Every time we are training here, we must look at it as a new building. We have never been in here, and we don't know what the structure of the building is. But as an assaulter, always clear your corners. You see a threat, and you eliminate the threat. You watch your muzzle. We don't go fast. We are not in a competition. We go slow. Slow is smooth, and smooth is fast." It was a saying I had learned operating with Navy SEALs, and it kept me and my team alive many times.

We did the same training but with NVGs during nighttime. The following day, we went to the range. We were shooting from different distances: ten, fifteen, and twenty-five yards. I asked the group leads, "What sort of shooting do we have today?"

They said, "We shoot two rounds at the targets, clear left, and clear right."

I said, "Are we living in the seventies? That tactic is old." I put six targets up. Each target had a hostage. The targets started from twenty-five yards. The closer the targets were, the smaller they would get, and the hostage would be covering most of the target. I told them, "Headshots are ten points, and chest shots will be five points."

We did that training, and the soldiers were content. They liked learning new tactics. We all enjoyed improving at our jobs. I would do research for new Special Operations training on Google and YouTube. I was learning new tactics too. I always shot the first magazine and last magazine on the targets to practice and show the soldiers that we were all doing the same thing. Later, I assigned one of the guys as my D-Com. He was an intelligent guy. He also used to work as a terp with U.S. Army Special Operations Forces in southern Afghanistan before joining the task force.

Chapter 11

It was almost 2014. This was a big year that brought a lot of changes for both the military and civilian sides. The United States and NATO were planning to withdraw troops from Afghanistan. That was big breaking news for the Afghans. Afghanistan had a big army, but we didn't have enough air support or heavy support. Back then, we only had a few Mi-17s (which were left from the Russian invasion) and some cargo planes such as C-130s. So, basically, we only had air transport. The Afghan people were scared. The Taliban were cruel in the past and present. No human wants to be oppressed. People want freedom of speech, freedom of expression, and in general just want to be free. And you are right—we have to stand and fight for it. That would just mean more killing.

By this point, our country had been at war for the past forty years. Everyone was tired of it and getting more tired of it. I had known nothing but war my whole life, like my father before me. When was it going to stop? We are going to be killing each other forever. Millions of Afghans had already left the country and gone to Iran and Pakistan. They'd moved from there to Turkey and from Turkey to Europe. It had all happened before the withdrawal was complete. The security conditions got dangerous, and the U.S. decided to postpone the withdrawal process. The U.S. and NATO maintained their presence until December of 2016. The ISAF mission was changed to Resolute Support (RS). Their mission was to advise and help Afghan forces with their logistics, and the U.S. left 8,400 troops. Most of the units had no advisors. Only a few Special Operations detachments were on the ground. They were just small teams, training and advising. A unit without advisors meant no air support.

Our unit advisors had to leave due to the new policy. My journey as the commander was different compared to other commanders. We had some British advisors from the U.K. intelligence services. I am not sure what department they were from, but when they were introduced to us by our chain of command, we were told they were U.K. intelligence service members. When they came to our unit, it took them two months to understand the whole process of the unit. I worked alongside their Special Operations Forces in the past. They were intelligent people, but, man, the advisors I was working with had zero understanding of the Afghan government, war, and the whole process we used.

These advisors would come to our training every day just to watch what we did. They were asking so many questions. It was funny. Of course, I am not complaining or saying anything bad. It's just that the U.S. advisors had a sound system and excellent support while advising the task force. One of the main reasons was that they were with the task force from day one. They built this unit alongside Afghans. U.S. rules and policies were different in terms of advising an Afghan unit, especially a Special Operations unit. The Brits had their own way of advising Afghan units, but the feeling wasn't there.

The first problem with the British advisors was they weren't operators. They were intelligence officers. They had a lot of restrictions on how to work alongside our unit. I became friends with one of the advisors. I told him, "You guys are operating so differently. You know we are not a regular intelligence operating unit. This is a Special Operations task force!"

He said, "I know, mate, but our rules are different compared to the U.S. We are only here to report the operations."

"Okay, but you know the advisor's role is that they are supposed to provide us with any support that the Afghan government can't while we conduct operations."

"I know, mate."

With that response I realized that relying on our current advisors to support us wouldn't do us any good. We were operating in a bigger circle with the air support we had from NATO when U.S. tier one units were advising us. But unfortunately, we couldn't get that support with the

British advisors. From the Afghan government side, we could only receive air transportation. In guerrilla warfare, it was vital to have eyes in the air. We were fighting an enemy that was using holy places, residential houses, and women and children as their shields. One of the most significant advantages we had with air support's presence was identifying movers in the vicinity of the operation area.

When there was a raid in the village, civilians didn't come out of their compounds because they didn't want to be marked as an insurgent. Therefore, the only movers were insurgents. Of course, air support didn't engage them unless the movers were armed. We took a lot of precautions. In most cases, an insurgent would be hiding their AK under their blanket called a "Pato" (a thin or thick piece of cloth the size of a small blanket that Afghan males use to cover themselves; thin cloth is used for summer and thick is used in winter). For that reason, it was hard to identify whether they were armed or not. Reporting movers is the least an air asset does for the troops on the ground, and it is one of the most vital parts of our raids.

At this point, I'd like to thank any air force pilot that helped us during our operations, regardless of whether you were Afghan, American, or any other NATO-allied nation. If by fate you are reading this, thank you.

When I became the Charlie Squadron commander, we had many successful operations. Of course, it was teamwork. I am and will always be proud of the things we accomplished with all the soldiers I have worked with. It was and always will be because of the team and, again, teamwork. I would have never been able to do it myself. If a soldier anywhere in the world is taking credit for the team's effort and claiming he has done it by himself, he is not only lying, but he also is betraying his team.

My first operation as a commander without air support was a big one. Our target was an insurgents' headquarters in the Safi Mountains (Kohi-Safi) close to Bagram Airfield. Due to a change of mission, U.S. or NATO troops weren't allowed to conduct this operation. Kohi-Safi was one of the locations that Bagram Airfield was getting indirect fire (IDF) attacks from. Kohi-Safi is a district located in eastern Parwan province. Since both Bagram and Kohi-Safi were located close to each other, insurgents of any network were using the high ground to shoot rockets at the airbase.

The intel we had on this target was that fifteen insurgent fighters were located on top of the mountain, and they were responsible for attacks on military convoys and Bagram air base. I never trusted an intel source to be 100 percent accurate. I always had to take it seriously, but in my personal experience, they were never 100 percent accurate. No matter how much money the source was paid, no matter what top secret intelligence agency collected the intel, I didn't trust it. I have seen a lot of paid informants. But man, I have never trusted any of them. They are like the sellers in the black market. They will even sell *you* if they get a higher offer on the table. My first question during a briefing was always, "How strong is the source, and what are the recent updates on it?"

For example, we had cases where the source wanted to kill his tribal opponents or enemies by giving us the wrong information. They wanted to use us as an unsuspecting weapon. I remember an instance from a raid we had previously in Logar province. We had a bunch of targets in the area. This compound we raided had an older man with three young daughters. The girls were between nineteen and twenty-four years of age.

As soon as the initial questioning started, the old man said, "I know who your source is. Tell him no matter what he does, I will not let him marry my daughter!"

As soon as I heard that, I said the source gave us the wrong information. One of the advisors got into an argument with me because this was a kill or capture mission. It was serious.

The advisor said, "This is a valuable asset for the U.S. military. He has given us good targets before."

I said, "It doesn't really matter what he did in the past. I am an Afghan, and I know my people. He lied about the current intel. I will detain the old man and take him to base, but he is innocent." I asked my intel officer to get me details on the girls' marital status and love stories. My officer found out that one of the girls had a lover and that he was with the insurgents. He also found out that the girl's father wasn't approving this marriage. I found more details about the source later. This young lover became a source and sold the military some intelligence to gain the trust of the in-

137

telligence officers. Then, he targeted his future father-in-law, saying that he was a Taliban commander in the area. He tried to kill him by using us.

I pulled the source aside and told him, "I swear to God. If I find out you lied about this target, you will be on my list as the next target, and I might not arrest you." We took the older man back to base and found nothing on him with the other agencies. We were only allowed to keep a detainee for seventy-two hours max. If no evidence was found on him, he would be set free. This is just one of the stories from fourteen years of nonstop combat and work in the Special Operations units.

Getting back to the mission, our Bagram package was ready for action. Because we didn't have eyes in the air, I had to bring in some changes to how we approached the target. I planned to use a sniper team to give us cover from the top of the mountain. But our snipers weren't equipped with night vision or thermal scopes. I requested some from the command and advisors, but unfortunately, the request was not approved. I had to use an Afghan trick. I went to some friends and asked them to get some. Those friends knew people in the black market. After one hour of calls, we found some thermal sniper scopes. I only found two. I bought them with my personal money. After the commander's approval, I took them in. We only had five hours to test the thermals and practice with them. It was a little challenging for the first hour. The buttons were in English, and my guys didn't know any English.

I told my recon team to work on it and not to come back until they were proficient. I told them, "Take whatever you need and as much ammo as you need to shoot. Get good at it."

The recon team worked with the thermals and shot with them for four hours. The team lead came back and said, "We are ready."

It's funny that I could find that kind of equipment at the black market, but I couldn't find it through the unit.

The briefing was complete. The departure time was 10 p.m. We wanted to go there in total darkness and raid this group while they were sleeping. The vehicles were lined up and ready to depart. The convoy departed from the unit. We arrived at the target destination and dismounted from the vehicles. I had my assault and security teams ready. I sent the recon team up front to set up their observation point. When I received the confirmation from the recon team, we started moving. The OP team reported a mining operation close to the target location building. It got me curious. I wondered if it was a cave or if the insurgents were mining gems or gold. The OP said, "We see no guns on the movers."

We got up there, locked down the location, and assaulted the target. As soon as we approached them, we could see them through our NVGs. When they heard us, they looked confused. Insurgent fighters were never like that. They would react and call in their friends for help. Even the look of these guys was different. They shouted, "Who is there?"

I told my guys not to say anything.

They repeated again, "Who is there? We will shoot!"

Usually the presence of a gun and voicing of a threat would be confirmation for us to engage them. I told my guys not to do anything. I said, "We are government forces. Don't do anything stupid."

As soon as I said that, they dropped their weapons and said, "Don't shoot us."

These reactions were never the reactions of insurgents. We told them to raise their hands and roll up their shirts so we could check for suicide vests. They looked clean. We approached them quickly, and as soon as we cuffed them, they said, "We have thirteen other guys inside the building."

We called them out. Every single one of them walked out with hands in the air and shirts up. We cuffed them all. They had a total of fifteen AKs and nothing else. Based on the intel we had received, there was supposed to be a weapons cache five hundred yards east of the building. We had the grid for it. We found the spot, and it looked freshly dug. Our EOD checked it with a mine detector. The detector started beeping. We slowly dug around the area and gradually dug closer and closer. We didn't want to hit an IED's wire or pressure plate.

What we found out made me more suspicious about the intel we received on the target. We found a bunch of old rusty rockets and grenades. Based on my experience, and checking with our EOD, the explosives weren't functional. During our basic questioning of the fifteen fighters, they said, "We own the AKs, but we have no clue where those old explosives came from. We have permits for our AKs, and we work for an Afghan parliament representative by the name of Haji Almas. Our job is to protect the mining crew and the mine itself."

I asked, "Who is your supervisor?"

One of them said, "I am the supervisor."

I pulled him aside and asked him how long he had been doing this job for. I also asked what they mined here.

He said, "It has only been three weeks since I started working as a supervisor, and before that, I was only a member. And we mine charcoal here."

I asked my intel officer to collect as much information as he could and informed him that we would be taking these guys back to base. After the basic questioning, we found a picture of the former supervisor. I gave it to our intel shop and told them everything that was sketchy about this operation. I also ordered the intel shop to work on this package as quickly as they could. One hour later, the intel shop came back with surprising news.

They said, "The old supervisor of the guards is our informant. Based on our basic analysis and information, the old supervisor was fired from his job three weeks ago and decided to take revenge by selling these guys as a terrorist network. We will try to do a forensic examination on the explosives to see if we can pick up his fingerprints on them."

It was later confirmed that the informant was behind all this, and he left the country to go to Pakistan. As a leader and commander, it was always crucial for me to analyze the situation and reactions and do everything I could to prevent civilian casualties and imprisoning innocent people.

Chapter 12

We only had the British advisors for one year. After the British left, the U.S. tier one units like SEAL Team Six and Delta Force started advising the task force again. We mainly did night raids on insurgent networks around the country. These were mostly around Kabul province. City operations were a lot more fun than night raids. Going out in civilian clothing and surprising enemies at a time and location that they didn't expect was always interesting.

Most of these operations were to target Afghan parliament representatives' guest houses. By "guest house," I am referring to a separate building that was inside the main compound of the parliament member. The only difference it made was whoever went in or out of that building wasn't the parliament representative's responsibility. The guest house would be used for the people coming from all over the country to meet with Afghan parliament representatives. These reps were sponsored by either Pakistan, Iran, Russia, or China. And we all knew these countries were not in a good relationship with the U.S. They were all happy to see the U.S. fail in Afghanistan.

Pakistan and Iran were interested and invested in keeping Afghanistan weak. It is pretty standard for countries to not want a strong government in their neighborhood. Nobody wants a nation that can challenge it on its border. Pakistan and Iran had seen what a strong Afghanistan had looked like in the 1980s and did not want that again. Sponsoring parliament representatives was a way for these countries to influence Afghanistan and have a concealed vote in the country's life-changing decisions. If the terrorists were in control of the government and had a claim to legitimacy, then these countries could declare they were merely supporting Afghanistan.

On these kinds of missions, we would go after suicide bombers who had come to Kabul and were staying in parliament representatives' homes. They were sponsored attacks. The bomber's mission was usually to attack U.S. convoys, U.S. bases, and other government officials. We would use the GSM system to track them down by their phones and hunt them. The task force's rule of engagement for suicide bombers was different because the risk was too high to try to take them alive unless we were sure they had no explosive vest on. This was still too much risk. The orders were to kill the suicide bomber on sight. This rule of engagement was only for the task force.

We received orders from our command that my squadron would conduct more operations in the city. We did a lot of operations in the city. I will mention some of the big ones; I can't fit them all here. Our first operation on an Afghan parliament representative was an exciting experience for me. From day one, I have never liked parliament representatives. They were very corrupt. I have seen a lot of cases involving parliament representatives, but the regulations normal units followed prevented them from taking action. I felt this when I was in Afghan Special Forces prior to joining TF-241. We mainly captured regular insurgent commanders during our city raids. Sometimes the city raids were on HVTs.

We lined up as we usually did with military vehicles. The briefing was short unlike the briefings for night raids. We rolled out of the base but did so not in a convoy. We kept seven hundred to nine hundred yards of distance between each vehicle. You wouldn't be able to tell we were going as a convoy, and we didn't want to look like a convoy.

Our target was in downtown Kabul. A suicide bomber was staying in a parliament representative's house in Police District 10, right in the middle of the embassies. This parliament house was close to the U.S., British, and German embassies, and it was being used as a safe haven for a terrorist. The suicide bomber's target was the U.S. embassy staff convoy that left every afternoon between 3 p.m. and 6 p.m. There was always a long convoy escorting all the personnel. Even though the area was restricted, the target managed to stay there. What that told me was that the parliament representative was definitely involved in this plan.

We arrived at the target's house. It was a lovely building with a lot of security around it. The first thing we did was lock down the building and surrounding streets. We tried to do this in such a way that civilians wouldn't notice something was going on in the area. Everybody was on standby mode and ready for action. I approached the house gate with five of my men. We were acting like there were only six of us here to do this job. The security guards stopped us. We told them we had an arrest warrant for the target and a search warrant for the place. The security guard commander asked us if he could check with the parliament representative as a respectful courtesy. We agreed.

It took him five minutes to open the gates. We entered the compound. Usually we had to deal with the parliament member's frustration and anger because we were searching his property. This representative was acting nice. It wasn't normal, and I got suspicious. I considered the idea that maybe there were some friendly representatives, but I was convinced something sketchy was going on. I told my guys to keep observing the compound, and said if they saw anything, they had to report it right away. The representative told us to do our thing, but we would have to excuse him because he was going to one of his ministry meetings. Since he was cooperative, we were nice to him in return. He got into his armored car that was parked there and left.

My team reported, "A car left the house. I think I see three people in it."

I said, "Roger, we are tracking that." A second later, I told myself, *If it was him and his driver, where did the third guy come from?* I ordered the GSM team to track the target again. The GSM team lead told me he would work on it, and it would take about ten minutes. The head of security stayed with us. We started searching the house, but we didn't find anything. The GSM team called and told me the signal had been popping up from the home before we entered, but they could no longer track him. I told the head of the security to take me to their room where they were controlling the security cameras from. I went through security camera footage, and I confirmed my suspicion. When we'd hit the first checkpoint on the road this representative was living on, someone had informed him about the raid. The footage showed our target was put in the armored vehicle lying down so we couldn't see him, and then he left with the parliament representative. He escaped with the help of the representative and his armored car.

I said, "Damn! The target is gone."

We wrapped up the operation and started moving back to our base. The signal popped up again, but this time, he was on the Kabul-Jalalabad Highway. We were on the same road. We kept tracking them and saw that they were headed our way. We put up a blocking position and checkpoints, then waited for them to come. We searched all the vehicles coming through the checkpoint, and we saw the parliament representative's car with the representative in it. We stopped the vehicle and captured our target. We detained him and the representative and took them back to base. We later found out that the representative was released by the National Directorate of Security (the Afghan FBI). When we asked why this happened, the government leadership told our unit commander that we couldn't arrest parliament representatives due to a policy they voted in for themselves. I was annoyed. After that, I knew big-time war criminals and terrorist supporters were walking freely at the highest levels of the government and that they were untouchable.

Parliament representatives were one of the most significant issues in the Afghan government. They would get support from and be paid by the Afghan government, but they wouldn't work for the Afghan people. During official hours, they would worry about their personal businesses and wealth. India built the Afghan parliament. I remember people saying that they wished India had made a cow ranch instead. A ranch would have been far more productive than the filth that walked the building's halls. A large amount of blame for Afghanistan's fall lay with the parliament.

The biggest lesson I learned that day was no matter how high in power these politicians were and how nice they were, we should attack their compounds with the mentality we had during a night raid in insurgents' territory. They looked like us and held positions in our government, but they were not for us. They served other masters.

—

In war, you cannot be successful all the time. Not every operation will go your way. In war, you will have a lot of ups and downs. Both sides will have casualties. Our daily training helped us to avoid losses as much as we could, but not every operation was clean.

One of the examples of an operation that didn't go well was one we had in Kabul city. We were going after four suicide bombers. According to the intel we received, they were planning to attack the center of the city. As always, I had my doubts about the source and the intel, especially with suicide bombers. The more accurate the information, the safer the operation would be. The intel shop gave me a strong confirmation about this intel. Don't get me wrong, I was a combat soldier from day one. Intelligence was never my thing, especially with the experience I had with the sources and their information. I never trusted it due to all the lies I was told by so-called sources.

We got ready at the gate and departed. This time, we had a six-vehicle quick reaction force (QRF) team to help with heavy engagements. The QRF team was set up in a location close to the operation area but away from civilian buildings. We arrived at the target location. We set up security around the perimeter and locked down the roads. The assault team was lined up and ready to breach. I double-checked everything with my team. Everything was good to go. Even the GSM team confirmed that the signal was coming from the target building. I gave the go-ahead, and we breached.

Our breach wasn't explosive due to our policy in Kabul city. A ladder guy jumped over the wall and opened the door. I was on the outside receiving reports from the breach point and passing it to the unit. We had Afghan and U.S. Special Operations leadership watching this operation from the air. I got suspicious due to the lack of gunfire. I asked myself why there was no engagement so far. We were all expecting the enemy to fight back, and we had orders not to bring them alive.

I was talking to the commander when I heard a massive explosion. Unfortunately, the house was booby trapped. Based on the information we found out later, the enemy had an explosive remote system installed.

It was three IEDs placed in three different parts of the house. The enemy triggered the bomb. It was rare for events like this to happen in the city. We'd never had an experience like this in Kabul city and the surrounding provinces. We weren't expecting it, and it cost us. We lost three of our best soldiers that day. They were amazing warriors. They were three of my best assaulters. May their souls rest in peace. Of course, as commander and leader, I could never let this go until I brought the responsible insurgents to justice.

Four other soldiers had minor injuries. We transported the wounded soldiers to Bagram Airfield. It held the best military hospital in the country. The three martyred soldiers were transported to our unit for a proper cere-mony with Coalition air transport. Unfortunately, we couldn't do a formal military ceremony in the soldiers' hometowns due to security threats. We didn't want any future threats to their family. The families would come to our unit to receive their loved ones and bury them in a civilian burial ceremony. We would send people from the unit and squadron leadership to attend the burial and funeral ceremony but with a disguise.

I put up my black turban to look like a Mullah (a Muslim priest) to not draw any attention. I went to one ceremony with my deputy, and other leads went to the other two. Because all three ceremonies took place on the same day, I could only attend one. We, as Afghans, don't keep the dead above the ground for more than a night max. It is a disrespect to our beliefs, and another reason is that Afghan hospitals don't have the facilities to keep them in morgue freezers. That is why we have to bury them as soon as possible. I introduced myself to the soldier's father and promised him that I would bring the responsible terrorists behind this ambush to justice. I quickly went back to the unit after the ceremony. I had to start investigating this intel and source as soon as possible.

The intel had looked promising because it had passed all the intel shop processes. The informant had been described as having exemplary achievements and a past record of giving good intel. I shook my head and said, "No. I don't care if he told us where Osama Bin Laden was. He is a terrorist, and I will do whatever I can to make him the target of a kill mission. I want a team on that informant. I need to find out if he sold us out or not!"

The team started investigating, and we later found out that he had sold us out. I asked the intelligence shop to prepare a target package for him. I wanted to find the network behind the bombing. Of course, it wasn't a one-man job. There was a group behind this attack.

The informant went rogue. He wasn't responding to his phone, and I am sure most of you have heard the expression "money talks, bullshit walks." Luckily, there were other informants who would quickly sell the rogue informant out. We located him five days later. I so badly wanted to send him to meet his creator, but I wanted names and locations of the group who ambushed us. So, we went after him and captured him while he was shopping. We brought him back for further investigation. He wasn't cooperating, but he slipped and revealed too much information. He told us that the Taliban's Red Unit (Taliban Special Forces) were behind the operation.

After a week of gathering intelligence, we found our target compound. It was a team of ten Red Unit fighters in Police District 13, which was a Hazara tribe area. The Taliban were using that area because there was less attention and focus from Afghan intelligence units there, and this district was very close to Wardak province. It also had a lot of routes that insurgents could easily use to commute.

We had strict orders to not bring in any Red Unit soldiers alive. We did the briefing and were ready to go after this group. The headline of the briefing was "KILL MISSION." We were prepared to depart. I called in, "Departing, departing." We didn't go in civilian vehicles this time. It was entirely a military operation. As we were en route to the target location, we received intelligence that they had four suicide bombers in the compound. We arrived and locked down the area. Nobody could get in or out. We'd hit the target at night in case a fight broke out. We always had the upper hand fighting at night due to our better equipment. Also, civilians were less likely to be out at night, which meant they were less likely to get caught in a crossfire. We cut their power off and used ladders to get over the walls. The team members on the ladders were giving us a structural description.

It was a two-story building. As soon as we opened the door, the Taliban started shooting through the windows from inside the compound. The ladder guys opened fire and kept shooting through the windows and doors.

One of the suicide bombers decided to run toward our soldiers. As soon as we saw him, we shot him in the vest. He exploded. It wasn't usual for a suicide bomber to explode after being hit. It took us a few seconds to find out what the heck had just happened. After regaining our situational awareness, we started engaging the building again.

We shot RPG rounds into the rooms. Bullets cracked overhead and zinged around the compound as they ricocheted off walls. We pushed toward the structure and threw three grenades in the room. We cleared and found three more suicide bombers. Fortunately, they were dead. We quickly collected intelligence from the building. We had to blow the explosives on the three bombers' chests. It was too dangerous to leave live, primed explosives behind. We didn't have good EOD equipment, and we didn't have the time or ability to defuse the suicide vests. So, we charged C-4 and placed it on each of their chests. We got to a safe distance and exploded their bodies. Due to a big blast from the explosives in the compound, the building collapsed on the insurgents. Fifteen terrorists were killed during the operation. The intelligence was good, and I asked the unit commander to give an extra bonus to the source for bringing such accurate information in a small window of time.

Unfortunately, the source who'd betrayed us was released on his first trial. This was due to the influence of parliament representatives. Fortunately, he was killed during a raid by Afghan security forces in 2019. From the establishment of the task force in 2001, we only had thirty-two martyred soldiers. Among the martyred soldiers, only a small number of soldiers were killed in close-quarters combat. Most, unfortunately, died from suicide bombings and IED attacks on our convoys. We were just better warriors than the Taliban, and the only ways they could hit us were these weapons of chance.

Chapter 13

Kevin King from the U.S. and Timothy Weeks from Australia were two teachers from the American University of Afghanistan who were kidnapped at gunpoint in August 2016. They were held hostage by the Taliban for three years. Our task force received the target package during the winter of 2018. We had a three-hour briefing, the most extended briefing I have ever been a part of. It was important for us to be accurate and not make a mistake. We never did hostage rescue missions. We had a four-day operation up ahead, and the operation was supposed to start in the next forty-eight hours.

The first thing I did after the initial briefing was give my team guidance on how I wanted them to prepare. The second thing I did was use Google to access the FBI's Hostage Rescue Team training videos. I saw one shooting drill that I really liked. It involved placing two targets on top of each other, one as hostage and one as the enemy. I put six targets with hostages in front of them in different positions. The first hostage was positioned close to the chest of the enemy. The hostages would cover more of the enemy's body until you could see only a tiny part of the enemy's head on the target number six. The first target was easy, and it would get more challenging by the last target. My boys knew how to shoot, and they were good at it, but our warfare was different compared to this operation. I wanted them to be the best at hostage situation shootings.

It was a long convoy. We had gotten into the vehicles and were ready to depart when I received a call from our intel shop to stop the convoy from leaving. The other commanders and I needed to go in for an update on the intelligence. We went in, and the new intelligence said there were three suicide bombers and an unknown number of IEDs prepared and waiting to be used on us. These suicide bombers weren't set up because of our hostage rescue operation. They were set up because of our nonstop raids in Wardak province, and we had to go through Wardak province to get to Ghazni province, where they were keeping the hostages. Wardak was our only option, but at the same time, we couldn't take the risk of traveling through there and putting our soldiers' lives in danger. We could take on the terrorists in Wardak, but that wasn't our mission. We had limited time to find the hostages and couldn't get bogged down in a different fight. We didn't want to cancel the operation either. It was a matter of rescuing two people.

We, the Afghans and the U.S. advisors, were discussing a better plan to conduct this operation, and we didn't have much time. I asked the lead advisor, "Can we get some air transport?"

He said, "We can, but we would only get three CH-47s."

"Perfect."

"But we can't fit all these soldiers in three choppers."

"I have a plan."

"What's the plan?"

"You can fly my squadron. That's about one hundred guys. After the choppers have refueled, they can transport the next squadron, then the third squadron."

"It might work, but let me get in touch with the Special Operations command and share this plan with them."

We received the approval. The plan was changed, and three hours later, me and my squad departed. We ended up receiving four CH-47s instead of three. It was an hour-and-thirty-five-minute flight. We had to stop at a U.S. base in Logar province to refuel. We arrived during a night with a full moon. As soon as we landed at the target, we got off the choppers running toward the village. The CH-47s left, and everything went quiet. It was so silent that whispering sounded loud. It was standard for us to start listening to ICOM scanners as soon as we got off the choppers. Surprisingly, the scanners were quiet—like absolutely quiet. There was no chatter. Everybody wondered why the Taliban weren't talking to each other. We thought that they had definitely heard the choppers! But we didn't know why they weren't reporting or checking with each other. It was very unusual!

It was a beautiful night, but everything was green through the NVGs. We started walking, but this was a quick kind of walking. Usually, our walking during operations was a bit slower. During normal operations, we would slow down because we wanted to carefully observe what was around us due to the high threat of explosives. Slow is smooth, and smooth is fast. "Don't rush to your death" is another SEAL saying. But due to the hostage situation, we had to be quick. If the enemy knew we were there, and we didn't close distance fast enough, they could move the hostages, and we would be back at square one.

We arrived at the target building and surrounded it. There were no movements and no movers in the area. Everything was quiet when I checked with our advisors. They said that there were three other operations in the area and that may be the reason. I later found out that the advisor was right. The building was isolated by the security teams. We breached the compound with explosives, then assaulted. We cleared the first building. It was a dry hole, meaning there were no people inside the compound. Again, we asked ourselves, "What is going on? Why is it so quiet? Did we get the wrong intel?" I talked to the intel team and told them to get in contact with the unit and its intelligence shop. I wanted to find out if there was some update to the info from the sources in the area.

The operation went on and on. We cleared the first village, then the second, then the third, and so on. We passed day three and still had nothing. There were no engagements. We had spread out in the area. We were spread so far that we often couldn't reach other squadrons on the radios. It was difficult. But even in the hardest of times, there are funny stories to tell. One we all laughed about was when we had to send nineteen men from one village to another village so they could be questioned. The problem was we couldn't send our men with the detainees. We didn't have enough manpower to go with this group to the next village, but we had to send the detainees.

My deputy came up with a great idea. He said, "Let me handle it for you, Commander. I will transport them with no escort." He lined up all nineteen guys and marked their hands with a black marker. Their hands were cuffed with zip ties. He told them, "Walk straight to the next village. We have a predator drone above your head, and we will be watching you from the air. If you try to run away, you will get killed, and if you get lucky and survive the airstrike, we will find you and you will be killed."

As soon as my deputy said that, I nearly laughed but somehow held myself together. I knew we didn't have air support. He used these words to scare them. They started walking in a straight line to the next village. We reported the prisoner transport to the squadron that was in the next village and explained the situation. The commander there laughed and said, "Let's see how it goes." Twenty minutes later, we checked with the other squadron. Their commander said, "They are not here yet. Let me send a guy to the rooftop to see if they can see them." Three minutes later, he reported, "We see a line of people coming this way. They are walking in a straight line."

I said, "Okay. Let me know when they have arrived." Ten minutes later, I received confirmation that they had arrived. It was all nineteen men. This was funny for all of us.

The operation went on for over one week. We still had no signs of the hostages or their captors. Then, we found this one room on the side of a mountain. We went in. We saw signs that people had recently been there. I told my guys to dig into this room. I told them to break walls if they had to. At the corner of the room, there was a wall cabinet. I told my guys to remove it and to check if there was any hidden room or door. We removed the cabinet. There was nothing behind it, but a carpet was underneath it. We moved the carpet aside, and there was a wood board on the ground. We removed it and saw a small doorway. We opened it and found a hole and a ladder going down. We started clearing the hole. When we got down there, we saw a room that looked like people had been imprisoned there. I have seen a lot of insurgents' prisons, but this one was better compared to others. There were books and dumbbells to work out with. In my opinion, it was confirmed that they had kept the hostages here.

I checked with my intel team to verify that this was the location. We received the confirmation for the area, but there was still no sign of hostages. Updated information came from the task force. We were told that a U.S. Special Operations command had had a raid in this area one night prior to ours. They'd gotten into some firefights. Then, the insurgents had relocated the hostages. So, we wrapped up the operation and joined back up with the rest of the squadrons. But of course, I couldn't leave the prison there like that. I asked my explosives guy, "How many explosives do you have?"

"Enough, Commander."

"Do you know what I am thinking?"

"I think I know."

"Leave no sign of this place."

The explosives were set with a ten-minute timer. It was a big explosion, and the whole thing collapsed. It looked like a big hole in the ground. The operation was over, and we planned to leave the area the following night. We returned to base. I wasn't happy with the result of this operation. I wish we could have saved the two teachers and sent them back home. It was unfortunate, but there was nothing we could do. They were released in a prisoner exchange in November of 2019.

—

The Taliban opened their official office in Qatar in mid-2013. Few people were hopeful about the peace talks that were about to start. The Taliban's demands were high, and on our side of the table, we had corrupt leaders negotiating on behalf of the Afghans. To be honest, I have never trusted any of the Afghan leaders. It didn't matter what tribe they were from. They have always fought for power and position and used the people as a tool to win. I was always mad at my people for supporting these corrupt leaders. I was especially mad at the youth because with every bad thing the Afghan leaders did, they still supported them.

There are as many as fourteen recognized ethnic groups in the country, with Pashtuns making up around 42 percent of the population. Tajiks account for about 27 percent, while Hazaras and Uzbeks are about 9 percent each. Then, there are a handful of other groups in smaller numbers, and there are few problems with these smaller ethnic groups. But the larger ethnic groups can't accept each other. If a Pashtun becomes the leader, the Tajik and Hazara tribes won't like or accept him. And if a Tajik or Hazara becomes the leader, other groups won't accept him. This was always the main problem, and this problem became greater due to widespread poverty, poor literacy, and bad parenting.

I can't put the blame on one ethnic group; they are all equally involved in ruining this beautiful country. We have had forty years of nonstop war. I haven't believed a word from our leaders in the past thirty years. They were all warlords and always killed innocent people to gain power. None of them served in the army. Every tribe makes a big deal out of their leader, but none of them genuinely served this nation. They all had personal interests. The sad part is that young Afghans killed each other for these leaders. Because of these corrupt leaders, people were born in war and were unfortunately killed in this war. Civilians were always the victims from both the government and insurgent side. Between 562,000 and 2,000,000 people were killed during the Russian invasion. Over six thousand innocent Afghans were killed during conflicts between U.S. and Taliban groups.

So, as soon as I heard about the peace negotiations, I knew it was all a big lie. Our warlord leaders didn't want to lose their current power and influence, and the Taliban on the other side had the same thoughts. But predominantly Pakistan and other countries were behind every decision that the Taliban were planning to make. Pakistan and other neighboring countries wanted a deal that benefited them in the long term. The first two main demands of the Taliban were the release of their prisoners and no more Afghan security forces. They also said we needed a new army. I mean, there were a bunch of demands.

I never trusted the Taliban, and I will never trust them. At first, when the Afghan government asked the Taliban why they were fighting, they said, "We are not fighting the Afghan government. We are fighting Americans." In 2019 and 2020, when there was no operational presence of U.S. forces in Afghanistan, they still attacked Afghan forces and mainly targeted civilians. When the Afghan government asked them, "Why are you fighting us now?" the Taliban leadership said, "Well, our fight is against the Kabul Office." (The Taliban called the Afghan government the "Kabul Office.") I have seen a lot of terrorists and dealt with a lot of them personally. I will tell you one thing: They can never be trusted. They have directly attacked holy and religious places, hospitals, and other buildings and areas crowded with civilians. When they were asked, "Why are you killing civilians?" the Taliban's answer was, "This is a holy war, and people need to pay some sacrifices too, and of course, all these civilians will go to heaven. Why aren't they happy?"

When I heard that answer, I was shocked and furious. I don't know where they came up with that crap. In the Holy Quran, verse 5:32, it says if you kill an innocent soul, it is as if you had slain mankind entirely. It is not only Islam. All religions are against killing people and against wars.

I will tell you a funny story I have about an insurgent leader who was recruiting suicide bombers to attack military and civilian locations. I had captured him for questioning. I have a mean face if I am not laughing. I grow my beard and sometimes keep it long and sometimes cut it short. I don't have a specific reason behind growing out my beard—I just like it. But I have a very thick mustache, and when it grows, the hair starts poking around my nose and gives me a hard time. So, back then, I used to shave my mustache. Basically, I would look like a Muslim scholar, even though I am not one. The insurgent had a long beard too with long hair.

The interrogation on this insurgent started. It was a long one, like twenty-eight hours of nonstop questioning. He wouldn't admit anything until we provided him with evidence. During this interrogation, I was checking in on him on some personal levels. This was one of the questioning tricks I came up with. I knew he would give himself away. I started with this story. "Man, I know you are right and your war is right, but I can't help you. You are caught now. I know a lot of your leaders." I mentioned some insurgent leaders' names and their personal stories from the information, intelligence, and investigations I did back at that time. This is how it went.

The insurgent said, "You know, you have the key in your hands to go to heaven."

"How? What do you mean? I am confused," I replied.

"You know, if you blow yourself up among the Americans, how many of them you can easily kill?"

"What is the point? Why would I want to kill myself?" I said this in a tone that implied I was scared to do so.

"Are you a faithful Muslim?"

"Yes, of course."

"How much do you know about the Quran and your religion?"

"I do not know enough. I do not practice enough."

"Don't worry. God is very merciful. If you do what I say, you will directly go to heaven."

"No way! I am a big-time sinner. God won't forgive me for the things I have done. I have killed so many of you guys. You think God will forgive me for that?"

"It is okay. We all make mistakes."

"What should I do?"

"If you kill these Americans or the Afghan commanders, either by blowing yourself up or shooting at them, you will be granted a castle in heaven."

"Wow, that would be great. I mean, heaven is such a nice place. I have seen it in my dreams. It is a beautiful-looking place. I would love to go there when I die."

"You see, that is a sign. God has shown you a sign. You have to act before it is too late."

"What sign?"

"Your dream was a sign to go there using a shortcut."

The conversation dragged on. I played it dumb and acted in a way so he felt that I was on his side. Everything was being recorded. One of my officers came to the investigation room. I quickly changed the subject away from the idea of me blowing myself up. Because the insurgent thought I was hiding the conversation from my teammates, it helped to gain more of his trust and showed him I was serious about my intentions. The officer left. I played it cool again, and we kept talking. I went out of the room a few times and used the restroom excuse. I wanted to get more information about his family and friends. I needed to play it as cool as I could with as much confidence as I had. After a long conversation, I asked the most important question of the day.

"Where would I get a suicide bombing vest from? It is not easy to find."

The insurgent said, "I will hook you up with the right people. Don't worry about that."

"Are you sure you can do that? I don't want to get in trouble before making any move. I am really tired of my life and my job, but there is nothing else to do."

"Trust me. I have done that many times."

As soon as I heard that, I left the room and went outside. With that subtle line, he'd just admitted to organizing and supplying suicide bombings. The other officers were watching the investigation. I said, "Did you guys get that on the camera?" The investigation team said they did.

I went back in and asked him, "I will go to heaven if I do this, right?"

The insurgent said, "Yes, of course!"

"Okay, can you do me a favor?

"Sure, anything. What do you want?"

"You go blow yourself up first, and if the heaven you are talking about is really nice, give me a call. I will come after you." I laughed and said, "You moron! You thought I was a dumb ass like you. God knows where the address is of this heaven you are talking about going to? If your address were real, you would have gone first."

"They need me on earth more than heaven."

"Zip your mouth before I break it."

I read some verses from the Holy Quran that proved him wrong, "And do not kill the soul which Allah has forbidden to be killed except by legal right. He instructed you that you may use reason" (6:151, Saheeh International translation). I continued, "If Allah ordered Muslims to kill the non-Muslims in the Holy Quran, he would have ordered Prophet Mohammad (peace be upon him) to do so when the Muslims had a big empire. The Prophet's neighbor was a Jewish widow. He even visited her when she was ill. When she asked, 'Why are you visiting me?' the Prophet (peace be upon him) said, 'As a Muslim, my neighbor has rights over me.'"

"You played me. I trusted you."

157

I left the room because if I didn't, I would have definitely broken his jaw.

This pitch from the suicide bomber was similar to one of their Taliban leader's. This leader was working directly for Pakistani intelligence services. He was motivating Pakistani and Afghani youth. He would say, "American women are invading your country with their guns, and you are going to Europe to clean their streets as their servants. Instead of working in the west, go fight Americans in Afghanistan." He said this while his children were studying in Pakistan's best schools and universities. Some young adults were getting motivated and were accepting his invitation to fight in Afghanistan in his gatherings that were held in Quetta, Pakistan.

Once, we captured a suicide bomber in Kabul city. We caught him while he was sleeping in the Pul-e Khishti Mosque in PD1. This police district is one of the most crowded parts of Kabul city. When we took him to the unit for further investigation, the first thing he said was, "I didn't want to do it."

We asked him, "What do you mean?"

"I was ready to blow myself up, but when I saw people praying and that they were Muslims, I changed my mind."

"What did they tell you?"

"That everybody that lives in Kabul are infidels and that they must die."

I found that there were a lot of similarly sad stories. These are just a couple from my experience. A lot of suicide bombers changed their mind and didn't want to go through with it. The number of them my team and I encountered was high, and this is just the number we know about.

Chapter 14

To be honest, there was a point that not only me but all the guys in the task force and Afghan armed forces were tired of this nonstop war. We always offered peace to the Taliban, but they never accepted it.

I remember, one night, we went on this operation in Parwan province, located north of Kabul province, and this village we went to was amazingly beautiful. It was up in the mountains. It was lusciously green with beautiful weather, and there were waterfalls all over the village. You always had fresh air blowing into your face. I remember talking to one of the advisors about the beauty of the village, and he said, "It is like heaven on earth. Something like Rivendell Valley from *The Lord of the Rings* movies. Not the housing but the valley."

While walking to the target, I thought to myself, *What an amazing tourist location this place can become. And the villagers would also benefit from it, but instead, they chose the wrong path.*

Frustration from this war was with us, especially after 2017, when we did more and more nonstop operations. While I was sitting with my soldiers, we would be talking about peace. My soldiers would swear and say, "I will work as a laborer in a market and will give away everything I have in exchange for peace."

The only break we had throughout all these years of fighting was when a ten days' cease-fire took place between the Afghan government and the Taliban. It wasn't just a relief for the armed forces—it was a relief for all Afghan people. Those ten days were an extraordinary experience for my countrymen. We knew the Taliban were not willing to stick to their word. They were supplying their comrades in different districts and locations throughout the country. We received a lot of intelligence reports about the Taliban stocking arms and planning future attacks. The Taliban were getting close to Kabul city. We ignored them all because we were hopeful that we might have peace.

I remember most of the soldiers were asking me, "If we have this much intel, why don't we take action on it?"

I said, "My brothers-in-arms, I know your frustration. I know when these ten days are over, we might get into bigger fights, but let's look at the bigger picture. If we, as a task force, do something about this intel, even though we all know the Taliban won't extend the cease-fire duration and they will fight us harder, the Afghan people will always blame us for making the first move against them."

The Afghan government was also in a defensive position. That made things really hard for the armed forces. The ANA soldiers were told to not shoot unless the enemy shot them first. They were told not to attack unless the enemy attacked them first. Basically, it meant, "Sit in your homes and wait for them to kill you."

As the task force, we were never in a defensive position. We constantly attacked them before they made any move, and that was one of the biggest reasons the Taliban hated us the most. The Taliban always said in their statements and gatherings, "If we catch conventional armed force soldiers, we might give them a second chance. But for the Special Operations soldiers, we will chop them into pieces. Afghan special forces are infidels."

In the Holy Quran, it has been written that no matter how many sins a Muslim makes, he or she will be a Muslim. He or she may not be a good Muslim, but he or she is still a Muslim. The only time you will be called a disbeliever is when you say there are more gods than the Almighty God (Allah and God are the same for Muslims, just different names). The Taliban never practiced Islam, yet they still claim to be the best of Muslims, especially among the Afghans.

At the beginning of the cease-fire, our advisors left the unit and went to Bagram Airfield. They had orders to leave the unit and would no longer be involved in our operations. They would visit our unit and meet with us regularly, but they wouldn't have any official presence in our unit or our operations. That made our job more complex because it meant not having air assets during operations.

Then, it was day ten. The Afghan government requested an extension of the cease-fire, but the Taliban didn't approve it. Lower-level Taliban fighters were also tired of fighting, but disobeying orders meant death to the fighter and his family. Taliban leaders were concerned that if they extended the cease-fire timing, they might lose a considerable number of their fighters. That was one of the biggest reasons for not extending the agreement.

We had received a lot of intelligence during the past ten days of the cease-fire, and we had a lot of target packages that were ready for action. So, on day ten, as soon as we received the confirmation that the cease-fire was officially over, we launched an operation in Wardak province. This time, we took the longer route going to Wardak. We wanted to do a show force. The Taliban didn't want to maintain the cease-fire, and they would pay for that decision. This was done for many reasons. First was to raise the Afghan people's belief in their armed forces. The second was to scare the enemy and deter them from launching any suicide bombing attacks in Kabul city. The third was to gain leverage so that the conditions might be favorable for another peace deal. If you want peace, be prepared for war. Wolves don't hunt wolves. They hunt sheep.

We received the briefing. This was going to be a clearing operation to disrupt enemy activity in the area. Shortly after the brief, we lined up all of the vehicles from every squadron. Almost the entire unit went on this mission. We were ready to roll out. There was a total of 118 vehicles, and the convoy was almost four miles long. We had sirens on and drove around in Hollywood style. It was supposed to be showing off. People were cheering on the sides of the road. They all had happy faces. They were wishing to be as cool as our guys, but what they didn't know was that a village was going to be raided, explosions would happen, and soldiers might get killed. This kind of job gets glamorized by the media, but it's not glamorous. It's a job I wish nobody had to do.

When we got close to the main gate of Wardak province, we went full blackout. We turned off all the lights that were visible to naked eyes. We had our NVGs switched on and drove in pitch black darkness. We arrived, and the Taliban chatter started. They were so mad, saying, "What is wrong with these soldiers? Leave us alone. Give us a break." The Taliban were tired of our raids. They were tired of this nonstop war and killing like us. But they had no option. It was fight or die. This wasn't the case with all of them, but it was with most of them. They were scared of getting captured or killed. Most of them weren't really holy fighters (ready to die for a holy cause) as they were claiming. Most of the ones who were ready to die as suicide bombers were very young. They were usually as young as teenagers. The old ones were smart. They didn't want to die. They just wanted to have the power. The leaders never participated in direct conflicts because they knew this was a wrongful cause. It wasn't a holy cause; it was fighting for the throne. It was just a game of thrones.

Our operation went smoothly. There was no fighting this time, and it was a quiet night. We captured twelve Taliban fighters in their homes. They were caught off guard; they weren't expecting this operation at all. We destroyed three Taliban headquarters and seized the weapons and equipment held inside during the raid. We were back in the city twenty minutes after the sunrise. We intentionally did that to show the people they have a strong military ready to operate at day and night. We did all that because the news and media never supported us. They always took sides with the Taliban. They did this because if they didn't, they would get attacked or their staff would be assassinated by the insurgents.

The media plays an important role in our daily lives. If our operation had civilian casualties, the media would show that for a whole week and give us a lousy picture. This would provide people with a really disconnected and pessimistic view of the Afghan armed forces. But if the insurgents did a suicide bombing, the news would be about the government and calling the armed forces incapable. There was no winning with them. Some of our operations were posted on the armed forces official page for the social media app Facebook. I created a fake Facebook account and went through the comments to see what people were saying about our operations. Most of the comments were negative. Some comments went like, "A whole operation and only killed twenty insurgents."

But people didn't realize they were playing a significant role in this war. If they would have helped the armed forces, this war would have ended long ago. But they did the opposite of that. People never helped or cooperated with the security forces. When we would ask them why they weren't helping the security forces, they would answer, "If we do that, after you guys leave the village, they will come after us and kill us."

Governments stand on people's support and tax revenue. If people don't support their government, that government will fall immediately. We all have seen examples of it around the world. The Afghan armed forces never had that support. I experienced a lot of hate when I was in the army Special Operations Forces. We had to go to work in full uniform, and I could see the looks people gave me and heard the way people talked about me. They didn't have the guts to throw their hate at me because of my mean face and because I was working out a lot back then. I was a muscular guy. But from their reactions and facial expressions, you could clearly see they hated me. Anyway, deep down in my heart, I tell myself that I still love my people, but most of them deserve the Taliban regime.

—

War is ugly. Civilians have never and will never support wars. At least the ones paying the costs of war never will. The costs are too great. Only the dead see the end of war. It is the greedy people in power wanting more power and money who want war. Wanting more is human nature. We will never be satisfied. Prime examples are billionaires still working hard because they are not satisfied with their wealth. If they helped all the poor people around the world, they would still have plenty of money to live a luxurious life without even working. There are rich and powerful men who want countries to be at war so they can make money from selling guns and drugs. I have seen many of them encouraging the Afghan war to continue. It was all done illegally, and the weapon dealers became rich.

When the Afghan-Russian war ended, those rich people were annoyed because they lost a big part of their income. Those rich people didn't care about the civilians getting killed because of their weapons. They didn't care about the houses being bombarded because of them. It was the greed that kept feeding this war. Being willing to kill and support killers out of greed for money can be dangerous. This love for money made people kill their own brothers. I will not go deep down that road. You might wonder why I am talking about wars in general here. You might think it is not related to the content in my book, but unfortunately, it is directly related to the Afghan War. You might even say this greed was the reason the war happened in the first place.

There are good and bad things about guerrilla warfare from an intelligence perspective. Whoever pays the big bucks wins the game. What is that supposed to mean? It means the fighters on the ground are in it for either power or money. The elements of power and money are almost the same thing, but they come in different shapes. They both go together and are bound together. From day one, countries supporting the Taliban were paying the Taliban one amount to conduct some terrorist operations against the U.S. and NATO. And the U.S. and NATO were paying another amount to counter those operations. Both sides had failures and successes.

The Afghan War was an intelligence war, and the superpower countries were playing the game. And Afghans on the ground were getting hurt. Unfortunately, it is true. The Taliban-supporting countries were paying the Taliban leaders to keep the fight going and kill the Afghan soldiers. And the U.S. and NATO were paying the government forces to fight back against the Taliban. Trillions of dollars were spent on the Afghan War. More importantly, people lost their lives or became disabled for the rest of their lives. Those people were Afghans or U.S. or NATO soldiers. They were humans who had families, had a wife/husband, and probably had kids.

One of the countries that was supporting the Taliban was Russia. We all know Russia and the U.S. have had their problems for as long as most of us remember. Russia supported the war against the U.S. invasion of Vietnam, and the U.S. supported the Northern Alliance in Afghanistan to fight the Russian invasion. Then, when the U.S. invaded Afghanistan, it was time for Russia to take their revenge on the U.S. I mean, this is what we call "COLD WAR." Since coming to America, I've been told that the Cold War was over and won. In my experience, I don't see how.

A question I don't see asked enough is, "Who are the Taliban?" Talib means "Islamic student," and Taliban is the plural form of the word. They also call themselves holy warriors or Mujahidin, meaning someone fighting only for the sake of God. In theory, they were not supposed to be fighters for money or power; rather, the reward would be given to them on judgment day. I don't want to get into too much detail from an Islamic point of view. I would need another book to talk about that. To make it simple, the Taliban are an extremist group of Muslims. They think forcing others to worship God is their job and obligation. Forcing someone to worship is not what Islam teaches us.

There is no verse in the entire Holy Quran that says you have to force people to worship what you believe in. What you can do is have good deeds and be a good Muslim. Other believers will have their own choice whether to accept your religion or not. You can do debates and preach it, but nothing by force. That was and is the problem with the Taliban. Forcing you to be a good Muslim will not make you a good Muslim. God wants you to worship him with your heart, not to do so to show off or because you are being forced to. All Afghans wanted and still want Afghanistan to be an Islamic country with an excellent Muslim ruling it based on what the Holy Quran says, not the leader's assumption about it. No one supports translating it in a way that benefits you. The Holy Quran doesn't have an old or new testament, and changing the words for your benefit is an unforgivable sin.

Most of the Taliban fighters were young and illiterate. They were born and raised in a village far from schools, technology, and a good understanding of Islam. Our Mullahs (similar to priests) preached in the mosques that because we had been at war for the past forty years, we didn't have good Islamic schools. That is why there was a wrong belief that the Islamic schools in Afghanistan weren't quality schools. Therefore, students believed they had to go to Pakistan to study. People were told by every Mullah leading a prayer in a mosque that they should go to Pakistan because those Mullahs learned there. They believed Pakistani Islamic schools were the best. The problem with the Pakistani Islamic center is that they teach Islam in an extremist way, and those Islamic schools are thoroughly influenced by the Pakistani intelligence service system. When our youth were going there to learn about Islam, the teachers were teaching them what Pakistan's version of the CIA wanted them to be taught, which was, "You have to join the holy war in Afghanistan. You have to kill Americans. They invaded your country. If you become a suicide bomber, you will directly go to heaven. Kabul's gates are heaven's gates."

Completing these Islamic schools would take years. You'd go there as a kid, and your teachers (who claim to be holy guides) would tell you that Afghanistan is a nonbeliever country, especially the government. You wouldn't just hear this once or twice. They'd keep telling you those lines for years. Not only would the teachers tell you that, but the whole society living there would tell you the same. It would definitely have an impact on you. A saying comes to mind: "Surround yourself with positive people because negative people will always push you down and make you believe you are not who you are."

Those Islamic students (Taliban) would come back to Afghanistan and start their schools in Afghan villages all around the country. Half of the day, they'd teach their extremist beliefs in schools, and the other half, they'd fight against the government. Those Pakistani-trained scholars preached against the government in all the villages throughout the country, especially when there was an operation done in the village or district. They were insurgents—not only in the eyes of the U.S. and NATO; we Afghans called them insurgents as well.

A Taliban is an insurgent. He can claim all he wants that he is a holy warrior, but the truth is he isn't. Taliban leaders wanted power and had no problem using the illiterate youth as a weapon to gain that power. There was a minority group of people that supported the Taliban. Most people didn't have any option because they were living in a Taliban-controlled area. They had to help them otherwise they would have been killed. The majority that didn't support them initially got involved with the group eventually due to specific reasons. One of these reasons was injustice (which was the primary one). Something was taken from these people by an Afghan warlord, and they felt powerless. The fire of revenge in most Afghans is hot and burning. To take revenge, they had to join a Taliban group. If they didn't have this sense of helplessness, they would not have entered into a war. Only fools want to go to war.

I mean, show me one single parent who wants their kids to go to war. The love of a mother and father for their child is something extraordinary, and this love has nothing to do with education or literacy. I myself am a good example. My mother is illiterate. She has not had a single day of school in her life, but her love for me and my siblings is something exceptional, even though we are almost a dozen in number. She still loves every single one of us, and she was always against me going to the military because of the danger and because I might end up getting killed. I have no doubt this was the same for the typical Taliban soldier. But because he wanted to take revenge on someone or something, he would risk his life and his family's lives by joining a terrorist network.

Contrary to popular belief, most Taliban soldiers were not believers of their cause. Some were brainwashed teens, but many were in it for practical matters. The trillions of dollars pouring into the country from all the powerful countries made the war what it was. This was illuminated by a conversation I had with one of my sources. He was excellent at what he did. He was collecting intel from most districts of the Taliban-controlled areas, which wasn't easy for other sources to do. He would say, "Just give me the money, and I will bring you info about the Taliban gathering in Pakistan."

As I said, he was excellent at his job, and that was what we wanted. One day, I asked him, "How did you join the Taliban?"

He responded, "I heard that the Taliban pays 300 U.S. dollars per month to their fighters, and the Afghan National Army pays $200. And I need to work to feed my family."

"Why not the army then?"

"There's lots of corruption and too many problems with the Afghan Army."

"Nah, as long as you are on the right path and know what you are doing, you won't face any problem!"

"Nah, there is power and no rules or responsibility with the Taliban. And if you play smart among them, you will survive and make good money when you reach the top."

"Okay, okay. No point disagreeing with you. Now tell me, how did you join?"

"As I said, I was looking for work. When I heard about the $300 salary, I went to a friend of mine that was with the Taliban. I asked, how do I join? My friend gave me a number and told me to contact him and tell him I knew this friend. I contacted the number. He told me to pack some clothes and go to our neighboring village. I was told to meet with the group in a certain location. After the meeting, I was given a radio and an AK-47 to start my new work as a member of the Taliban. We were doing some random stuff, nothing special. It was the end of week two, and it was a Thursday night when our commander came to our location. We were in a cave on top of a mountain. The commander said, 'I received a call from our leader that we need to send a suicide bomber to hit center of the city.' He referred to the bomber as a 'Holy Martyr.'"

"But how did you pick who to be the suicide bomber?"

"Give me a minute. I will explain it to you. Our commander came and asked, 'Who is volunteering for this holy mission?' Everyone was quiet. I was definitely quiet because I didn't sign up for this! Then, he quickly changed his question with this sentence: 'I know you all want to go on this mission, but we will let destiny decide who that lucky holy warrior is.'

"I am thinking what is the Taliban commander planning to do? The Taliban commander said, 'We will write every fighter's name on a small piece of paper, and we will put all the names in a bag, then shake them. We will pick one of the papers. Whoever's name is on that paper is selected by God.'

"I was like, Holy cow!? I hope they don't put my name on the paper! The Taliban commander started writing the names. He looked at me and said, 'You are one of us now. I trust you as much as I trust my senior warriors!' I couldn't say no because I didn't want to look like a guy that was in the group because of money.

"The Taliban commander said, 'Okay, names are ready.' He told me to pick one paper. I picked one and gave it to the commander. The commander started crying! As soon as he started crying, all the fighters started crying too. I thought his name was selected. The Taliban commander said, 'Looks like I am not worthy of this holy mission,' and he read the name! When he read the name, I was shocked. IT WAS MY NAME! And I noticed they were all crying, but I couldn't see any damn tears on their faces. It was all fake.

"The Taliban commander said, 'Let's do it again. Maybe God changed his plan and made one of us worthy of this mission.' He shook the bag and told me to pick a name again, and what I saw almost gave me a heart attack. MY NAME AGAIN! But how? The Taliban commander continued, 'No, God decided that this young man is the only man that is worthy of this mission.'

"We prepared a good dinner, and our guard shifts were about to start. The shifts were four hours and sometimes longer. I was thinking to myself and asking myself, 'Why did I sign up for this?' I was kind of suspicious of this name selection. I did a smart move and told all the fighters, 'You all go to sleep. I can't sleep tonight. I am going to heaven tomorrow.' When everybody went to sleep, I started looking for the bag that had our names in it. Thankfully, I found the bag. I started going through names, and guess what? The Taliban commander wrote my name on all those papers. It was 2 a.m. when I packed my clothes and fled from the area. Since that day, I have been playing with the Taliban system."

A contractor's vehicle was blown up by an IED in 2008 while I was working as an interpreter for Canadian special forces. Surprisingly, the driver and passenger survived.

Out on a mission as a combat interpreter with Navy SEALs in Kandahar in 2010.

Sleeping on a mountaintop with Navy SEALs for
over two days after receiving a large gash in my
skull from a vehicle rollover (2010).

Meeting with locals and village elders after a mission
with Navy SEALs in Kandahar province (2010).

Joint mission with the Green Berets and Navy SEALs in 2013.

Handing candies to kids in a village located in one of the southern provinces. This was taken in 2011.

Taken in 2014 in Wardak province during a mission that
killed eighteen Taliban commanders.

Posing for a photo with an Australian special forces
operator on a hilltop during a mission in Kabul in 2015.

The base of TF-241 right before I headed out on a mission in January of 2016. It was freezing.

Conducting close-quarters battle and breacher training before an upcoming raid.

Coming back from a mission in September of 2017 and arriving at FOB Shank.

Providing security to the chief of the CIA, the U.S. ambassador to Afghanistan, and numerous generals during a visit in 2019.

August 18, 2021, at 0200 hours. I hopped into some Afghan Air Force planes because I'd never get the chance again.

August 21, 2021, during a resupply mission from Eagle Base to Kabul Airport at 0331 hours.

Hamid Karzai International Airport, August 23, 2021. A commercial plane was evacuating people behind me.

August 24, 2021, around 0500 hours. Two planes are filled with passengers and ready to take off.

Eagle Base, August 24, 2021.

August 26, 2021, on the tarmac of Hamid Karzai International Airport moments before Abbey Gate was hit by a suicide bomber.

August 27, 2021. These were our living conditions during the evacuation. We didn't have access to much food.

Chapter 15

The Taliban were receiving financial, logistical, and training support from neighboring countries, including Pakistan. The Taliban would go to Pakistan during wintertime for more training. Most of the Taliban had families living in Pakistan, so winter was a time for them to visit family and learn new ways to kill people. It was a two-for-one bargain. The Afghan armed forces killed or captured many Taliban fighters with Pakistan residency identification cards. Another country that was supporting them was Iran. They were recruiting Afghans as spies for their country through a system called the Khomeini Committee (Khomeini was Iran's first supreme leader). They were helping some poor families and at the same time recruiting Afghans to achieve their purposes in Afghanistan. Most people who were getting aid from this Iranian program were Shia Muslims. Ninety percent of Afghans are Sunni, and 10 percent are Shias. Iran is 90 percent Shias and 10 percent Sunni. Russia was also financially supporting the Taliban.

Around May of 2020, the number of terror attacks increased overall in the country, especially in Kabul province. We were still going after all types of terrorist networks in the area, but we couldn't stop all of them. We received intel from the head of the Afghan intelligence agency that there was a network that was doing assassinations for money. We knew that they were getting financial support from one of the neighboring countries, but we weren't sure which country, and we weren't certain how they were supporting this network. The intelligence was passed to our intel section, and the TF-241 intelligence officers started working on this target package.

These officers were good at what they did. As combat operators, we wouldn't be able to do much if it weren't for these intel officers. They had many ways to collect more information on this assassination ring. Other intel departments, such as Afghan ministries of defense and interior affairs, were also trying to gather information on this ring. After two months of hard work, we had something. It was handed to us to take action on it. This operation was one of the most secret that we ever did in Kabul. This ring had been suspected of assassinating U.S. and Afghan soldiers, government officials, and civilians.

There are a lot of examples of them conducting assassinations. One was when they placed a magnetic mine on an Afghan Army vehicle that was transporting five Afghan commando officers. Another attempt by this network hit a U.S. Special Operations convoy by using a suicide bomber carried by a vehicle. This happened about 500 to 600 meters away from the Russian embassy. A lot of people were killed in that incident. The U.S. convoy had casualties, but I do not know to what extent. Another attempt occurred when they placed explosives on the vehicle of a female Afghan parliament member by the name of Shukria Barakzai. She is well known in the country. She was lucky that she survived, but her bodyguards were killed. The explosion happened in front of a private university, and unfortunately, lots of students were killed and injured due to the size of the blast. After the incident, she retired from the parliament and later went to the U.K. as the Afghan ambassador. She is currently living in the U.K.

So, one day around 12:30 p.m., I was called in to come to the task force's TOC. I knew this call was different compared to other calls that I would receive about an operation. I would usually know about a target at least two or three days prior to operation day. I hoped it was not an emergency call. I walked into the TOC and saw just three people sitting around the briefing table. It was our lead advisor, the head of the intel section, and the operation commander. As soon as I walked in, the lead advisor said, "Commander! What we talk about here must stay a secret till this op is done."

I said, "Okay," and pulled up a chair and sat down.

The lead advisor stood up and positioned himself next to the briefing screen. He started by saying, "Gentlemen, this is operation Black Snake. Our target is an assassination network that plants sticky bombs on cars and assassinates Afghan government officials and military personnel. They are located in Police District 6 of Kabul city. This network is responsible for the death of many soldiers and officials. We have limited information on how they operate and how many people are in this network, but we do know their location, and we are going after them today."

I raised my hand.

"Go ahead, Commander. What is your question?

"So, this is another Taliban or ISIS network? What makes this op so secret?"

"No, Commander, this is not a network like the Taliban or ISIS. Actually, they don't even have a lot of connection with the Taliban. This network is working for foreign intelligence agencies, and they get paid per assassination. We are not sure for which foreign agency they are working, but our main guess is the Russian KGB."

I said, "We knew all along that Russians were behind some terrorist attacks, but no one did anything about it."

"You are right, Commander, but this is only an assumption so far, and that is why it stays a secret until we see the result."

The brief was similar to other briefs but with one difference: We were told to do a detailed SSE and look for documents related to assassination and terrorist activities in the country. The briefing was finished, and everyone left the briefing room, but I stayed and reviewed the briefing once more.

The intriguing part was the area where the organization was operating. I used to go to an English language course in that district and had a lot of friends teaching English language courses close to the target building. I had been in that area frequently, but I never suspected any crime and never spotted a suspicious family or individual on the road that the target was on. The target house looked simple compared to the rest of the homes in the area, and it was an affluent area. A lot of foreigners used to live there, but after multiple terrorist attacks, they left the country. That was sad to see. As an intelligence operator, I never heard a word about it and never noticed anything suspicious, even though I'd regularly gone through that area for the past six or seven years. I am obsessed with my work, and I strive to be the best at everything. If I didn't notice these guys, then they were good at hiding in plain sight. I took it as a chance to learn and get better at spotting signs of suspicious activity.

In the past, I had many encounters with lousy intelligence. I had developed a sense for it by this point. I could feel when intelligence was fake as it was getting briefed. This operation didn't feel that way. My sixth sense was telling me that this was going to be a good operation.

The target house only had one floor. It didn't have any tactical structures like barricaded positioning, too many trees, or two or three floors, and it wasn't connected to any other streets. It was a four-thousand-square-foot house, which was expected in the area. It had a small garage entrance, a huge yard, and a few trees inside the yard. The house only had five rooms, which were all at the rear part of the house. It was surrounded by walls that were six feet tall. This was noticeable because Afghan walls are mainly eight feet tall.

I left the TOC and went to brief my soldiers. I briefed with a lot more detail due to my personal experience in the area. I did not tell my soldiers that this target was suspected to be working with foreign agencies. After the brief, I told my joint terminal attack controller (JTAC) to bring his small drone, which we never used in the city missions. The soldiers were told to be on a five-minute recall.

It was close to sunset when I received the approval from the advisors that the operation was a go. I called in my soldiers, and we were ready to roll. We were in civilian vehicles because of the city environment. We drove to the main gate as a convoy but couldn't depart as a convoy. We left the base with a two-minute gap between each vehicle. We started departing from the base one by one. The target was twenty miles away from our base, but due to bad traffic in Kabul, it took us about two hours to get there. Since we were going as civilians, we couldn't do anything but be patient.

I told my deputy to move close to the target building and to lock down the area. I knew about a small park located close to the target building. We needed to watch and see if there were any movers going in or out of the building, so I took two vehicles, and we drove to the park. We got out of the vehicles, readied the drone, and flew it over the target building to watch for any activities inside the building.

There was one car parked in the yard, and a couple of kids were playing there. Seeing kids inside the building was a good sign because it meant that the chances of a gun fight were significantly decreased. When people are going to put up an armed resistance, they don't bring their kids or their nieces and nephews. The kids being there offered a hint regarding the mentality of the people in the target building.

I told my JTAC to keep watching the house and report suspicious movement to us. I drove back to join the squad and prepare the team to raid the building. I drove close to the target house and parked five yards away. I called in one of my teams to lock down a section of the street to stop incoming and outgoing traffic. Another team prepared to assault. After three minutes, we were all ready to enter the building. Ladders were up and watching the building. The street was blocked. People slowly gathered and started watching, wondering what was going on. The JTAC and the ladder team reported that everything was normal. The ladder team called the kids playing in the yard to come and open the door. One of the kids, a thirteen-year-old boy, did so. The first thing we did was pull him off the entrance and ask him who was inside the building. He told us that his dad, two of his uncles, and the rest of his family were inside.

We got the kids out of the way. I gave the order, and the assault began. In seconds, the first room was breached, and in minutes, the whole house was cleared. Nobody fired a shot. The questioning team was inside the building, and they started their investigation. The women and children were put in one room, and men were lined up in the yard. There were eighteen men in total. The rest of the squad started the SSE process. The tech team found contact numbers that were in our watch list. Some communication on WhatsApp looked sketchy.

The SSE team leader called me on the radio and asked me to come to the room that he was in. I quickly walked in and saw that he was holding a bundle of 100 U.S. dollar bills. There was a ripped pillow lying on the ground next to him. I asked, "Where did you find the money?"

He pointed at the pillow and said, "It was stashed inside."

I called on the radio and said, "Check every single blanket, pillow, and mattress and rip it apart if you have to." After twenty minutes, I was called back to the room. As soon as I walked in, I saw ripped blankets, mattresses, and pillows, and my deputy was holding a stack of U.S. dollars.

"Did you count it?" I asked.

"Yes, and we are still counting."

"How much is it so far?"

"450,000 U.S. dollars."

"Quickly count the remaining money and wrap up the operation. Bag and tag the money and cuff and blindfold the eighteen males in the house. We are returning to base in ten minutes. The rest will be done there."

My deputy called me ten minutes later and said, "Commander, 800,000 U.S. dollars was the total count."

"Good job, Deputy, and good job, everyone else. Get back into your vehicles. We are leaving in a convoy. Be ready for any sort of suspicious activity on the way back to base."

We departed in a military mood; barrels were out of the windows and ready for any sort of engagements. It was dark, and the roads were quiet. We got back after twenty-five minutes. When we drove in, I received a call from the TOC saying to go directly there. My driver dropped me off at the TOC, and I told him to go back to the barracks and rest. I walked in and saw a lot of advisors sitting in the briefing room. I didn't know most of them, and I was the only Afghan in there. The lead advisor stood up and told me, "Commander, good job!"

I said, "Thank you, but all the credit goes to my team and their hard work." The first question I asked was, "Is it confirmed? Are these guys getting support from the Russians?"

The lead advisor said, "Based on the results of the questioning and what the tech teams found, there is a high possibility that they are being supported by the Russians, but we will find out after investigating them tonight. Be ready! This might lead to other operations."

"We are always ready. Bring it on."

After fourteen hours of nonstop investigation, the result led to three other operations, two in Kabul city and one in northern Afghanistan.

A total of thirteen members of this network were captured, and they all confessed to getting support from Russians. It had been done through corrupt politicians.

This network was getting paid for each assassination. The prices for each kill ranged between 1,000 U.S. dollars and 20,000 U.S. dollars based on the target. Their assassinations ranged from hitting Afghan officers and Afghan politicians all the way to killing U.S. soldiers and personnel.

From my experience, this wasn't the only foreign intelligence-supported network in the country. On December 27, 2020, ten Chinese spies who were working directly for the Chinese intelligence agency were captured. These spies were Chinese nationals, unlike the Russian-supported network who funded a proxy to do the dirty work. Seven of these spies were caught in Police District 17, and three were captured in Police District 10. These spies were caught by a sister unit that went by the name NDS 901. They performed a unique function similar to but different from Task Force 241. The Chinese spies were caught with sticky bombs that were being used for assassinations. They also had pistols and homemade explosives. They were responsible for espionage and hacking Afghan and NATO security systems. They were imprisoned for twenty-three days and were released after China publicly apologized for sending the spies into Afghanistan.

Neighboring intelligence agencies had been backing and supporting different terrorist networks in the country throughout the past two decades of war in Afghanistan. NATO and the United States knew about it, but nothing was done regarding these networks.

Afghanistan was influenced on all four sides. Most of the north was controlled by Russians, and some northern parts were controlled by China. The southern and eastern parts were controlled by Pakistan. The western regions were controlled by Iran. The focus of all the neighboring countries was on Kabul province. They didn't hold these areas with armies and hard power but with influence campaigns and intelligence networks. They were embedded so deep in the Afghan communities there that these countries could achieve their objectives without having to resort to the use of much military force. We are not talking about only the Taliban or ISIS. These influencers controlled parliament members, government officials, generals, and other people in positions of power.

Because the type of combat was guerrilla warfare, that also made it easy for those countries to influence Afghanistan. Guerrilla fighters all join the fight for different reasons and have little loyalty to a singular cause. Many are in it for the power and money. They will join whatever side they need to so long as they get the money and weapons to achieve these two goals. These countries didn't have to risk their own citizens. They just had to arm and fund the proxies that would do the dirty work for them and give them deniability. If it weren't for the support of these countries, we would have won the war on day one.

When examining the war, it is essential to ask these questions: How does a simple farmer with an AK-47 fight NATO and the U.S.? This farmer doesn't even have a TV, a computer, or a smart phone in his house, but he knows what to wear to not get spotted by a drone's thermal imaging system. How does this simple farmer know how to build different-sized remote-controlled IEDs that are specially designed to destroy various types of U.S. and NATO armored vehicles? How does this simple farmer get weapon supplies when he doesn't even have food in his house to feed him or his family? How does this simple farmer know how to build a suicide bombing vest and use it in a well-planned attack and hit places that are impossible for most Afghans to access? How? My own village didn't have enough food to survive, but when some of the villagers joined the Taliban, they bought heavy and light machine guns! The money was always coming from different sources outside of Afghanistan.

—

One afternoon in 2018, I took a taxi. I commonly used the service because of my brain injury. I can drive, but it comes with a risk. If my brain decides to seize at the wrong time, I could end up losing my life, so I made a habit of using taxis. I was leaving the unit's base and heading home. I had already changed into civilian clothes. The first rule of the task force was that you were never to disclose who you are. We never wore military uniforms when we were not training or on mission. The Taliban had no issue targeting us if they could find out who we were. My civilian disguise was impeccable. Because I grew my beard long and wore a turban, people would look at me and wonder if I was a terrorist. It helped that I could put on a mean face. I enjoyed this reaction because it meant that I was blending in very well. This is what I wanted.

I had a method when it came to picking my taxi. I never chose the first taxi because it always made me feel suspicious about it. I would wait for the second, third, and sometimes fourth to come by. I did this because I never really knew if my identity was safe or if someone had an intent to assassinate me. It's the kind of thought that can drive a man crazy if he overthinks about it.

On this afternoon, I jumped into the second taxi. I could have ridden this taxi to my final destination, but I decided to get out and get into another cab. I didn't have a specific reason for this other than it was just good protocol. It was just past 3:30 p.m. local time. This was when official hours ended; 4 p.m. was the downtown rush. You can't find taxis or buses during that time. There are too many people trying to get home. It gets incredibly crowded in the area in front of the Presidential Palace. The Presidential Palace, Ministry of Affairs, and Ministry of Defense are extremely close together and share the same entry point to their parking lots.

Whenever I got close to this area, I always wanted to go faster and get away from there. If there was a traffic jam, I would get out of the car and walk. I didn't want anything to do with that place. It was nicknamed the dead zone due to the history of bombings there. In the taxi, I was kindly yelling at the driver to speed up.

It was 3:45 p.m. We passed through the zone. Thirty seconds later, a shockwave ripped through the air. Rocks flew in the sky, and mangled cars caught on fire. It was a large explosion. Due to its size, I knew it couldn't have been a magnetic mine. It had to have been a suicide bomber. I quickly got out of the taxi and looked toward the direction of the explosion. A cloud of dust filled the air. I dialed 102. This was the emergency number for the ambulances. I told them what happened, then took off.

Around fifty people were killed in that explosion, and another ninety to one hundred were wounded. It was pretty average as far as suicide bombings go. People in other countries might see this and mark the day as a day of remembrance or make a memorial. For us Afghans, it was just another day. I was thirty seconds away from dying in that explosion, and I survived by mere chance. All the methods I used to keep myself alive during my civilian life didn't matter. I wasn't the target of this bombing. The Afghan civilians were. This was just the situation all Afghan civilians inherited when they were born. This was just one of eight times I almost died in this way.

—

The Taliban never had a problem attacking civilians in the most brutal of ways. In March of 2017, a group of Taliban killed the few ANA soldiers guarding a large hospital and entered the building. The hospital was known as the Charsad Besttar (which translates to four-hundred-bed hospital). When the Taliban entered, we could only assume their intentions. The ANA had attempted to enter unsuccessfully, so my squadron and an Afghan SWAT unit landed on the roof of the building by helicopter. We split in two directions, and each began clearing a side of the building.

We had to clear the hospital room by room and floor by floor. I stacked up outside of the first room with three more of my soldiers. I was the first man. The third man moved forward and tossed in a flash-bang grenade. This is a device that is nonlethal but releases a bright flash of light that temporarily blinds everyone in the room. The grenade went off. We went in. I cleared left to center. The second man cleared right to center. The third cleared center to left and the fourth center to right. There were no Taliban. We moved to the next room.

We stacked up. Again, I was the first man. We threw another flash-bang grenade and moved in. This room also had no Taliban, but their carnage was left behind. There was an elderly woman who had been receiving care in this room. The Taliban had taken knives and stabbed her repeatedly while she could not move. They took hatchets and chopped away on her sternum and decapitated her head. The sheets of her bed were completely red from all the blood.

We moved to the next room and continued clearing. We reached a room that felt different. As we approached, I heard one Taliban in the room. The third man threw a fragmentary grenade in the room. It went off, shooting steel fragments throughout the room. We pushed in. As I cleared left to center, I saw a Taliban on the ground in pain from the wounds caused by the grenade. I shot him in the head four times. I usually stopped at two, but the brutality of the situation motivated me to shoot more. His skull was a cluster of dark red chunks that had splattered across the floor. By 2017, I had killed so many of them that I didn't think twice about it. It was second nature, and I felt no remorse. It was no different than killing a rabid dog.

The squadron killed six to eight Taliban that day. I am not sure how many Taliban the SWAT-like unit encountered. Almost every room we cleared had a hospital patient brutally murdered with hatchets and knives. Severed limbs, heads, and pools of blood were everywhere. The Taliban had used knives and hatchets so that they could save ammunition for the fight against us. A few of the victims had been shot point blank in the head with a pistol. They were all defenseless.

It was the kind of scene that would rival the most brutal horror movie villain in Hollywood. But unlike the movies, the villain didn't die in a lengthy battle with an underdog protagonist. Here, the villains of this massacre died a pitiful death, and their worthless lives ended leaving behind nothing but an unrecognizable corpse.

—

Another day in 2018, I was sitting in my room at the task force reading the news. I received a call. I was being called to the TOC. I walked there and made my way to the briefing room. It was common to receive a mission after this kind of call. Usually, I went to these meetings with my deputy, but I wasn't expecting to be on an operation, and he wasn't present at the time. This was a bit of a surprise. In the briefing room, I saw some of the advisors sitting there. We went through our customary greetings.

"How quickly can you have your men ready for a mission?" the advisor asked. His face looked blunt, and he appeared unfazed.

"It depends how quickly action is required. If it's an emergency, then five minutes. If it's a regular operation, then fifteen," I replied.

"Okay, Commander. We have the HVT package ready for action. There's just one problem. The target moves around a lot. He is not stationary for long."

"So, what should we do then?"

"We will have to wait until after midnight, until we have a confirmed location for where he will stay overnight. As soon as we have a confirmed location on him, we have to be ready to depart from the unit in a maximum of fifteen minutes."

"Okay. Great! I just need as many details about this as you can give me so I can develop the plan." The advisor gave me all the details. "Who is this guy we are going after?"

"He is the guy who runs the Taliban's financial system. He is very important to the operation of their network. He runs the money, and that money hires fighters. If he is out of the picture, it will disrupt their entire operation."

"Perfect. We are going to get him tonight."

The briefing was different compared to other operations. We weren't going to land far away. We were going to land a few hundred yards from the target and take the compound by surprise. This guy was important, so we already expected to face a higher caliber of Taliban fighters. During the last three years of the conflict, the Taliban had been using more advanced equipment. The most important of this was NVGs. We'd started fighting an enemy that could also see in the dark. That meant our tactics had to change a little. We had to limit the use of our infrared lasers. These can only be seen by NVGs. We had to use more caution, but we were still far better trained and more experienced, and we got to pick the time we went in.

I started briefing my guys. "We will infil by Chinook and land just 800 meters away from the target compound. We will run quickly and as silently as we can. As you know, the Chinooks are loud, so they will know we are coming once we land. We have two buildings to raid tonight. The assaults will be simultaneous like we always do. Explosives will be placed at the breach points and explode at the same time. We will breach at the same time. As soon as the buildings are cleared, and we have our target, we will exfil and leave the area. This quick assault is not something we normally do. Stay flexible if things go south. We are on an eight-minute recall. Be ready to load the Chinooks in eight minutes at any point you're called."

You might ask why I said eight minutes when the advisor had said fifteen. I know Afghans. Afghan people are not really good at being on time. That's why I gave them a shorter hit time. Better to be five minutes early than two minutes late.

It was 9:45 p.m. when I received another call from the lead advisor. I went to the TOC for an update on the operation. The advisor showed me a couple satellite images. They had been captured while the target was on the move to the place he would sleep for the night. The pictures weren't clear, but it looked like they had two hostages. This made our job a little more complex. We wanted to get this HVT, but trying to rescue hostages while doing so would split our attention. To make it worse, intelligence came in that the target was protected by twenty Red Unit fighters (the Taliban's Special Forces). They were likely better equipped, and we were going to be in for a big firefight. The last update I got was to be ready at the HLZ by 10:15 p.m. (in less than thirty minutes). I called over the radio and told my guys to be there by 10:10 p.m.

The information didn't change the plan. Whether they were Red Unit with NVGs or they were eighty-year-old farmers with a few pistols, we were going to get this guy. By this point in the war, we were all well aware of how to win these battles. I personally had been on about 550 missions with the task force by this point. We had all been there, done that, and few things surprised us anymore.

We staged ourselves at the HLZ. Four Chinooks came to pick us up from our base. They were special mission unit (SMU) Chinooks. SMU Chinooks had armor on the bottom of their frame and were heavily armed with mini-guns and 50 cals. All four landed at the same time. We had a concrete HLZ, so there was no dust, but it was always windy. When they pass overhead, it's like you're in the middle of a storm that's beating on you. When you are inside the helicopters, it is deafening and hard to hear. We loaded in, and the Chinooks took off.

I had a habit of taking a nap while flying to the target area. It was an hour-and-twenty-five-minute flight. Some soldiers were napping on the floor, and some were on the benches leaning against anything they could find. I found my spot lying down on one of the benches. You might judge me and think, *Who takes a nap while going to war?* I do. I mean, we were in the air. There was nothing we could do. The pilot and the gunner needed to be awake, but I didn't. My job was on the ground. And most importantly, if we got shot down, I wanted to be at peace when it happened. This was just my nature. I had been doing this job nonstop for the past fourteen years. I didn't really care anymore.

So, I was taking my lovely nap when I heard a scream next to me. The crew yelled, "TEN MINUTES!"

I woke up groggily. I pointed my finger up and yelled, "TEN MINUTES!"

All the soldiers who were napping woke up. The next call came from the flight crew. "FIVE MINUTES!" Everyone locked and loaded their weapons. We all double-checked our equipment. The last call came. "ONE MINUTE!" We all looked to the exit and got ready.

We landed. The rear ramp lowered. I was at the rear side of the Chinook, so I was first off. I ran straight ahead, and my guys followed me. We spread out and established 360-degree security (meaning we had eyes and rifles pointed in every direction around us). The target village was dark. They didn't have any lights. The moon was half full, and the weather was a bit chilly. It was the standard kind of night for an operation. My American advisor stayed next to me. He had a short beard and long hair, and he had been in this line of work for a long time.

I asked my communication guy if there was anything on the ICOM scanner. He said there wasn't anything significant. The Taliban had their usual chatter about the raids. Like always, they wanted to figure out where we were going. We started moving very fast toward the target compound. This wasn't putting our heads forward and sprinting. We were just walking fast, keeping our heads up and rifles scanning. We had to constantly watch our surroundings and stay alert.

We had a breakoff point midway to the target. One group went toward the first compound, and the other went toward the second. Based on our intelligence, the target and his men were split into two groups. It took us around ten minutes to get to the target compound. As soon as we arrived, the security team locked down the compound, and ladders went up. I was talking to my breacher at this point and instructed him to place the charge on the door. Suddenly, my ladder guy started shooting. I quickly checked with him over the radio.

"What is going on? What are you shooting at?"

He responded, "Commander, as soon as I went up on the ladder, there was an armed fighter inside the compound. He was pulling down his NVGs and was about to reach for his gun, so I engaged him. He is down."

"Okay, good job. Keep watching and reporting. We are placing the charge. What does the structure look like?"

"There are two separate buildings in this compound. There is a car garage on the right when you enter the building. Then, there is an open space and three rooms connected to each other based on the windows. There is a half-constructed building on the back side, and a path to that side of the building is through the open space between the car garage and the other rooms."

"Where was the guy that you just killed?"

"He was on the half-constructed part."

"Roger. When we breach in, you move to the rooftop with your team and cover the other side of the building, and if you see any armed mover, engage him." Next, I spoke to my breacher. "Place the charge."

"Roger," he responded. A minute later, he told me, "The charge is set."

"Assaulters, ready to breach in 5…4…3…2…1."

The explosive went off. A giant blast kicked the door in, and dust filled the hole. The assaulters began the assault. After the fifth guy went into the building, I followed and stayed on the left side to clear the way for the rest of the assaulters. I had to be inside to give better directions. My advisor followed. We had to stay close to each other so that he could report up and coordinate air support, which we had to be on the same page for. As soon as the garage was cleared, the assaulters moved to clear the rooms. That is where the target was staying, along with some of his fighters and the hostages. I heard more gunshots.

"What is going on?" I said over the radio.

The ladder team responded, "We saw two more movers on this side of the building. One is down, and the other is still alive, but he is behind cover."

"Keep shooting at him. Don't let him move."

The assaulters went inside the individual rooms to clear them. More shooting started. I went on my radio to get an update.

The assault team responded, "We got shot at from the inside of the room. One of us got shot. It went through his body armor, but the armor grabbed it along the way. Just the tip went through. He says he will be alright."

"Okay, clear the room. Do what you need to do. Try to save the hostages, but if there's nothing you can do, then that's that." They knew what I meant by this. I was saying win the fight and don't hold back.

We shot rounds of M203, a grenade launcher, at them. I was staying on the ground behind cover as much as I could. My advisor was right behind me. He was behind more cover and standing on a concrete floor that was one foot above the ground. We were both shooting. I told one of my guys to throw a fragmentary grenade inside the building. He pulled the pin, then threw it like someone lobbing a baseball and yelled, "FRAG OUT! FRAG OUT!"

It was at this moment that my advisor yelled, "GRENADE! GRENADE!" and pulled me by my vest toward him. I couldn't step back because of the concrete behind me. I thought to myself, *Better to get hit in the legs than the face*, and I got low and moved my head away from the direction of the grenade. It exploded. I was lucky and didn't get hit. I got up and started shooting again. I questioned why I'd only heard one explosion. *If we threw a grenade, and they threw one, there should have been two. Where did our grenade go?* I moved forward to closely monitor the assaulters' progress inside the room. I checked in with them.

"Commander, we can't go into the rooms. They are too small, and they are barricaded inside. What are your orders?"

I responded, "If you have no other option, throw in the frags" (meaning more fragmentary grenades).

I heard over the radio, "Frag out! Frag out!" then an explosion. Again, I heard, "Frag out! Frag out!" and another explosion. For the third time, I heard, "Frag out!" and the final blast. They'd thrown three grenades in the room. I heard a few more gunshots. Then, it all went quiet.

"Assault team, report!" I said over the radio.

"All three rooms were cleared. We have four enemy KIA, and our target is among them. We have the two hostages."

"Roger. Bring the two hostages for questioning."

I talked to my advisor to coordinate an airstrike on the half-constructed building. We did not know how many more Taliban soldiers were in there, and I didn't want to bother fighting them again.

The second assault team also engaged targets in their compound. They had it easier, finding just four fighters there.

We had to exfil because the airstrike was going to be close. We wrapped up, checked our equipment, made sure we had everyone, and rolled out to our HLZ. I thought about the grenade situation. I still didn't know where our grenade had gone.

On the way, I talked to my advisor. "Hey, bro. Thanks for saving me back there."

"No problem. We are a band of brothers from different mothers. You have my back, and I have yours."

"Do you know where our grenade went?"

"Oh, you didn't see it?"

"No? See what?"

"When our guy threw the grenade in, the barricaded fighter threw it back out at us."

"Oh, damn." I'd known from the first moment we engaged them that these guys were well trained. I was amazed he'd been able to see the grenade with the type of NVGs he'd had on. They were the version that only cover one eye and are notoriously hard to play catch with due to the lack of depth perception and a narrow field of view.

We regrouped with the other team and waited for the Chinooks at the HLZ. I saw the airstrike come in. I could hear the whistle of the bomb, and the explosion lit up the night sky. The flame had to have been a hundred feet high. It was the kind of thing that would have given me a rush of adrenaline years ago. But as I said, by this point, I had been there and done that. It was routine. We had no casualties other than a few superficial wounds. We had air support providing eyes in the sky to warn us if anyone was coming. No one was. As long as the Chinooks were coming (and they were), as a leader, I didn't have much to worry about at that point. I was just looking forward to my next nap.

When we got back, it turned out that there weren't two hostages. There was one hostage, and the other guy was keeping him hostage. The second guy was a Red Unit fighter. He was the one who'd taken the hostage from a wedding party, which is why he knew the full story of how the hostage had been taken. Initially, we thought they'd been taken together because they had the exact same story. When they were questioned separately, my intelligence officer figured it out.

This Red Unit fighter was not a good guy. Since he was taken captive and was a prisoner of war, he was treated like so in accordance with international norms. We didn't just execute people—we weren't the Taliban. It was his right to be prosecuted according to the law, which meant he would be freed quickly by our corrupt system. This was why we didn't take in Red Unit fighters alive. This one was lucky and would get another chance. We knew that if we crossed paths again, he wouldn't get so lucky.

Chapter 16

The Afghan government's fall was way different from what people in the west understood it to be. First, it is essential to note that the Taliban didn't win this war through military means. It was more of an inside job. During the last presidential election in September of 2019, there was a dispute about the results. Ashraf Ghani was declared the winner, but the supposed runner-up would not accept that. His name is Abdullah Abdullah. The election was a mess, and both sides had frauds. It became a rivalry between the Pashtuns and Tajiks, with each tribe wanting the candidate from their tribe to win. It resulted in protests and riots. Neither could prove they won fairly.

Because Abdullah was not budging, the U.S. got involved and gave Abdullah half the power of the president. He didn't have an official chair, but he had the ability to assign certain governors, ministers, and key officials. You can't have two presidents. It doesn't work. Neither of them had the authority necessary to make decisions.

When the peace talks among the Afghans, U.S., and Taliban began, they didn't include Ashraf Ghani and his team. He didn't matter because the goal was to get rid of him. Ashraf Ghani's great achievement was removing Afghan warlords from their power, and for that reason, they wanted him out.

—

The war had been going for almost twenty years when the peace talks were scheduled in Doha. There were four parties deeply interested in the outcome of these talks: the United States, the Taliban, the so-called Afghan leaders, and the Afghan people. What each party wanted is important to note.

—

The United States.

The United States wanted to leave this war. They had been in it for two decades, lost two thousand soldiers, and had another twenty thousand wounded during the conflict. They had also spent over two trillion dollars ($2,000,000,000,000). The U.S. was done with it, but they also didn't want to leave it to the Taliban. This would be considered not only a loss for the U.S. but also a victory for Russia, the U.S.'s longtime rival. In the end, the U.S. would be just another name in the graveyard of empires that failed to win in Afghanistan.

—

The Taliban.

The Taliban wanted control of the country. At this time, their high-level leaders were not even living in Afghanistan. They were enjoying a wealthy life in other places around the world. For them, this was about power. They also wanted an Islamic country based on their understanding of Islam, which meant an abolishment of women's rights and a return to the kind of living I experienced as a child in the village. A key thing they emphasized was wanting to dismiss the current armed forces in Afghanistan and build a new army from scratch. More was talked about behind closed doors, but these were the key points.

—

The so-called Afghan leaders.

The so-called Afghan leaders consisted of Abdullah Abdullah, Hamid Karzai, and their inner circles. They wanted to maintain their current power in the government. They also wanted to maintain their wealth and influence. They did not care who was in charge so long as these two expectations were met. These two politicians would play a key role in Afghanistan's fall.

—

The Afghan people.

This is the party that should have mattered most. The Afghan people had nothing to do with the Afghan government. The people were all tired of this war. The war had displaced families; bombarded homes; killed men, women, and children; created more poverty and starvation; destroyed literacy, education, and jobs; and, most important of all, kept people from feeling safe in their own country. Every citizen who left their home in the early morning didn't know for sure that they would see their family again that day. At any moment, you could suddenly lose a loved one. I walked everywhere with a loaded pistol and three magazines. Whether military or civilian, you couldn't go anywhere without having a reasonable expectation that any moment could suddenly be your last.

This is a tricky subject to convey to an audience that has mostly experienced peace. I remember this old widow who was living on the same street we did in Kabul. She had three sons that were all in the Afghan National Army. All three of them were working on the same base in western Afghanistan. When the Taliban ramped up their attacks on the armed forces, the army brought her three sons back to her covered in white cloth. The government didn't supply any coffins, so this white cloth was all these boys got. All of us neighbors rushed to help and be there for her. When she could finally bring herself to words, she said, "They came from the almighty God, and they went back to him." That family was done. The deaths of those young men were the last hopes for the family whose mother was so old she wouldn't survive the shock of such news. That family tree ended there. I cannot explain in words how painful it was to watch that scene. It brought tears to my eyes. It brings tears to my eyes even now.

We are all human and want to live in peace. We don't want to immigrate to other countries where we might get called out due to our race, color, and religion. This war was ugly. We just wanted our country to be at peace. The Afghan people wanted to be able to finally live and didn't care who was in charge so long as they could finally provide stability.

—

The Doha talks continued but saw no progress. Eventually, in 2020, the U.S. released five thousand Taliban fighters back into the wild. This was done as part of the negotiation process. That was the stupidest decision the U.S. and NATO ever made during the last twenty years of war. As soon as they were out, they were greeted with honor in their villages and became leaders for different Taliban groups.

I was sitting in the DFAC at lunchtime, watching the news and discussing the mistake that the U.S. had made on releasing these fighters. We saw that a TV reporter was interviewing some of the prisoners while they were being processed to leave Bagram prison. Most of them were saying, "Long live the Taliban! We will win this war, and we are ready to fight again!" They were saying it right before they were released. Imagine it yourself. What does that tell you? Were they not going to rejoin the fight? I mean, they had no option. That was what they were doing all their life, and they were addicted to it. Killing is a bad addiction. Releasing those prisoners was a terrible mistake.

We received a lot of intelligence that the released prisoners were recruiting and gathering more fighters to attack provinces in northern Afghanistan. Most of the Taliban fights were in the south until 2014. After 2016, withdrawal fights pushed into the north of the country. With the prisoner release, the number of attacks went up in northern Afghanistan. The soldiers and commanders in the task force were angry and sad. We'd lost so many good warriors and spent sleepless nights to put these people in prison. And now they were free. We were all furious. Not just the Afghans in the unit but also the military advisors that were working with us too. But these decisions were made above our pay grades. We had no say, no input.

The Taliban offensive campaign started on May 1, 2021. From the start of the new government, the Afghan security forces didn't receive enough support and authority. From May, the security in the country started to get worse and worse each day. The one big problem Afghan security forces had was always being in a defensive position. You can't win a war always staying on defense. You have to attack them before they attack you. Reaction cannot beat action. Therefore, it was necessary to act proactively instead of reacting to the enemy.

A small number of security forces were doing night operations. This was mentioned in the leadership-level meetings. Out of the entire Afghan armed forces, only 5 percent of them were Special Operations, and this 5 percent was doing all the fighting. I saw the official document myself back in 2017. Night operations were the most successful operations in the country, and the army wasn't doing enough of them. Night raids had the highest success rate in guerrilla warfare. During the daytime, the enemy couldn't stay in the village, but they usually came back to visit their families during the night. And with good intelligence, we were able to capture or kill them. But night raids needed assets like accurate intelligence (which required funds) and air support (which Afghans didn't have). The task force's air support was directly provided by the U.S. Air Force because of our advisors. The Afghan Air Force was new, and we didn't have experienced pilots. And most of our aircrafts were logistical aircrafts like Blackhawks, Mi-17s, and C-130s. These couldn't be used as air support unless specifically modified to do so. We had a small number of A-25 jets, and those jets could only support certain provinces. Air assets were critical. Most of the missions accounted for in this book showed the many ways that eyes in the sky and firepower from above saved the lives of my men and myself. It's completely different.

In addition to all these challenges, we had corrupt commanders and leaders. There were soldiers that couldn't go home for over thirteen months despite living in the same country they fought in. This was due to bad leadership or sometimes just not having a safe transportation system for the military. The risk of ambushes, IEDs, and suicide bombings didn't go away whether on mission or traveling home. We had so many cases where new graduates from the police academy were hit by a suicide bomber after graduation on the way back home. This would happen even though they were being escorted by a military convoy. It was almost impossible to prevent suicide bombings inside a crowded part of the city.

—

Bagram Airfield closed on July 1, 2021. It was unexpected, and it was handled horribly. There had been rumors that the U.S. would withdraw its troops. Even with these rumors, we never suspected that America would abandon Bagram. Bagram was like a small city in the north of Kabul province. It had so many lights, you could see its glowing essence from many miles away. It was huge. It had over one hundred parking spots for just its fighter jets. You could see Blackhawks, Chinooks, Apaches, C-17s, C-130s, drones, and AC-130s (the monster gunships) coming from this base. The airfield had two runways. One was around 12,000 feet long (~2.2 miles). This base had a huge hospital and giant hangars full of equipment, armored trucks, and (most important of all) the famous Bagram Prison where those five thousand fighters were imprisoned. Most of these prisoners were leaders in the Taliban network.

When Bagram Airfield went dark that night, 90 percent of the lights were suddenly turned off. This had never happened before. We didn't know what was going on. When the Afghan people in the area figured out it was abandoned, civilians raided the airfield to loot what they could. There was a company of ANA soldiers that were there to protect the prison, but they did not have nearly enough manpower to guard the entire airfield.

I was in my office going through some documents when the lead advisor at the task force came to me and told me to prepare a small undercover team to go to Bagram. The team was supposed to collect as much information as they could. We didn't know that the U.S. was gone.

Bagram had a famous black market that was selling the supplies and equipment that got smuggled out of the airfield. You could buy gun parts, military equipment, and much more. That was where I found my thermal scopes for a previous mission. I picked soldiers for the team that were very familiar with Bagram district and told them, "Your job is to go and see if Bagram is looted." If it was looted, it meant that people had broken into it, and everything was gone. If it wasn't, then we still had time to save billions' worth of equipment paid for by U.S. tax dollars that had been left there.

The team wore their everyday Afghan clothing with guns and gear hidden in their clothing. They went to check Bagram Airfield, the most extensive, now abandoned, U.S. military base. It was a one-hour-and-thirty-minute drive from our location. They were reporting back every thirty minutes.

Fifteen minutes later, I sent a QRF team to Bagram Airfield in case the first team needed support. They stayed in the vicinity and were on standby. As soon as the recon team arrived, they called and said, "The whole Bagram Airfield is on display in the black market."

"What do you mean?"

"Commander, the whole base was looted, and the ANA couldn't control people looting the base. The ANA also said the Americans didn't hand it over to us. All this equipment is up for grabs."

"Oh, man." I took a deep breath and said out loud, "What the hell did you just do, America? That equipment will be sold to Pakistan, Iran, Russia, and China. Those countries could use that gear and equipment to analyze the American military systems and create a counter version of it."

We had already started having to overcome the Taliban acquiring NVGs. Now that they had the entire American arsenal, they would be a far more significant threat. That was one of the most shocking things the Afghans witnessed before the fall of Afghanistan. Unfortunately, it was too late to do anything about it, and all the equipment was already in the process of getting smuggled to the neighboring countries. Twenty-four hours later, we received confirmation through our sources and intelligence that the equipment was already being shipped to Pakistan, Iran, and China.

When the withdrawal happened, our task force advisors had to leave like the thousands of other advisors. These weren't good signs. It doesn't matter how large of an army you have if you don't have the support to back them up. The military just becomes a number of bodies at that point and not a capable fighting force. It is always about the support that comes with it.

Task Force 241 was a good example. We were small in number, but because of the excellent support we received, we accomplished a lot more than what we were built for. The task force was still in contact with the advisory team. The advisors were still in the country; they'd just moved to Kabul Airport.

We had a similar experience back in 2014 when the U.S. announced that they would withdraw its troops. Back then, people were scared and were leaving the country. That is when millions of people migrated to Turkey and Europe.

I am not blaming only the U.S. for everything wrong that was happening in our country. We had corrupt leadership, and the worst of all was that the country was in a nonstop war for over forty years. We were all tired of dying every day. We just wanted to live in peace.

Tensions started getting higher and higher every day—more attacks were happening, people were dying nonstop, the media was siding with the Taliban, and people were already tired of the corrupt government and leadership.

Chapter 17

It was August 6, 2021, when the first Afghan province in the southwest fell into the hands of the enemy. We heard this through the news and our sources. I was mad at the Afghan commanders for not fighting. I felt like we, as the task force, needed to do more and more.

The task force's operation tempo increased from conducting operations every other night to every night. Our undercover operation increased to two to three operations a day. We were hitting Taliban gatherings in Kabul and raiding Taliban-influenced districts of Kabul province. We knew it might not make a big difference, but it would help slow the Taliban from achieving their goals.

District after district in the southwest started falling into the hands of the Taliban. The task force couldn't do much other than conduct raids. Our operations couldn't do much but keep the Taliban in Kabul under pressure. We were too small to make a major impact. We also had no one to support us. We received news that the Afghan soldiers were not putting up a fight due to the orders they received from their chain of command.

I personally had phone conversations with some of the commanders I knew. They were part of the Afghan Special Forces, and they said, "Our commanders told us not to fight."

"But why?"

"We don't know. We just don't know."

I realized at that moment that we were in this fight alone.

By August 8, the task force operations were restricted to only Kabul city and the surrounding districts. We all understood that Kabul's fall would mean the Afghan government's fall. We were doing as much as we could to stop that from happening, but slowly, province after province kept falling.

It was Thursday, August 12, and by now 80 percent of the provinces had fallen into the hands of the Taliban. It was a week of nonstop work. None of us had the thought that the Afghan government would fall into the hands of these animals. Despite our feelings of betrayal and exhaustion, we were still hopeful about the situation.

We didn't have any operations for the following night. I decided to take it off, and I sent half of my soldiers home and told them to enjoy this break as much as they could. I didn't know when we would get another break. I followed my own advice to the soldiers and went home for the afternoon. I was exhausted and disappointed with what was happening in the country. I was disappointed but still carried hope with me. I took a cab and started a conversation with the cab driver. I wanted to hear civilians' thoughts on the things happening in the country.

Just like us, the cab driver was disappointed in the Afghan government. I remember him telling me, "Brother, this is a corrupted government that has been occupied by a bunch of greedy warlords. They don't care about their people, and of course, their own families are already out of Afghanistan living in the U.S. and Europe. If something happens, it will be the poor people that will suffer any hardship that will come to this country."

He wasn't wrong. We all witnessed bad leadership and corruption. I couldn't disagree. I got out of the cab at my usual spot. The city looked quiet and sad. It wasn't as crowded as it used to be. When I was walking to the next station, I was demoralized, and I was talking to my God. I said, "My dear God, why can't we live in peace?"

I saw beggars on the side of the street. Not just one or two but ten to twelve in that five-minute walk. They were poor people, old men, ages seventy to eighty, dragging a cart around, trying to make some money to feed their families.

It always took me five minutes to walk to the other cab station. These stations were for line cabs, the ones that go specific routes similar to buses. Cabs were just faster.

This time, I was tired and told the cab driver, "I will pay you extra if you drop me off close to my house." I didn't want to walk the distance I walked every day. We agreed on a price and departed.

I arrived home, and I was tired. My kids went to their grandparents' house with their mom. These were my wife's parents. Afghans live in big families. My brothers and I were all living with our parents in one big house. I sat and talked with my parents. I enjoyed the moment. I always discussed politics with my father, and we spoke about the country's situation for twenty or thirty minutes. The government could do better to change the living conditions. I remember my father said, "Son, God is not cruel. If we don't change ourselves, no one will ever do it for us."

After the chat, I went to my room. I checked my phone and went through social media, then fell asleep.

—

This time around, I only spent one night at home. I woke up early that Friday, maybe around four in the morning, and I started to prepare myself for the morning prayer. After the prayer, I decided to go back to the unit. I was just bored in the house and wanted to get back to work. I had some stuff to do, like checking the performance records for my soldiers so I could prepare a list of promotions for my guys. This was my day off, but my mind was restless. I usually said goodbyes and asked for my parents' blessing before leaving the home, but because it was too early, I didn't want to wake them up. I quietly left the house. It was still dark.

Everything was normal, and because it was early morning, it was tranquil. I arrived faster due to the empty roads. I showed my ID and went onto the base.

The guards at the gate joked with me and said, "Commander! Did your wife kick you out of the house?"

I laughed and said, "No! I was bored and wanted to come back early. That is all."

I had a 2009 Toyota truck parked in the unit's parking lot. These were vehicles we only drove around on base. The base was also quiet at that time of morning, so I started the car and drove back to the main part of the unit. I arrived inside the unit and went directly to my office. I changed into my uniform, grabbed my radio, then walked to the TOC to see if we had any plans for today. I got on a computer to check if there was any email from the advisors. I saw a new email that said, "Call us as soon as possible."

We had satellite phones that were more secure. I called the advisors, and they told me to prepare my team for new tasks. There were a lot of changes suddenly happening. The first task was to take my squadron and go to the Kabul-Wardak gate. The gates were just a huge metal arch with an Afghan armed forces outpost. The area was surrounded by a desert. There was a village that could be seen from the outpost, but it was at least a few miles away. We were to stay in the ANA outpost and take over security. We were to prevent any Taliban groups from trying to enter Kabul city.

All of the combat soldiers were called to return to base. My squadron's day off got canceled. I went to Wardak with the Charlie Squadron, and another squadron went to the Kabul-Logar gate. Everything was normal on our side. There was no Taliban movement. Our squadrons were doing twelve-hour shifts and rotating our position with other squadrons. Two squadrons were at these two gates, and two squadrons were back on base to resupply and conduct missions in Kabul city.

Some provinces were keeping up a fight, but unfortunately, most provinces didn't put up any fight. It looked more like we were handing over the cities to the Taliban. When the Taliban's attacks increased, they were sending village elders to tell the Afghan armed forces outposts to surrender their weapons and go home in peace. They relayed that if the people at the outposts tried to fight, they would not be given any second chance, and the Taliban would kill every single one of them in the worst way possible. Most of the small outposts surrendered their weapons and their gear, then walked away with a written note from the Taliban. The note said: This soldier was cooperative, and he has been forgiven.

—

Just one day later, Saturday, August 14, 2021, the Taliban were controlling 90 percent of Afghanistan. Logar province had fallen. This is one of the closest provinces to Kabul province. Ghazni province (another of Kabul's neighboring provinces) had fallen too. On this particular day, the tensions were very high. The Taliban were taking over province after province. The Ghazni governor surrendered without a fight, and later, he was escorted safely halfway to the gates of Wardak province by the Taliban. He was given back to the Afghan government before the Taliban returned to Ghazni province.

There was a video of him getting escorted by the Taliban that was leaked all over the internet. When I saw the footage, it boiled my blood. I was mad as hell, saying, "Why didn't you put up a fight?! Why did you hand over the province so easily?! What kind of a loser are you?!" The vice president ordered to detain him and hand him over to the Afghan police command. After arriving in Wardak province, he was detained in the center of Wardak province by the police forces, and he was taken to police headquarters. He'd committed a big, unforgivable crime—the crime of helping the Taliban.

Fights were happening in the big cities like Herat, Balkh, and Kandahar, as well as in Nangarhar and Helmand provinces. The generals were getting replaced during the final minutes of the Afghan government. The president was making his last moves.

Our outpost was close to the gate. It was 3 p.m. when the Taliban started shooting at us with light and heavy machine guns from the nearby hills. After marking their locations, we hammered them with 120mm mortar rounds. This fight lasted about thirty minutes, and we dropped around forty 120mm rounds on them. The Taliban chatter was minimal. Then, everything went quiet. No more shooting. The next squadron came to replace us after the handover was done. We returned to base, and by sunset, we were inside the base and getting resupplied.

We didn't have any intelligence coming in. I was told all the sources were off the grid. This wasn't good news, but it meant I got a chance to get some rest and save some energy for the upcoming days. I had a feeling that these next few weeks would be some of the worst I would ever have.

I went to bed thinking, *It all happened so quick. What will happen? We can't just surrender ourselves, especially after we have killed so many of them. How is nobody fighting back? How did they take over the provinces so quickly? What is going on? Why are all the soldiers saying that they had orders to not fight? Who is giving these orders?* Since I was exhausted, I fell asleep quickly.

—

It was now Sunday, August 15, 2021. It was four in the morning. I woke up, still tired and still worried about the future of the country and my people. I took a shower and prayed the morning prayer. During my prayer, I prayed to God, "Dear lord, please help me. Dear lord, don't fail me in front of my soldiers and the people. If my time is up, please forgive my sins. Dear lord, I have no bad intentions for my people. You know this better than anybody. Please help me help the poor and the oppressed."

I wore my uniform and went to the DFAC to eat my breakfast. It was around six in the morning when I walked into the facility. It was quiet. There were just a couple of soldiers having their breakfast.

The TV was on, and the six o'clock news had just started. I don't like the news, and I especially didn't like the news during this time. News organizations are never there to benefit the people. They don't want you to hear what you want to hear. They want you to hear what they want you to hear.

I only watched the headlines. It was all bad news. Headlines were all saying that Afghanistan was about to fall and that 99 percent of Afghanistan was in the Taliban's control. The TV remote was sitting on the table. I grabbed it and turned it off.

I looked around. The soldiers were exhausted. We were all tired. We had no appetite to eat. Our minds were busy with horrible thoughts about what would happen to the country. What would happen to us? What would happen to our families? We had done some bad things to these guys, and no matter how "nice" the Taliban had become, they would still try to kill us. We were all thinking about whether we were going to fight to the death or we were going to hide in a safe place and leave the country later.

After breakfast, I walked out and went to my office to grab my gear. Charlie Squadron was going to go back to the Kabul-Wardak gate. I called my team leaders and told them to gear up and be ready. We were going to depart at seven o'clock. I was in my office going through the squadron's documents. I had to collect any documents that were related to the personnel and the task force in case things didn't go as we planned. We were still hopeful that we could save this country. But if we couldn't, I didn't want to leave anything that could reveal us so the Taliban could track us or our family members.

It was fifteen minutes prior to departure when my team leaders walked into the office. They asked if I was free to talk. When they said, "Can we talk?" I knew they were worried and wanted answers.

"Sure. What is going on?"

One of my assault team leaders spoke first. He took a deep breath. "What is the plan, Commander?"

"What do you mean? The plan is the same as yesterday. We will go to the gate, stay in the outpost, and prevent the Taliban from coming into the city."

My mobility commander smiled and said, "Commander, you know what we mean when we ask what the plan is. Please tell us if you heard anything. The soldiers are worried. They all have questions, and they need answers."

I looked at them and responded with a cold smile. "I don't know, guys, I don't know. Nobody knows. We will fight them, and we will safely come back to the unit, and if we are overrun, then we will fight until the last drop of our blood has been spilt."

I put my gear on, and we all walked together to our vehicles. Soldiers were standing beside their vehicles. I knew what they meant when they asked if I knew about the plan. They wanted to know if they were going to survive this. They wanted to know if they were going to get evacuated or if the government was going to turn this war around. They were expecting answers that I didn't have. Nobody had those answers.

We all got into our vehicles, and the convoy started driving. Our feelings were different on this mission. In the past, soldiers had hope that conducting a mission might help the security of the country. But this time, the soldiers were sad. They worried about their families and their future.

I rolled my window down, and I put my gun's barrel out of the vehicle's window. I was trying to show that we were still ready to fight and die for this country and its people. The wind was blowing into my face and hair. I had to look strong. I had to show that I still had my morale, and I had to keep a war face.

The city was very crowded. People were driving, walking, and running to Kabul Airport. People were trying to escape the country. Not only politicians—almost everyone that had some money, passports, and some sort of visa or residency of another country was trying to leave. Cars were jammed. It was like a movie scene where the world is ending, and everyone is running to get to a shelter.

My deputy always loved politics. I called him over the radio to ask him about the situation. I checked with him to see if he had any update on the last two provinces, which were Logar and Wardak provinces. He responded with a sad voice. "Commander! The Taliban are at the gates. The last two provinces have fallen!"

I took a deep breath and said, "I could see that coming. Thanks, Deputy."

The feeling was something different, something I had never felt before. It was worse than the devil staring directly at your soul. It wasn't just about me—it was about my beloved Afghanistan. It was a country that was in the process of getting better and becoming developed only to jump right back to 1996. All these sacrifices, endless nights, fallen soldiers, wounded soldiers, and risked lives amounted to nothing.

A thousand concerns about my family went through my head when I heard that news. There were only a few of us in the leadership on that channel. I don't know how many soldiers listened to that, but it was something that would get leaked very soon. As a leader, I had to stay strong and focus on the squadron. I grabbed my radio and pushed the button to talk to my guys, "Net call, net call. Be ready to kill some bad guys. No matter what happens, we are strong. We have always crushed the enemy, and we will keep doing that."

The thing I feared most was the soldiers not putting up a fight—giving up. I mean, in that moment, I wouldn't have blamed them. It was like a sinking ship. You can resist by getting water out of the ship bucket by bucket, but you are only buying time.

One by one, the team leaders responded over the radio. "Roger, Commander. We have no fear. We will crush them with God's help!"

That response gave me extra life and courage. I said, "Screw it. If I die, I will die next to my warriors." It was a great feeling, like being in the middle of nowhere with no food and no supplies, knowing you might die in the next twenty-four hours, then hearing the sound of the rescue team.

We arrived at the outpost. The other squadron was functioning on little to no sleep; one look, and you could feel their weariness. I talked to their commander to see if there had been any action since last night.

The squadron commander responded with a smile. "Bro, you know the Taliban. They bluff and bluff. They knew I was here. That is why they didn't show up. They didn't want to mess with me!" We both laughed, and they departed back to base.

I remember looking up at the sky. There were no clouds, just a warm sun glowing on us. I made a joke with our guys. "Absorb as much vitamin D as you can! If we die, our bone quality will be good." All the soldiers laughed. Humor was a welcome distraction.

There was a small hill behind our outpost. I sent a team of snipers to give us overwatch and observe movements on the highway. Everything was abnormally quiet. There was no Taliban chatter.

It was just 9:50 a.m. when I received a call from the task force command, and I was told to return to base. I asked the commander, "Is everything all right?"

"Have you not heard the news?" His voice was filled with disappointment.

"No."

"Looks like the Taliban has entered Kabul city."

"But we are at the gates! How did they enter?!"

"We don't know. We have no contact with our sources on the ground. It is best for you guys to return to base. We will decide what to do from here."

Despite all that was happening, I never expected to hear that. It was one thing to hear about the Taliban taking over distant parts of the country. It was another thing to hear that they were in Kabul. This was home, and now they were here. The previous Taliban era had been the darkest time of Afghanistan, and I couldn't imagine my country going back to that.

I was sitting in my vehicle when I received that shocking news. I opened a bottle of water and drank a sip. I started to stare at the water. It took me to a deep train of thought. It was the kind of feeling you get when you hit a dead-end road, and you don't know what to do. I was in thought for a brief moment, then grabbed my radio and called my team leaders. "Wrap it up and get ready to return to base."

The team leaders asked, "What is going on, Commander?'"

"Let's just go back to base until we see what happens next. We don't know what is going to happen even in the next few minutes. Let's focus on regrouping with the other squadrons."

The vehicles were lined up and ready to roll. The convoy started moving. The Kabul-Wardak gate was close to our outpost. When we arrived at the gate, we noticed that nobody was there. The Afghan security forces had abandoned the gate. I told my guys, "Barrels out of the windows. Be vigilant. The city might be overrun by the Taliban. We don't want surprise attacks."

We had been on the road for five minutes when we passed the gate. The lead vehicle hailed me on the radio and said, "Commander, we notice a big group of people holding Taliban flags in their hands. They are screaming and cheering. Should we engage them?"

"Do you guys see any guns with them?"

"Negative. They don't even look like the Taliban. They look more like civilians."

"Roger. Do not engage. I repeat, do not engage them. Watch them carefully. If you see any one of them armed, stop him, and report quickly if you see anything suspicious up ahead."

"Roger, we will. Out."

Our convoy was right next to the group of people. When they saw us, they started cheering. I felt a wave of disgust. I looked at them and said, "What are you cheering for? You are holding the flag of this country's enemy." I grabbed the mic for the loudspeaker that was co-located with the siren in the car. "You people need to pray to God that he helps you know what is right and what is wrong. You can stay a sheep, or you can stay a lion. You can't be both."

The crowd was just looking at us. They wanted to say something good about the Taliban, but they were scared of us. This area was called District 5. Because it was close to Wardak province, and it had a lot of uncontrolled routes to Wardak province. The Taliban were in full control of that city. Most assassinations were happening there too. It was fully influenced by the Taliban.

I looked at them angrily and said, "You people don't deserve one minute of my service. I am ashamed of the service I did to protect people like you."

We drove off. Most of the city was empty. Shops were closed. Military- and government-registered vehicles were abandoned on the side of the road. The houses looked empty. Some parts of the town looked like a ghost town. It was like one of those movie scenes when everyone is leaving things behind and just trying to get to a shelter or an airport. It was terrifying. The only busy parts were Kabul Airport and the surrounding roads. All the police checkpoints were abandoned. It was like nothing I had ever experienced before. We arrived back at the unit in forty minutes.

As soon as we were back inside, I told my guys not to unload their weapons. I told them to refuel and stay on standby. I talked to them with courage and confidence in a tone that suggested that we could still control the situation. Then, I told my driver to take me to the TOC. He did. I got out of the vehicle and walked in. The other squadron commanders were there too.

As soon as I walked in, I said, "What is the plan? But before you say anything, I will not surrender, and I don't care what the orders are. I will not surrender to these animals."

The task force commander said, "Don't worry. We won't."

With strong determination, the squadron commanders wanted to take Kabul back. "We will crush them as we always have. Surrender is what they want us to do so they can execute us later."

Even though the Taliban's spokesman had stated that they would forgive the former military personnel, we knew them better than anybody else. The Taliban could not be trusted. We wouldn't trust them. In the heat of the moment, we received a call from our lead advisor. I looked at the phone and said out loud as it was ringing, "It is either good news or bad news." We didn't have any plans yet, but this phone call would determine our next move. I answered the phone because I was the only one that spoke English in that room. I would interpret everything for them during the call in case they had any questions.

The advisor started in a calm voice. "Commander, are all of your guys inside the base? If they are not, call them, like all of them, no matter their position or job. Tell them to come to the unit as quickly as they can."

"Yes, everyone is inside. We already called everyone back to base yesterday. They are all here."

"Okay, perfect. Collect all of your computers, printers, radios, sensitive documents, anything related to the task force or its personnel and take as much ammunition as you can and don't worry about the rest. We have plenty in this location. Commander, you are a smart guy. Don't leave anything important for the Taliban. I will send you the grid and location of another Special Operations unit located close to the airport. Me and my team are here. I want you guys to move here too."

"Roger, but first of all, we are planning to take Kabul back from the Taliban, and we have the forces to do it."

"Commander! Commander! I know you and your unit love your country, but it is too late. You guys did what you could. The president is gone. Let's say you guys took the city back. Then what? We are soldiers, not politicians, and it is too late for any political act. This country needs a president to run it. We are not the president. And besides, the Taliban took over the whole country. There is no way we can win this fight with just the task force. We can take over Kabul city, but the Taliban will block the incoming food and supplies, and people will starve to death. The whole Afghan military is gone. The U.S. has left. The Afghan Army is gone. There is no way we can win this thing. Commander, I know, I am disappointed like you, but it is what it is now."

I thought about it for a minute, then replied, "Roger. We will pack as soon as we can and will leave as soon as possible. We won't leave anything for the Taliban. Out."

"Good luck, Commander. See you then."

Personally, for me, this was good news. It meant there were still people out there that were willing to put up a fight. We could regroup and see what other units' thoughts were. Then, we could make a plan. If the other units were not going to stand with us, then we had to find another plan. But if they were in agreement, then we might be able to start taking Kabul city back. These were all assumptions and ideas. We didn't know what was going to happen minutes from now. Making a plan that everyone might not agree with couldn't be good. We had to be all for this or not at all.

Chapter 18

I told the squadron commanders to start packing up anything important. It didn't matter if it was weapons, ammunition, documents, or anything else related to the task force. I said that we would destroy them all at the location we were going to. When we checked it on our map, we saw it was the location of another Afghan armed Special Operations unit that we had been to in the past. The base was called Eagle Base. We started packing everything we had. We broke the TVs, office doors, windows, and pretty much anything that would have been usable. We left as little as we could for the Taliban.

I went to my office and geared up, but this time, it was different. I always carried five mags during operations, but this time, I packed eight magazines in my vest, eight in my assault bag, and another six hundred extra rounds for my rifle. My sidearm had five magazines of 9mm rounds. I had over nine hundred 9mm rounds in my office. I left three hundred 9mm rounds and six boxes of AK rounds in my office. I also left one grenade and some old C-4 charges. I had a plan for it later. Then, I walked out of my office to check on my soldiers.

It took us about forty-five minutes to pack all the stuff we needed. I was disheartened. I had to make the sorrowful goodbye to the base. We had thousands of memories here. We had done so much, and it was coming to a tragic end. The unit commander called everybody to our formation area. It had a small elevated platform. Underneath were the pictures of the task force soldiers the unit had lost over the twenty-year war. Close to the platform, we had the Afghanistan flag waving in the wind. It was beautiful and elegant. Green, red, black, and the seal of the Afghan government all waved against the blue backdrop of the sky, as if saying its own goodbye to us. Everyone gathered in front of the flag, and the unit commander gave us a motivational speech and ended by thanking us for everything the task force and its personnel had done throughout all the years. He then asked the squadron commanders if they wanted to say anything. I looked to my left, then to my right. I saw all hands were down. I raised my hand. The unit commander called me up front.

I walked to the commander. I saluted him and turned around to face the soldiers. I stared at their eyes for a few seconds. They all looked devastated. You could see the tears on their faces. They all looked tired, and they were worn out. I started to get some words off my chest that I'd never publicly said in the past.

"Warriors! Mark this day and always remember what I am about to tell you!! No matter what happens after today, you were, are, and will be the lions of this country! You will be the unknown heroes! Tell your stories to your children and grandchildren. Don't let these sacrifices that you and your brothers made die within you! Be proud of what you did throughout all these years. Remember we did not lose this war! We were sold out by corrupt politicians! Long live Afghanistan! Long live the brotherhood!" I saluted all the soldiers. They all applauded, and that brought tears to my eyes. With blurred vision, I walked back to my spot, and the unit commander started the ceremony of pulling the flag of Afghanistan down from its post. I could hear the soldiers crying. I tried to hold myself together, but tears were rolling down my own cheeks.

After the ceremony, I stayed there and looked around the formation area. The memories I had there came to my mind. I thought about all those friends I had lost and the friends I had gained. I thought about both the happy and sad times. After a few moments of deep thought, I heard the unit commander tell us to get ready to leave. The convoy was ready in fifteen minutes.

I called six of my soldiers. "Grab three jerry cans of gas and come with me."

"What is going on, Commander?"

"Let's burn this place down."

We couldn't destroy the whole unit, but we could destroy some of it. I sent three soldiers to the TOC and three soldiers to the place where the offices were located, and I went to my office with a can of gas. I started pouring the gas all over my office. Then, I poured the gas on the ammunition and the explosives I'd left earlier and set the jerry can next to it. I walked out and saw the soldiers standing outside. "Are you guys done?"

"Yes, Commander, we are ready."

I called my mobility commander and told him to send us two vehicles. The vehicles arrived, and at the same time, I heard the task force commander say over the radio, "Depart, depart." The convoy started moving. I started the fire, then we got in our vehicles to catch up with the convoy. As we were driving off, I looked back at the unit one last time and saw the smoke coming out of my office.

The Taliban and opportunist civilians were looting Afghan military outposts and bases as soon as they saw that the military had abandoned it. I said to myself, *By the time those rounds and explosives catch fire and are ready to go off, I hope some Taliban are inside my office and see the surprise I left for them.*

—

We caught up with the convoy, and it took us twenty minutes to get to the base we were planning to go to. Before we arrived at the gate, I called my advisor and told him the exact number of vehicles and personnel that would enter the base. We had around 105 vehicles and over 600 combat soldiers coming in.

The advisor said, "We are expecting you, Commander."

When we arrived at the gate, they automatically opened it. The unit at Eagle Base had been the topic of unfair press releases in the past. They weren't known to boast about their successes, and because of this, they weren't able to defend themselves in the court of public opinion. But they were great warriors, and I was lucky to be with them in the end. We used to conduct some joint training there.

It was a massive base that stretched probably thirty square miles. There was a stretch of mountains that composed its northern and western borders. There were guard towers and outposts on each peak that could observe anyone trying to climb the mountains to gain access. On the southern and eastern sides, there was an eight-foot wall. On the outside of this wall, there was a ditch that was another four to five feet deep. This wall ran along a highway that connected the Kabul and Wardak provinces. The gate to Kabul was right next to this base. This gate consisted of an outpost and various buildings. Cars would be required to stop and undergo a security check when passing in or out. Because the base was so huge, it would take miles of walking to get from the exterior wall to the buildings in the center.

When we arrived, there was a vehicle waiting to lead us inside the base. Once we entered, we lined up our vehicles and parked them all in one spot. The task force commander went to meet with their unit commander. The other squadron commanders and I went to meet with the advisor. We walked to their TOC, and when we arrived, I saw the advisor standing by the door. He said, "Hi, Commander," with a smile on his face. I'm guessing he was trying to comfort us in a way from all that was happening.

I said hello. After the greetings, I just wanted to get right down to business. I asked him, "What is the plan? You said we are not fighting, so then what are we doing?"

"Commander, take a deep breath. Let's go in, and I will explain everything to you."

We walked in and sat around the briefing table. Then, the advisor started to explain. "Commanders: We are working on a plan to get you guys out of Afghanistan. We have talked to our chain of command, and they talked to the leadership back in the U.S. We are just waiting for approval. Nothing is clear yet—it might take some time. It may be hours, days, or weeks. And don't worry—we have the ammunition and food to fight for weeks. There's nothing to worry about. We are the task force. We won't let it last weeks. The Taliban are scared of us anyway. They don't want to die at the start of their glory days."

We had no plan other than to go along with our current advisor's plan. We wanted to negotiate with him and his leaders, but there was nothing on the table to negotiate with, and getting us out of the country wasn't confirmed yet. We were still waiting for approval from the U.S. leadership. About 95 percent of our soldiers had the proper documents from the U.S. embassy to get an SIV. Some were waiting for their visas to be issued, and some were in different levels of the process. This process takes years and is unreliable, which would cause catastrophic problems—but we'll discuss that more later.

We had only been at the base for a couple of hours when, around 12:30 p.m., we heard over the radio that the unit's guard force was reporting that the Taliban fighters were trying to take over the Kabul gate that was located right next to the unit's wall. We were under attack.

I had to be real quick. As soon as I heard this, I called my assault team leaders to get the soldiers ready to fight in case more help was needed. A squadron was prepared to go to the gate. The guard tower reported, "Shots fired, shots fired." The TOC gave the instructions to engage them. The guard tower started shooting just as the squadron arrived at the gate. Since friendly forces were in their line of fire, the tower stopped the shooting. The squadron took over and started engaging the Taliban fighters too. The fight had begun.

We shot at the fighters with RPGs, grenade machine guns, 82mm rocket launchers, DSHKs, PKMs, and AKs. We fired almost every kind of weapon we had to kill these Taliban fighters. There were around twelve fighters that had come to the base's gate, trying to loot the weapons and equipment left from the Afghan armed forces. They weren't expecting to see our guys after the country had fallen into their hands. It took about twelve minutes to clear the gate. All enemy fighters were killed. We were on the defensive, and our orders were different now. We had no intention to capture any of them.

While this fight was in progress, we heard another tower reporting three movers coming up the mountainside toward the guard towers. These three movers were each covered in a Pato. Another team went to help these towers. They got in a car and sped off the base to the mountain. They had to climb the rest of the way. As they were on the move, the guard tower reported that these three movers had pulled AKs from under their Patos.

The guard tower had to engage them. The assault team that was en route to clear the area arrived, and in a matter of a couple of minutes, those three armed men were killed.

The Taliban fighters were only fifty meters from the guard tower. After the fight, the assault team went forward to check the dead bodies of the three fighters. They found three suicide vests strapped onto the chests of all three of them. We couldn't disarm the bombs on the vests, nor could we leave them there. We had to come up with another plan. We placed C-4 on the vests and blew them in place.

We were in complete offensive form now. The commanders decided that we should engage any armed Taliban we saw. We were all tasked to patrol the four sides of the base. We had to show our presence in the area to the Taliban to avoid unwanted casualties. I was given the east side to clear. I knew that part of the city very well. We prepared a team of six vehicles and thirty assaulters. We used to roll very fast when going out of our gate, but this time, it had to be done slowly with caution and good observation so we could be more efficient and more vigilant.

We were on the road for about three minutes when we encountered the first Taliban checkpoint, which was controlled by five Taliban fighters. When they saw us, they blocked the road to stop us. We were three hundred meters away when the lead vehicle asked me, "What should we do, Commander?"

"You heard the new order. If they are armed, engage them."

"Roger, Commander!"

"Lead vehicle! Speed up so we can have enough people to engage them, and watch your line of fire!"

The lead vehicle sped up and turned away from the checkpoint to free up space so the following two vehicles could engage. The gunners on the vehicles turned their PKMs on the checkpoint and unleashed hell on the Taliban. The sound of our guns rang through the town.

All five fighters were killed. We didn't give them any chance to fire back at us. We got out of the vehicles and quickly checked to confirm that they were dead. After the check, we grabbed their guns, which were four AKs and one PKM machine gun. We had a point to patrol to and then returned to base. We didn't have any more encounters with the Taliban on the way back.

The team that went south had some engagements too. While they were patrolling on their assigned route, they noticed three fighters were walking on the side of the road. They started walking toward the convoy. Their bodies were covered with Patos. The patrol team couldn't see whether they were armed or unarmed. The patrol commander told his guys to be ready. They preemptively pointed their guns at these three men, something we'd never done before.

The area was quiet. Before the team approached these three men, they started waving their hands down. It was a signal to stop. We used to use that body sign to stop cars in police checkpoints. When the team stopped for them, they started by saying, "We are the Taliban, holy warriors. Hand over your guns and vehicles and walk home. We have taken over this country."

The patrol commander replied, "Do you even know who we are? Do you even know who you are talking to?"

"We don't care. Stop wasting our time." Then, they pulled the guns out.

"Bro, I feel bad that you have to die on your first day of your glory."

"What!? What did you say!?"

Since the guns were pointing directly at these three fighters, the patrol commander ordered, "Engage! Engage!" Our guys started popping rounds. The fighters went down instantly. We had all seen the effects of shooting an AK at close distance, but the soldiers on this patrol told me that those kills were nothing like this. A few AKs and two PK machine guns bursting through bodies of these three Taliban fighters was a different situation to experience. It is too graphic to describe in detail, but I can tell you that what remained didn't resemble a body. It was more like multiple pieces of one. That is how those three fighters' lives ended right there on the first day of their so-called kingdom. We no longer had the luxury of giving the Taliban any second chance. We would engage each one of them in accordance with the rules of war.

The assault team was still at the gate when the base started to get hit with mortar rounds. It was hard to locate where the mortar was coming

223

from. The team that had cleared the gate was tasked with going farther down the road to clear the areas that we suspected the mortar rounds were coming from.

Passing this base, there was a big Afghan bazaar. It was a very crowded one where nearby people were operating their small businesses. The team was told to patrol around it. They were instructed to engage any Taliban they saw. The bazaar was a three-minute drive from the gate, so our guys got there quickly. They were in the middle of the Afghan bazaar when they noticed some Taliban fighters standing behind a shop. As soon as they saw the fighters, they asked the commander whether or not they should engage.

The commander got mad and said, "How many times do I have to tell you? You see these inbreeds, you smoke them!"

We were listening to the conversation over the radio in the TOC and watching them with a small drone that was flying above them. As soon as the commander said that, the soldiers started engaging them. A fight broke out with the Taliban in the bazaar. Around thirteen Taliban were in the bazaar. They were willing to fight, but they didn't want to die at the end of their conquest. They wanted to live to reap the rewards. They also realized that we were not messing around. Their happy times of getting captured, being sent to prison, and later getting released were over. After a fifteen-minute fight, all of them were killed. After checking their dead bodies, the team found communication radios, AKs, and PKMs with these fighters.

The team returned to base after the fight. There were no civilians around the place. It was just them, the Taliban, and us. The Afghan Special Operations unit that owned the base had two more engagements with the Taliban during the patrols with a total of forty-nine Taliban fighters being killed. The Taliban understood that they shouldn't mess with us from that moment on.

The reason we changed our rules of engagement was to show the Taliban we were not the kind of people to mess with. A wolf is a lot more dangerous when it's trapped in a corner, and we had our backs against the wall. Everything was happening on the first day of the fall. It was sometime around noon when prisoners broke out of the most prominent

Afghan prison called "The Pul-e Charkhi Prison." This prison was built to hold around five thousand prisoners. There were a variety of prisoners in that prison, ranging from minor-time criminals to mafia members and terrorists. They all broke out. We first saw the video on a social media platform. A live video was on from one of the prisoners that was recording the prison break. It wasn't hard to break out. The prison had no guards; they just simply walked out with their belongings. There was nothing we could do about it. We just had to continue our day.

When the prison break took place, I said, "This city is doomed." But the Taliban are cruel, and dictators will execute a criminal if they are presented with the slightest reason to do so. I figured the criminals would lay low because the risk of committing crime at this moment was too great.

The rest of the day was quiet. There was no Taliban activity in the area surrounding the base. We were still doing our patrols around it. I assigned my deputy to run the squadron while ten guys from the mobility team and I started destroying documents, computers, printers, and anything related to our task force and personnel history. We created a big fire. First, we shredded all the documents, then threw them in the fire. The computers were smashed, and their broken hard drives were taken out, shot, and then thrown in the fire. We destroyed as much as we could and made sure we didn't leave anything behind. The only things we kept were weapons and ammo. We knew that it would be needed until the end. Everything else was normal for the rest of the day.

We had no clue what was going on in most parts of the city. We had no assets on the ground, no sources, and all the phones we used to communicate with our sources had been destroyed. Most of the soldiers were awake until three in the morning. I went to bed after the sunrise to just get a couple of hours of sleep. I needed to be fully awake to think better and make better decisions.

Since this base was huge, we didn't have people close to us for miles and miles. All of the city was quiet, but the surrounding area of the Kabul Airport was active. Thousands and thousands of Afghans were trying to get out of the country. A C-17 took off from the runway with Afghan refugees on board and clinging to the outside of the plane, and the video went viral on the internet. After that, more people started rushing to the airport. Friends called and texted each other to get themselves to Kabul airport to see if they could jump on one of those military flights.

There were an estimated ten thousand American citizens on the ground at that time in Afghanistan. Some of these ten thousand people were U.S. passport holders, and some were green card holders. There were an estimated eighty thousand Afghans who had directly supported the Coalition by working with NATO forces in the past. This number included their families. Due to threats by the Taliban, they had to leave the country. Many were already in the process of moving to the U.S. with their SIV. The visa process for this takes a minimum of three years and a maximum of five years. Sometimes your visa would get denied, and you would have to start over. That was one of the reasons that so many Afghan allies were still in Afghanistan.

Based on my personal experience, this visa process was probably the slowest and most complicated visa system that had ever existed. Applicants couldn't trust the system until they actually entered the U.S. There were cases where families were returned from Dubai, Turkey, and even U.S. airports. This bureaucratic process is a problem and annoying for all those who use it. But in the case of Afghanistan, this sluggish process proved deadly and set the stage for what came next.

—

On the fifteenth of August, after the fall of Afghanistan, people rushed into the Kabul Airport. There were an estimated six hundred U.S. troops still on the ground to help U.S. diplomats who were still in the country. These soldiers were in the Kabul military airport called Hamid Karzai International Airport (HKIA).

HKIA had a single runway, which was 3,500 meters long and fifty meters wide. It also had fourteen taxiways. This included civilian terminals, U.S. and NATO terminals, and the Afghan Air Force, which was also located in HKIA. They were all using the same runway. HKIA had six gates. These gates were going to different locations in the airport. Each gate had its own restrictions and rules. These six gates were South Gate (which was known as Abbey Gate), East Gate, North Gate, West Gate, Kabul Terminal Gate, and Afghan Air Force Gate. South Gate, East Gate, and North Gate were controlled NATO forces, and they required a specific ID or badge that was issued by the U.S. military. The only people who had access to these gates were the U.S. and NATO, foreign diplomats, and local employees who were working inside the base.

West Gate, Kabul Terminal Gate, and Afghan Air Force Gate were previously controlled by the Afghan armed forces. The civilian terminal was close to Abbey Gate. The civilian terminal was only used for commercial flights. It was located on the south side, and the U.S. military terminal and base were on the north side. NATO and civilian terminals were separated by the runway. Under normal circumstances, the Afghan border police were responsible for the security of the Afghan terminal. West Gate and the Afghan Air Force Gate were used by the Afghan air force, and both were located on the west side of HKIA.

Chapter 19

The initial plan by the U.S. government was to evacuate Afghan allies who had worked with the U.S. government and had done so with honesty, integrity, and loyalty. But the problem at the start of this evacuation was not expecting that the Afghan government would fall this quickly. The U.S. didn't have enough boots on the ground to carry on this massive evacuation plan. Some diplomats and citizens were airlifted out on the fourteenth of August. But on the fifteenth, the Afghan terminal was overrun by the civilians.

We witnessed civilians rushing to the airport when we were coming back from Wardak gate. There were three types of people rushing to the airport. The first type were U.S. citizens or green card holders. The second type were Afghan interpreters or allies and Afghan government officials. The third type were the people who were just going to take the chance to go to the U.S. Most of the Afghan allies, government officials, and Afghan Americans were told by their families and friends to just lay low.

The estimated number of civilians in the Afghan terminal was between seven thousand and ten thousand people. These people slowly started to take over the runway. Eventually, flights couldn't land or take off due to the civilians blocking the runway. This information was reported through our advisor's chain of command.

U.S. leadership decided to send more troops to help with the evacuation. In the initial plan, they sent three thousand U.S. Marines to help, but they couldn't land. The new troops were supposed to arrive sometime around midnight, but it was postponed. The U.S. had to start its evacuation with or without the additional troops.

It was around 2 a.m. when we received a call on the radio to move our guys to HKIA to help the U.S. troops. That was a call I wasn't expecting, but I was happy we were in a position to help the people. Even at the collapse of Kabul, we were still at people's service. After all the backstabbing by my people, we were doing something to help them one last time.

I called my deputy and told him to prepare the squadron to move to HKIA, and I explained the whole plan to him. I had trusted him with every assignment I had ever given him. Our soldiers got ready in a matter of minutes. This convoy wasn't small. Over six hundred men prepared to go, including my guys. We were all going to help with the evacuation process in HKIA. I kept thirty of my assaulters at the base in case things went south. A commander is nothing without his guys.

We departed from the base. HKIA was less than a ten-minute drive from Eagle Base. The roads were quiet. The route itself was not commonly used during nighttime because it was way outside of Kabul's downtown area, and it was a route usually used by the truckers. On our way, we saw a Taliban checkpoint, but it looked like as soon as they saw us, they ran away and left their equipment on the side of the road. We didn't have time to deal with that. We kept going until we were by North Gate. It wasn't very crowded. A small number of people were in front of it, maybe around three hundred to four hundred people. Our plan was to first enter the airport and clear the people out of it. After that, we would decide what part we might take to use as a barracks until the evacuation was done.

It was quiet past North Gate. That road wasn't used a lot, especially at that time of the night. Most people also didn't know about the North Gate entrance. We kept going until we arrived at the Afghan Air Force Gate. There had once been an army checkpoint, but it was abandoned. The gate itself used to have a lot of security (mainly Afghan Air Force personnel). It too was abandoned.

There was a Taliban checkpoint close to the entrance. As soon as we saw them, we engaged them. We didn't stop. The first vehicle turned its PKM left, and soldiers put their AK barrels out the windows. They unloaded on the Taliban at the checkpoint. The second vehicle did the same, and each vehicle followed suit until the sixth vehicle passed. By that point, they were all dead. We didn't stop to check; we didn't have time for that. The last three vehicles in the convoy stayed at the gate and prevented anyone else from entering.

A team of assaulters and a security team started clearing the abandoned Afghan Air Force buildings. These buildings were on our left side. The rest of us kept going on the runway in our vehicles. I could see the big crowd from far away.

We arrived in a long convoy of about one hundred vehicles. We brought over six hundred soldiers. The soldiers were all fully geared for war with NVGs on, light and heavy weapons, and most faces covered by a thin gator neck in case any footage got leaked (we were always restricted on letting the public film us). First, the U.S. soldiers were happy and surprised to see us. They were delighted to see an Afghan task force showing up to help with the evacuation and security. They were so overwhelmed that I think they would have been ecstatic to see anyone coming to their aid. Most of these soldiers had never been to a combat zone. They weren't Special Operations Forces. They were conventional units who usually stayed on base and held the security there. As the U.S. withdrawal had happened, the U.S. military had continually limited the areas where it conducted missions and rarely left their bases.

What we saw was a crazy scene. There were women and children in bad condition, scarred for life. This was the edge of the world for them, their last chance. Everyone was looking at us, scared and surprised because they were not expecting any Afghan unit to be around. They'd thought that we had abandoned them, but they were happy to see their Afghan soldiers. I felt terrible that we were about to kick these people out of the airport, but that didn't mean they couldn't come back in. First, we had to clear the runway so we could start flights. That way, we could help them to get out of the country. When I looked at the people, they all reminded me of family and friends. The kids reminded me of my own kids. It was difficult to watch.

These people didn't want to die. They came from all ages and all walks of life. None of them knew what destiny had assigned for them. None of them looked happy leaving the country. Most of these Afghans left luxurious lives behind and grabbed a backpack with some clothes to step in an unknown journey. Most of them brought only the clothes they were wearing. They didn't know where they were going. Nothing was clear. They were just asking the U.S. military to take them out of there. Even the U.S. officers did not have much information about what would happen to these people. Nobody knew who would be flown out of Kabul. Nobody knew what the plan was.

This situation made it hard for the security teams. You, as a soldier, are kicking all these people out of the airport and don't know who will be let back in. If something terrible happens to them outside of the airport, you'll feel guilty. Something like this had never happened before.

I do remember I saw an old man, maybe around the age of eighty, who had an oxygen tank next to him and was breathing through the mask. He was with this young girl who looked around eighteen. The old man was in a wheelchair, and the young girl was pushing him around. I felt so bad that I walked toward them. As soon as I asked the girl where she was going, she started crying and said, "This is my grandpa. We are Afghan Americans. We are just trying to get out of here."

I said, "I am so sorry, I can't let you in right now. But I will tell my soldiers to help you once this mess is cleared. I am helping not because you have an American passport. I will help you because, as a father myself, I know how hard this situation is for you."

Oh man, everything out there was hard to watch. I have seen horrible things on this earth about which I will never speak or describe. The images that haunt my mind make the horror genre look like a kids' show. When a man like me says it is hard to watch, it is. I had seen countless people die in front of me, but the terrified and hopeless looks on the faces of these people were hitting me right in the heart. The kids were crying. I saw kids from newborn to ten years old among them. This is not something you want any kid to experience.

The task force commander got out of his vehicle and met with the U.S. military commander who I think was a colonel. I later walked toward them to see what the plan was. After we exchanged greetings, the first thing the

U.S. commander on the ground said was, "Thank you for coming. Things were getting out of our hands."

The plan was to move all these people out of the airport. Then, they could go to either Abbey Gate or North Gate to enter the military airport. These were the only two gates that had direct access to the U.S. military part of the airport. People could go there if they had the proper documentation, which was a visa, a green card, a western passport, or any documents that proved that they were eligible for a U.S. or allied country's visa. These were countries such as the U.K., Germany, Canada, and other NATO countries that had presence and their allies in Afghanistan.

I didn't have much involvement in this process though. I had to return to base and stay there to help coordinate future plans. I also was going to destroy documents and run supplies from Eagle Base to the airport. So, I had to leave my deputy to run the squadron at the airport.

I told my D-Com the whole plan in detail, and I said to him, "You are in charge here, and I am proud and honored to work shoulder to shoulder next to you."

Before I left, I helped push people out of the airport to clear the runway. We told the people that the Afghan terminal was closed, and they had to go to Abbey Gate or North Gate if they had the proper documents. But unfortunately, they weren't listening.

"Don't use violence unless you have to," I told the task force soldiers.

Still, civilians weren't listening.

I was using the megaphone on my vehicle. "Do you know who we are?! We are not joking! If we have to shoot, we will shoot! Don't force us!" We were never going to shoot at them. I was hoping the fake threat would get them to move. They still had no reaction. People were just standing there, begging us to allow them in or showing us the documents they had. But our job was to move them out, and if they wanted to leave Kabul, they could go to the military gates. We had no involvement in processing documents. Our job was to just clear the area, but still, nobody was moving. I told my guys, "Throw some smoke grenades toward the crowd." These are harmless grenades that release a cloud of smoke of different colors.

My soldiers pulled the pins for the nonlethal grenades and threw them into the crowd. The concussion blasts and unpleasant smoke changed their minds, and the crowd started moving back. Some people were screaming, but they were being too soft about it. It was just a harmless smoke grenade.

There were some minibuses that the Afghan terminal had. My D-Com took the responsibility of controlling the vehicles and moving people off the runway and out of the airport. We had to use our soldiers to drive them. We transported them to the civilian terminal. The civilian terminal was totally abandoned with no employees or crew to run it. Some were dropped off at the Afghan Air Force Gate, and some were moved to the Afghan terminal and dropped at the exit gate.

It took a few hours to kick everybody out of the airport. We had the airport secure. We put as many people as we could possibly fit in the buses. Priority was given to families with kids, females, and older people. The first few buses were challenging, but it went smoothly after a few rides. They were asking the questions about when we would let them through to the other gates. We told them that the evacuation was not our job, and we didn't know who would be evacuated or when it would happen.

After we cleared the airport, we put security on all gates, which was a mix of Afghan forces with U.S. and NATO forces. The evacuation started after the airport was cleared. Every gate had the U.S. embassy and Department of State representatives to help with identifying the correct documents to let the right people in.

The U.S. embassy and the Department of State came up with a plan to send emails with a gate pass to the people who used to work for the U.S. forces and those that had an SIV in process. Unfortunately, that was a big failure. People started copying these passes, and some started selling them in the black market as if they were a U.S. visa. The price was 5,000 U.S. dollars at first and went down to 300 U.S. dollars after a week.

The problem with the gate pass was that it did not have a picture or any of the pass holder's info. It was similar to a U.S. visa, and "visa" was written on the top left corner of the pass. The text on it said in both English and Pashto, "Show this to the security at the gate. You will be put on a flight to the United States." Who doesn't want to get out of a warzone and come to the United States for free? It was a once-in-a-lifetime chance. I am not blaming anyone for trying to get on a plane at the airport. I know it was a highly complex situation, but things could have been done a lot better.

The mess created by the gate pass resulted in a chaotic situation for the next few days. Nobody was standing in line, nobody was listening, everyone wanted to leave, and everyone wanted to leave right away. All our soldiers were screaming, "Sit down! Get in a line!" When everyone wants to be first, that makes it very hard to check everyone and process them into the gate. If an Afghan didn't have the proper documents and wasn't eligible, he wouldn't leave even after he was told that we couldn't take him. Based on my experience, the plan was a total mess from bottom to top.

After the initial push, I had to go back to Eagle Base to work on re-supplying and keeping the support moving. I planned to keep visiting my guys every night for as long as this mission went. I told my deputy this and asked him to keep me posted and send me updates about the progress at the airport. Then, we got ready and departed from the airport. I needed to go back to base to see what the plan was. The country was lost, and we were a bunch of soldiers with an unknown future. We took the same route on our way back; it was the fastest route. We were ready to engage any Taliban checkpoints. The Taliban were lucky that we didn't see any of them on our way.

For us, the TF-241, nothing was clear. The soldiers were asking questions to my D-Com every day, and he was asking me. Nothing was clear for us. The plan kept changing every day. When I was visiting them at night, I would tell them if there were any updates, but unfortunately, there weren't any specific plans at that point. Even the advisors were not sure what would happen. I would receive just general updates through my guys on the ground but nothing specific about the evacuation. We didn't have much involvement inside the U.S. part of the airport.

The evacuation had been going on for about six days, and after the initial shock, it was going smoothly. We were evacuating about eight to nine thousand Afghans every day. I was checking on my soldiers at least once a day. My soldiers were just holding the security of the airport, the gates, and the towers on all sides of the airport. Some towers and parts of the base were held by U.S. troops.

I would jump on a supply convoy every night and visit my guys. The nights were quiet until we got close to the airport. We had to go through the crowd to get to the Afghan Air Force Gate. Every night, more and more people were coming to the airport gates. Everyone was trying to test their luck. We were taking food and water to our soldiers. The food wasn't good at all—it was just something to eat. Most of the stuff was raw. There was a shortage of supplies, and they didn't have anywhere to cook something for themselves. They were all worn out and tired. They didn't sleep most nights. Some had been awake for thirty to forty hours.

The airport was huge, and we didn't have enough men to cover it. Soldiers were doing twelve- to eighteen-hour shifts on guard posts. The U.S. troops were doing their own security. When I went to the airport, I would tell my soldiers, "Don't lose hope. Good news is on the way. We just have to wait." Their families were concerned about them, and they were worried about their families. They would talk to their families when they could talk over the phone.

I was keeping my soldiers posted about any significant news on whether they would get evacuated or not. We didn't have much positive information. We were hopeful that we wouldn't be forgotten and that plans were forming to get us out. Our help with the Kabul Airport changed some decisions made high up in the U.S. chain of command.

It was August 22, 2021. The evacuation had been going as smoothly as it could for a week. We were still running supplies to our guys at HKIA and would engage any Taliban we saw on our way. After the first two days of the fall, we didn't encounter any other Taliban. They would hide when we went through their checkpoints. Then, we received an unexpected letter from high-level U.S. leadership. It was given to us by our advisors. The letter stated something along the lines of, "There is a truce agreement between the U.S. and the Taliban. We request that you stop killing the Taliban. If you don't stop, it will break the agreement we have with them."

Through the chain of command and the advisors, I heard that the Taliban had sent a warning to the U.S. commander in charge of the evacuation process at Abbey Gate. The warning was, "You have twenty-four hours to end whatever you are doing and leave our country." The U.S. talked to the Taliban and requested more time. The Taliban wanted to show power even in the last days, which is why they'd sent this warning to U.S. command on the ground.

I was furious. I spoke to one of our advisors, "Bro, some inbred morons with AKs and turbans are telling the U.S. what to do."

The advisor said, "I know, I know, but we have to obey these rules now. I am frustrated too, but there is nothing we can do about it."

We were doing our patrols around the base when I left for the airport with the supply convoy. When I arrived, I called my D-Com to pass him the news. When I passed the message to my D-Com and the soldiers on the ground, they laughed and said, "The U.S. became so weak that a bunch of Taliban are giving warnings to them." With what we saw, this news was kind of expected.

It was now August 23, 2021. The days were coming by fast, and it just seemed to be getting worse and worse. Everyone was sad, and the depression was ambient. We now had no hope. We still had zero information about whether we would be evacuated. There were different rumors about the advisors and their plan. We had a lot of Blackhawks and Chinooks landing and taking off from Eagle Base. Our biggest fear was the advisors leaving the base at night. We trusted our advisors, but what happened with Bagram Airfield had created some trust issues between us and the U.S. We didn't want to come back and find that the advisors had flown out with no notice.

So much was happening around us, and so much more was about to happen to me. This day was the saddest day of my life. It's a day that is forever embedded in my mind.

It was around 4 p.m. when I got a call. It was from my father. "Son! Are you coming home?"

"No, Father, I can't. I want to, but I can't. We might leave the country and go to the U.S., or we might be in another country for some time until we get a U.S. visa. We are still not sure, but this is the plan. And if we don't get evacuated, we will stay and fight. We are not surrendering. It doesn't matter what the Taliban says about mercy and forgiving us. They won't forgive us, and we are not asking for forgiveness." I said the Afghan phrase "Ya marg Ya zindagi," which means "life or death."

"Okay, son. You are a smart guy, and I am proud of you. Can we come to see you for one last time and say goodbye?"

"Yes, of course you can. But can you guys come here? There are Taliban checkpoints all over the city."

"Yes, we can, and we will. I will give you a call once we are close to your unit. See you soon."

"See you soon, Father." I hung up. This call saddened me, but there was nothing I could do. I went to the TOC to tell them about my family visiting me at the gate. I gave them the car details and number of people in the car. The TOC called the checkpoints on the base and gave them the details. They told the guards to let the car pass once they arrived.

I found things to keep me busy at the TOC; otherwise, it would have felt like a yearlong wait to me. I needed a distraction. Two hours later, I received another call from my father. "Son, we are a few minutes away. We passed your checkpoint."

I quickly went to the room that I was staying in and grabbed whatever snacks, candy, and drinks I had. I put them in a plastic bag. I did this as a matter of hospitality and also to give something to the kids who were coming with my parents. They were my little kids, nephews, and nieces. I grabbed the key to my car and started driving down to the gate. It took me about three minutes to get there. I parked the car, grabbed the plastic bag, and started walking to the exit gate. While walking, I prayed in my head, *My dear God, please give me the strength not to cry in front of my family. If this is going to be the last time I see them on earth, I want them to remember me with a smile on my face and be proud of the things I have done in this life.*

I walked out of the gate and saw some of our soldiers standing on the right side. They were observing the road. They looked at me and said, "Hi, Commander. Your family is there." One soldier pointed with his hand to the left. I saw my parents and siblings standing next to their car and looking toward the gate. As soon as they saw me, they started crying. Oh

237

man, goodbyes are hard, especially in situations like this. This journey had started with a goodbye. I didn't want it to end with one.

I took a deep breath. In my heart, I said, *God help me.* I started walking. This was the most arduous walk of my life. I held myself together. I started greeting my family with a smile on my face. I then gave the snacks to the kids—my kids, nephews, and nieces—to keep them busy and occupied. I started hugging my father, then my mom and siblings. My mom and sister were crying, and they couldn't stop. I said, "Ma! What are you worried about? I am going to the U.S. very soon." I still didn't know if this was true. "I will be safe. Don't worry, Mom."

I had hidden some stuff from the rest of the family to give them less worry, but I could tell everything to my dad. I had a personal chat with my dad for about thirty minutes. We talked about family, relatives, and what had been happening in the city.

My father said, "Everything is fine for now."

"Does anyone know about me? About my job? My location? Does anyone ask about me?"

"Nothing so far."

"Okay, Dad, let's keep it that way. I don't want any sort of threat coming your way, especially with the type of job I had."

It was getting dark, and we had to say our final goodbyes. I didn't want them to be outside after dark. The security in Kabul was terrible, and I didn't want anything to happen to my family on the way back.

I hugged my father and told him, "Forgive me if I wasn't a good son to you."

He choked up and couldn't talk.

Oh man, that was excruciating. My father, the toughest man I knew, didn't cry in the worst situations. But now, nonstop tears were coming down his face. It was unbearable to watch.

I hugged my mom. She pulled off a ring that I had in my hand and replaced it with another ring. She said, "This ring was left to me by my father. You keep this, and I will keep yours."

I couldn't talk too much—I had a lot of emotions. I just smiled and shook my head in appreciation. I gave the watch I had in my hand to my younger brother who was a former Special Forces officer in a different unit. I so wanted to leave something with everyone, but that's all I had on me.

One by one, I said my last goodbye to every member of my family. I was struggling to hold myself together. I watched them get in the car and drive back home. They were looking back and waving until they turned onto another road. I knew that there was a possibility that I wouldn't see any of them again.

I walked back, and as soon as I sat in my car, the tears started coming down my face. I think it is good to cry. Sometimes it works like a pain-killer. I have cried in the past but only when I was alone. It was between me and my God.

Chapter 20

It was August 25, 2021. I went to HKIA with another supply convoy to visit my guys. When I arrived at the gate, I saw soldiers were sad. Usually when they saw us, they were happy, but it was different this time. I said, "What is going on?"

They didn't say anything.

"What is going on?" I asked the supply convoy commander. "Did anything happen here today?"

"There was a rumor that the U.S. soldiers at the gate shot three soldiers of a sister unit. One was killed and the other two were wounded."

I was shocked when I heard that! "But how?! When?! Why?!"

"I know, I know. I am shocked like you are, but it happened. It wasn't intentional. Whatever happened, the U.S. soldier got scared and started shooting at our guys."

I was livid. "Damnit! Damnit!! Those poor guys. That is very messed up. May God bless the dead soldier's soul, and we pray the other two are not in a bad condition."

When we went into the airport, I asked my D-Com if he knew about this.

He said, "We were on the other side of the airport, and I unfortunately just heard about it this afternoon."

"Be very careful with U.S. soldiers. Most of them are very young and new to the armed forces, and most have not seen combat. They have a terrible understanding of Afghanistan. Just be careful with them. I don't want to lose any of my warriors, and I don't want to see any other misunderstanding. We are almost at the end. I will have a chat with the lead advisor when I get back to base."

We had zero info on the soldier who had done it and why it had happened. I later learned from a source that it was German soldiers who had shot our guys. This is how chaotic things were.

After dropping supplies at the airport, we returned to base. As soon as I got back, I called the lead advisor over the radio and told him we needed to meet.

The lead advisor said, "Okay, let's meet in the TOC in thirty minutes."

Thirty minutes later, I walked to the TOC and saw the advisor standing at the door. He said, "Commander, let's go in."

When I walked in, I saw the commanders of the unit that owned Eagle Base and the other task force squadron commanders sitting and waiting. I said hello to them and sat down.

The lead advisor started. "I am sorry for what happened today. We don't know how and why it happened, but unfortunately, it happened. Everything we have planned has changed. We are leaving the unit tomorrow. We will explode as much as we can. We won't leave anything useful for the Taliban. After we go to the airport, we will start evacuating our guys. We will get you and your families out of this country."

We had to keep it a secret as much as we could, though it was kind of impossible to hide, but this wasn't the type of news that I wanted to pass to my soldiers during that sensitive period of time. The two wounded soldiers were evacuated to Germany. One recovered fully, and the other had to have his arm amputated. Both made it out alive. The dead soldier's body was given to his family at the gate. The family took him home for a burial and funeral ceremony. He never left Afghanistan.

I was awake the whole night, going from office to office in that unit to destroy as much stuff as possible, and I didn't go to sleep until morning. I was so tired that it took me a few seconds to fall asleep, but I only got a couple of hours of sleep. It was August 26, 2021: the last day of Task Force 241.

The first thing we did was take all the vehicles that we weren't planning to take to the airport and park them in one of the ranges that was used for RPG training. There was a total of 160 vehicles. We poured gasoline on them. Then, we shot them with an RPG. Moments later, most vehicles were on fire. I gathered all the extra weapons and ammunition we had. I put them all in a truck, set some explosives inside, and exploded the entire thing. We destroyed every piece of functional military equipment we had, from small items like pistols to bulky items like rocket launchers and explosives.

I had to go back to HKIA again to run some supplies for our guys there. The plan was for me to come back to base, but the plan changed later, and I stayed in the airport. I was very, very tired. My eyes were black, and I had not eaten for the last few days. I was hopeless, I felt betrayed, and worst of all, I had to leave my beloved country. I had planned to stay forever, die and be buried here, but it looked like God had other plans for me. I only packed a sleeping bag and some snacks with me.

It was around noon. The weather was hot. I left with the convoy. We took my team of assaulters that had helped me destroy all the stuff at the base. Thousands of people were standing at the gate when we arrived. It was a lot more than the first few nights. I was up front and had six other soldiers moving people out of the way. I didn't want to shoot rounds in the air because of the kids and women there. I had to scream. My voice was already cracked due to screaming every other night. "GET OUT OF THE WAY!" I said. "Don't make me get violent!" Most were listening, but some weren't. Because of the kids and women, I kept myself calm.

I kept yelling at people, and it was at this moment when I saw a car coming on the wrong side of the road right at us. I noticed it was a Ford Ranger, a former ANP vehicle. It was green and had a white Taliban flag attached to the back.

A fire was ignited within me. I pulled my gun up. "Get out of the way! Get out of the way!" I walked toward the Taliban vehicle and pointed my gun at the driver and his commander sitting up front. There were another three fighters in the back. He stopped. I told him, "Move the hell back before I smoke all of you here!" We stared each other in the eye. My barrel was pointed at the driver's face. "MOVE BACK! MOVE BACK!"

At this moment, my soldiers arrived next to me and pointed their guns at the Taliban inside the vehicle. My assault commander was one of them. He asked, "What is going on, Commander?!"

"I am about to do some *Sicario* stuff here." This was a reference to the movie *Sicario*. There is a specific scene where the actor engages five gang members sitting in a car on the U.S.-Mexico border. If these Taliban made any move I didn't like, I was going to kill all five of them. When the Taliban saw my guys next to me, they drove in reverse out the way they came in.

The people started praising us by chanting, "Long live our armed forces!"

I looked at them angrily. "Stop this fake celebration. When we were killing these guys, you were the first people to walk in the street protesting us. You were calling us criminals for being too violent. Now it is too late. I will never forget and forgive how you treated the Afghan armed forces. You will miss us, but we won't be here when you do."

They all looked sad, and some of them said, "You are right, you are right. We didn't know your worth and the sacrifices you guys made. We are sorry!"

I had no words left for them. I had given everything for my people and my country. Even when they didn't want us, we were there fighting at the battlefront, risking our lives to bring peace for the old and young. I shook my head and walked away. The crowd parted to the side. I told my guys to get back in their vehicles and start moving. We were just two minutes away from the gate. We arrived at the airport gate, but this time, we saw no American soldiers at the gates. There were a few Special Forces guys in the back waiting on some people, but there were no soldiers from conventional units pulling security on that specific gate.

While going through the gate, a soldier came to me and said, "Commander, Commander! I need to talk to you! It is urgent."

I said, "Sure. What's up?"

"Commander, a Taliban patrol vehicle came in earlier, and their commander said, 'Be careful. ISIS wants to hit one of the gates with a suicide bomber.'"

"Did you push it to the Americans at the gate?"

"Yes, we did."

"Okay." I contacted our TOC and told them to pass this to our advisors also. Spotting a suicide bomber or preventing a suicide attack is the hardest thing to do. I actually couldn't do anything to protect us from it, and I felt powerless.

We went in and dropped the supplies. Then, I called my D-Com. "Hey, bro, meet me. We have to talk."

When I saw him, he looked worn out and tired. His throat was sore from yelling at people. He was doing a lot to organize the civilians so we could process them faster. He and the other soldiers at HKIA hadn't gotten a lot of sleep, and some had been up sixty hours during the early stages of the operation. I told my D-Com the plans for the next few days. "We will eventually get evacuated with our families. I just wanted to keep you updated. Tell all the soldiers to call their families and tell them to be ready. We don't know who will leave first. Actually, I changed my mind. Give me your radio. I want to tell the guys myself."

I took his radio. I called, "Net call, net call for the last time. Remember, I am very proud of you guys, especially my D-Com for handling this process these last two weeks. Remember, you are leaving this country proud and a hero. If it wasn't for your sacrifices, this evacuation might have not happened. Be proud of what you did and everything you have done. I have good news for all of you. You all will be evacuated in the next forty-eight hours. You will be out of here. but we still have to keep this place secured till we are officially out of here, Thank you for everything. OUT." This was the last time I spoke to my entire squadron. This was the end of Task Force 241.

—

It was close to sunset on that same day. I was at the Afghan Air Force section of the airport, which was located on the northwest side of the base. I was sitting on a chair, tired and sleepy. The weather had turned nice, and a soft wind was blowing in my face. It felt good. It was a moment of freedom where I didn't have to care about what was happening and what had happened in the past couple of weeks. I decided to check what was going on outside of the airport with the Taliban and their new kingdom. I turned my personal phone on. There were a lot of emails and messages from friends who were checking on me. I went to check the emails to see what they were about.

I remembered applying for Canadian and U.S. visas at the same time a few months earlier. I wanted to get out of the armed forces for a few years and come back to Afghanistan with a new identity as a civilian. I wanted to permanently delete my past career and never talk about it again. But God had something else in mind for me. I was going through the emails when I noticed some emails from the Canadian immigration center that I'd received August 25, 2021, at 6:37 p.m. They were saying to not go to Kabul Airport due to high security threats. The body of the email stated:

Because of security threats outside the gates of Kabul Airport, we are advising you to avoid traveling to the airport and to avoid airport gates at this time.

If you are not already near the airport, we recommend that you stay away and do NOT travel to the airport until further notice.

If you are already waiting outside the airport, we recommend that you leave IMMEDIATELY and find a safe place to stay.

—

The threat wasn't the Taliban—it was ISIS (Islamic State). ISIS is another terrorist network that mainly operates in Iraq and Syria. A branch of it is in Afghanistan, and it is called ISISK (Islamic State of Khurasan). ISIS is more cruel and has way more extreme beliefs.

We had a lot of fights with them throughout my career, but they didn't have a big presence like the Taliban network. Most of the ISISK members were former Taliban members. For various reasons, they'd joined ISISK. As they say in my country, "Same donkey, different blanket."

It was 6:28 p.m. I was standing and facing the south side of the airport. I was looking at the mountain view south of Kabul city when I heard a big explosion. I looked around to see where it was. I grabbed my radio to listen to any reports about it. It sounded very close. I was holding my radio and looking around when I saw the black smoke going up at Abbey Gate. This was one of the most crowded gates of the airport, and it had a high security threat. I called my D-Com. "Do you know where that explosion was? Do we have any guys over there?"

"Negative, Commander. We don't have any of our guys at that gate. It was controlled by the U.S. Marines."

When I heard that, I quickly opened Facebook and logged in with my fake account. People were posting about the suicide bombing at Abbey Gate, and the initial estimates were over one hundred people dead and wounded.

A great gloom overtook my body. I mourned for the soldiers and civilians who were killed. They were all human and wanted to live a peaceful life. They had families, kids, and someone who cared for them. This world is cruel.

Why can't humans live in peace? Why do we have to kill each other? Why can't we focus on ourselves instead of competing with others and wanting to overpower others? Why do we have to be cruel? God is kind. He created us to be kind to each other, Muslims, Christians, Jews, and Hindus. If God still loves all of us, why do we have to kill each other? The way the current world works saddens me.

Chapter 21

I had this strong belief that I could change the situation and bring peace. I knew I was only one man, but I was a leader. If I could change myself, I could change my soldiers too, and they could change their families. But unfortunately, God decided something else for me.

The last couple of weeks were the dreariest of my life. I didn't want to leave my country. If I'd wanted to, I could have been in the U.S. in 2013 when my SIV was approved. I might have been a U.S. citizen by 2019. I could have been a Canadian citizen with an SIV back in 2012. One of the Special Air Service Regiment (Australian Special Forces) commanders I'd worked with in the past had emailed me in 2016 and told me that I could apply for an Australian version of an SIV too. But I'd decided to stay in Afghanistan out of love for my country. I wanted to do my part to make it safe and welcoming as I dreamed it could be. But the situation in my country and my career was forcing me to leave.

My soldiers started getting evacuated. One after another, they boarded planes with their families. It was time to go. It was time to say goodbye to my beloved home. It was time to leave all these beautiful memories and joyful times. Other countries are beautiful, but home is home, and nothing can replace it. I was born in this land, and I was hoping to die here too and be buried next to my deceased family members.

I started walking to this hangar that was mostly empty. I was going to drop my gear and gun. It was so quiet that I could hear the sound of my footsteps. In that hangar, I saw all these guns and equipment that had been dropped by the TF-241 soldiers and the guys from Eagle Base. I looked at my AK-Draco and said, "Goodbye, old buddy. You have been a great help throughout this journey. I will surely miss you."

I stared and looked at it for a couple of moments. All the times I had carried it on operations flashed through my head. I slowly placed it on top of the other guns. "I am happy that I am not leaving you for the Taliban." The plan was to destroy all the equipment before we left. I walked out of the hangar and looked back one last time.

I had already made calls to my brothers. I'd asked them to bring my wife and kids to West Gate. I knew a spot that I could get my family easily in. We still had U.S. security there, but I had already coordinated with them. My brother called me and said, "We are three minutes away from the gate."

I started my vehicle and drove to the gate. When I arrived, I called my brother and directed him to the secret way into the airport. There was a small door that had been used by the Afghan air force base and the Ministry of Interior Affairs in the past. The only people who knew about it were the military personnel who had worked in these two places or government officials. I had been to these two places a lot in the past. I had come there for command meetings at least once a week.

The security force at the door opened it for me, and I saw my family standing one hundred yards away from the door. I waved at them and motioned them to walk toward me. When they got close, I saw two of my brothers were with my wife and kids. I hugged them and asked, "Are Mom and Father okay?"

"Yes, they are fine. Don't worry about them."

I said to my brothers, "Goodbye. I hope to see you guys soon." I knew it might be a decade before I could see them again. I drove back inside with my wife and kids, and two hours later, a C-130 military airplane landed to pick me up, along with some other soldiers who were still there. We still had a small number of people left in the air force section of the airport where we had been stationed for the past few weeks. They were there to destroy the equipment that had been left behind. This would be the last mission of TF-241.

I was with my kids and my wife, and we only had one piece of luggage. The whole group getting on the C-130 was around one hundred people in total. We started walking to the plane. We had our advisors around the plane helping with the boarding. The advisors were counting the people getting on.

I was at the ramp of the plane when someone tapped my left shoulder. I looked and saw one of the advisors who had worked with me for the past year. He said, "It was a hell of a ride. Good luck with your new chapter."

I said, "Thank you." Then, we got on the plane. The plane didn't have any seats. It was just a hollow body meant for transporting supplies. I put the one bag of luggage on the ground so my wife and kids could use it as a seat. I was looking back through the door. As the ramp raised, it was the last time I saw my country. We took off.

It was August 29, 2021, when I left the country. It was one day before the last American evacuated at HKIA and left Afghanistan on August 30, 2021. We flew to Qatar on a direct flight. Then, we flew from Qatar to the United States of America. My family and I were sent to Fort Bliss, Texas, where we were put in a refugee camp at a training camp called Dona Ana. The desert of Fort Bliss looked very similar to Kandahar. Some of us were probably wondering if the U.S. had played a joke on us and flown us back into Afghanistan. To make the camp feel more inclusive, the U.S. Army soldiers renamed it Dona Ana Village (DAV). There we stayed in giant white tents that could sleep one hundred people. We set up makeshift structures with metal and plastic poles and hung large sheets to make family rooms inside the giant tents. It wasn't great, but we were well taken care of.

A little over a month later, we were resettled in California, where I reside today. Over 122,000 people were airlifted from Kabul during this operation. I am happy with the efforts of my unit and myself that contributed to this. Hopefully they will all find success wherever they landed.

—

As an Afghan, I am heartbroken about what happened at the fall. We already had millions of Afghan people as refugees all over the world, and millions more were added to them. If I was given the choice of peace, even if it meant working for the Afghan minimum wage and struggling to get by, I would take that deal in a second. As they say, war is hell.

The Taliban may have been cruel, but many of them were still Afghans. An Afghan soldier getting killed and a Taliban Afghan getting killed were both a loss for the country. I can only imagine what Afghanistan might have looked like if we had focused our energy on building the country instead of killing each other.

This war has been going on for about four decades. In the history books, the Russian invasion and the American invasion will seem like two distinct events. For Afghans, it felt like one long war. A lot of Afghan men, women, and children were born in this war, and unfortunately, a lot were killed in this war. It was a somber ending for my country and my people. All these years have been for nothing. All those lives, both American and Afghan, were lost for nothing.

—

The Taliban made some false claims after we left. When they saw that we had destroyed every piece of our equipment, they were mad, and their commanders said, "We gave these soldiers a chance and showed them mercy, and in exchange, they should have left us their equipment."

When I saw that interview, I said, "Bro, you can claim all you want, but we all know the truth. You tried to kill us a few times, but you failed, and that failure forced you to sign a truce and deal with NATO in the end."

It annoyed me enough to set the record straight. We could have stayed in Afghanistan longer, but that would have meant more senseless deaths for the Taliban and any civilians caught in between. It was the right decision to leave when we did. The Taliban should be happy that we chose the path of peace in the end. A lot more of them are alive because of it.

I am currently living in the U.S. I received my Canadian visa when I arrived here, but I decided to stay here in the good ol' U.S. of A. I know that the USA is one of the greatest countries on earth. I tried to join the military here, but due to the brain injury, it looks like I can't. I am planning to study and become someone useful for this country or whatever country I go to in the future.

I do miss my home a lot. No other place can be home, but I am happy my family and I are safe and living in peace. And I am hopeful for the future of Afghanistan. Based on the phone conversations I've had with the people I know who are in Afghanistan, it sounds like the Taliban have changed compared to the past. They are less dictatorial and cruel. They want to bring changes, but there is no budget to do so.

Whatever happens, I will stay hopeful. Hope is the only thing that kept me alive for the past thirty years, and I am sure it will stay with me until I die of (hopefully) old age.

Later, I had to get the rest of my family out of the country. They are currently out of Afghanistan, somewhere in the neighboring countries. They had no option but to get out due to my work with the U.S. and Afghan government. Eventually, we will reunite when we are able. Until then, we will remain apart for many years to come.

—

When the Taliban advance happened, no one was expecting the provinces to fall so quickly. We expected it to be a normal attack. The Taliban would take ground in some areas, and we would take it back in a counteroffensive. We were confident that everyone would fight back. From my vantage point, the morale of the Afghan armed forces was that of a force willing to kill the enemy. The most shocking moments in the fall of Afghanistan were the calls we received from friends and colleagues in the Afghan armed forces informing us that they were ordered not to fight. It broke people who desperately wanted to defend their land from the Taliban, which had been merciless and indiscriminate over the past decades. Grown men cried because they couldn't take the idea that their generals had told them to surrender.

The will to fight is key in a soldier. But that alone cannot win a battle. War is a team game. The soldier is only as capable as the weapons and supplies he is given. Once the supplies of water, food, and ammo stop coming, the soldier cannot win. War requires large-scale coordination. Because the generals and high-level government officials had decided to surrender before the offensive began, the Taliban had already won. A few provinces and a few units didn't surrender, and I assume their leaders refused to go along with the coordinated plan. In the end, it just wasn't enough. We had been sold out.

Writing this in August of 2022 (one year after the fall), I do not know what exactly was said in the Doha peace talk meetings. In the future, this information may be released, and I hope it will be. Something happened in those meetings that set the stage for my country to quickly come crashing down. At this time, all I can do is try to put the pieces together from news reports.

The Associated Press published an interview with Hamid Karzai on December 15, 2021. In it, Karzai stated that he and Abdullah met Ghani, and they agreed that they would leave for Doha the next day with fifteen others to negotiate a power-sharing agreement. As the former president, Karzai had lots of influence on the corrupt politicians, and Abdullah, as the co-president, had some claim to office. They proved to have more power than the so-called President Ghani. The Taliban were already on the outskirts of Kabul. Karzai said that the Taliban leadership in Qatar promised that their insurgent force would remain outside the city until the deal was struck.

Early on the morning of August 15, the capital was fidgety and on edge. Rumors were swirling about a Taliban takeover. Karzai was putting together the list of the fifteen others that would go to Doha. He called Doha and was told that the Taliban would not enter the city. By about 2:45 p.m., it became apparent that the Afghan President Ghani had fled. Karzai called the defense minister and the interior minister and searched for the Kabul police chief. Everyone was gone. Ghani's own protection unit's deputy chief called Karzai and asked him to come and take over the presidency. Karzai declined, saying that he had no legal right to. Instead, Karzai made a public statement on television with his children beside him to try to calm the city by showing that he was still there. Karzai adamantly stated in the interview that a peaceful transfer of power would have occurred had Ghani remained in Kabul.

A book written in Dari by Fazal Ahmad Manawi (a former senior Afghan politician who continued fighting the Taliban after the fall) offers another piece to the puzzle. In this book, Manawi describes an interaction with Abdullah Abdullah. It was the morning of August 15 when he visited Abdullah, and Abdullah told him, "Karzai and I are leaving for Qatar this afternoon to talk with the Taliban leadership to transition the power from Ashraf Ghani to the Taliban."

Manawi responded, "But, sir, the Taliban are at the gate."

Abdullah continued, "Don't worry. The Taliban agreed during the talks that they would not enter Kabul city for two weeks until everything is officially handed over to us."

It was past 2 p.m. when Abdullah received a call from Karzai. "Our guy [Ashraf Ghani] has left the country."

"That is not good. What do we do?"

"Nothing. We will wait for the Taliban leadership in Kabul city."

Moments later, Abdullah received a call from Zalmay Khalilzad (the U.S. envoy in the Doha talks). Khalilzad informed Abdullah that President Ghani had fled the country, to which Abdullah replied, "You damn Americans. You ruined everything and this country." The conversation ended.

Ashraf Ghani did not give the order to the army that made them stand down. People under him or in an adjacent position of power or influence made that decision for him. Ghani knew that he had no power, and the memories of what happened in 1996, when the Taliban tortured and killed former president Mohammad Najibullah, haunted him. They hung his body in the street. Ghani did not want to suffer the same fate. Ghani fled because of this, and he held little power after elements of the government had executed what was essentially a coup.

Abdullah and Karzai wanted to retain power, wealth, and influence through the Taliban by voluntarily ceding power in a peaceful exchange. Had their plan gone as intended, the Taliban would have gained greater legitimacy. The Taliban want to be recognized internationally as an official government because they need to be plugged into the currency system and because they are currently out of money. They can't even pay their soldiers at the time of writing this. This exchange would have given world powers

253

an excuse to recognize the Taliban as an official government instead of an invading army or a terrorist organization, as they are currently listed.

Another exchange happened publicly that showed that there was some kind of deal that involved the U.S. and the Taliban taking over. In July of 2022, the Taliban interior minister (and leader of the Haqqani Network, a notorious pillar of the Taliban) said in a speech spoken in Pashto, "We promised and agreed that we [the Taliban] won't be a threat to the rest of the world and proved it throughout fourteen months of tests from the day of the agreement. The U.S. must recognize us as an official government. If it wasn't for us, they wouldn't have been able to do evacuations. There are still American civilians living in Afghanistan, but they never faced threats from our side. Isn't that enough?" He smiled and said, "Don't make me open my mouth. There will be a lot of untold secrets laying on the floor." This again suggests that there was a secret deal made by the U.S. and the Taliban with Karzai and Abdullah also involved.

On August 15, 2022, Zalmay Khalilzad gave an interview to Radio Farda in Dari. As the U.S. special envoy during the Doha talks, his statements were nothing less than stunning. Khalilzad stated that the Doha agreement had three conditions. First, the U.S. and NATO troops would leave in fourteen months. Second, the Taliban and Afghanistan would not be allowed to be a haven for terrorist networks. Third, the Afghan government would be handed over to the Taliban during an official transition so that the rest of the world could recognize the future Taliban-led government.

The reporter asked if Khalilzad and the U.S. had considered the girls who finally had access to schools and the advances in women's rights. Khalilzad replied, "That was up to the Afghans, not us." He continued, "Ashraf Ghani ruined our plan after he left the country. If he would have officially transitioned power to the Taliban, we wouldn't have had the current problems."

The reporter asked, "Why didn't the Afghan troops fight?"

Khalilzad replied, "I don't know. I mean, there was an agreement that the Taliban would come to Kabul's gates, and then Karzai and Abdullah would go to Qatar to talk about the new future ruler of the country. But the chaos and Ashraf Ghani's plan wasn't predicted. The Afghan leaders shouldn't have left the country since there was a deal. Everything would have been fine."

This deal wasn't voted on by the people. We never had a say. We were kept in the dark as we became pawns in a game of power grab. Soldiers died fighting the Taliban to the very end. And they did so while getting stabbed in the back by the so-called leaders that claimed to represent them. In the end, all of it was for nothing.

The European embassy is effectively open right now in Afghanistan, but the European countries cannot publicly recognize it yet. The U.S. embassy is still closed, but my sources on the ground have told me that the doors to the U.S. embassy and the surrounding U.S. bases are still locked and the Taliban has not touched them. This suggests that the U.S. will be opening an embassy soon. It will be hard to sell to the public and the world, and that is why the U.S. is acting slowly.

—

There were many strategic mistakes made by the U.S. during the evacuation. The biggest blunder was pulling out the U.S. military before the U.S. civilians. The Taliban had an agreement with the U.S. that they would not be attacked and had to leave within fourteen months. The U.S. government should have known that the Taliban offensive would be fast and their takeover swift. They were involved in the talks, and they knew the deal. The State Department knew how many Americans and SIV holders were in Afghanistan. They chose to move the military assets out knowing that Americans and SIV holders could be stuck there.

The second biggest blunder was pulling out of Bagram Airfield. Bagram was less than an hour north of Kabul and was strategically placed to be easily defended. Bagram had air assets, and that alone would have kept the Taliban at bay. A few thousand troops and air assets would have kept the Taliban out of Kabul just by their mere presence. This would have also provided a safe passage out of the country for people, as NATO troops could have secured the routes to the airfield with far less civilian intervention. Once the Taliban were at Kabul and the U.S. chose to begin evacuating from HKIA, the U.S. was stuck. That airport was embedded within a city of millions. Air support was no longer an option, and space was limited. After this string of bad decisions, there were no more tactical moves to make.

—

If there was one factor that contributed the most to the inability of America to secure victory in Afghanistan, it was that the high-level U.S. officers had no idea what was happening on the ground. Messages get politicized as they go up the chain of command. Often, a soldier on the ground will make observations and send up reports and suggestions to solve the problems they see. At first, these messages are relayed with some accuracy. As they travel up, though, the inconvenient details get removed, and the message gets changed due to the politics of the rank structure. Nobody wants to tell their boss the blunt and candid truth. Stuff gets added to soften the blow, and by the time it gets all the way up, the message loses its honesty. From my perspective, the U.S. generals did not know what was going on.

One general whom I admired and respected was U.S. Army General Scott Miller. He is the example I wish all officers would follow. General Miller visited the provinces himself because he wanted to see what was going on with his own eyes. He was not afraid to go where the conflict was, and the decisions he made benefitted from this.

My advice to the politicians is to always listen to the guys on the ground. They are close to the locals, and they know what is going on. My advice to the guys on the ground is this: Listen to the locals. Analyze it and don't trust everything, but listen to everything anyway. You will learn something that might save your life or change the course of a war.

For the future army officers, this is my advice: Always sit down with your soldiers weekly and have meetings with them. Just hear them. Don't make it an official ordeal—just interact. These experiences matter, and they might save your life. Every soldier matters, and every soldier has experiences that help the team. Do not discount anyone. You respect them as a soldier, and you listen to them. Always give the credit to the soldiers and work to get them promoted. They take pride in their rank. If you highlight a soldier's mistake, but you never highlight the good things he has done, you will lose the loyalty of this soldier, and it will cause resentment. Every soldier does things worth praising. If they aren't getting that praise, that is a failure of leadership. Always be willing to fight for your soldiers, and they will fight for you. The little stuff matters.

—

To conclude this, I have one last thing I would like to get off my chest. Many of you who are reading this have fought in my homeland. Many of you have known someone who has. Some of you may have lost loved ones. All of you have lost countrymen. I need not explain the fantasies of war. War is hell, and one should never wish for it. But it takes men of great character and resolve to know what war is and still choose to stand in defense of a greater good, knowing fully the consequences of such a decision.

To those who placed their barrel next to mine, you have my respect. It wasn't your fault. Your bravery will not go unnoticed. These stories and the countless other memoirs about Afghanistan will live on. The soldiers who died in combat or died at home from the trauma of war will not be forgotten. I pray that God shepherds the souls that have passed from this world, and I pray that God brings peace to all who might need it. Thank you for your efforts. Thank you for your support, and may God bless you all.

Printed in the USA
CPSIA information can be obtained
at www.ICGtesting.com
LVHW090437081223
765728LV00061B/1296

9 781955 026901